THE DIVORCED PARENT

ALSO BY STEPHANIE MARSTON:

The Magic of Encouragement: Nurturing Your Child's Self-Esteem

THE DIVORCED PARENT

Success Strategies for Raising Your Children After Separation

Stephanie Marston

WILLIAM MORROW AND COMPANY, INC.
NEW YORK

It is the policy of William Morrow and Company, Inc., and its imprints and affiliates, recognizing the importance of preserving what has been written, to print the books we publish on acid-free paper, and we exert our best efforts to that end.

Library of Congress Cataloging-in-Publication Data

Marston, Stephanie.
The divorced parent: success strategies for raising your children after separation / Stephanie Marston.
p. cm.
Includes index.
ISBN 0-688-11323-0
1. Single parents—United States. 2. Parenting—United States. 3. Children of single parents—United States. I. Title.
HQ759.915.M36 1994
306.85'6—dc20

93-15847
CIP

Printed in the United States of America

First Edition

1 2 3 4 5 6 7 8 9 10

BOOK DESIGN BY MM DESIGN 2000

To my brother, Marvin Arthur Small,
one of the most caring, sensitive men I knew,
whose love and friendship enriched my life.
Your love and memory will live forever in my heart

&

To my parents, Leon and Selma Small,
who gave me the gift of life and have always encouraged me

&

To my sister, Marian,
who has provided grist for the mill over the years
and has been a staunch fan and supporter

Acknowledgments

A book is a collaborative effort. As a writer I have depended on the generosity of the hundreds of parents in my support groups, clinical practice, and seminars who have freely shared their struggles, turmoil, and successes. This book would not have been possible without you.

I am deeply grateful to the people who supported me through this long, and at times arduous, process:

A special thanks to my daughter, Ama, for her love and friendship. It means everything to me. Thanks, Fez, for keeping me laughing.

To my parents, Leon and Selma Small, for being loyal cheerleaders and for all that you have taught me over the years. I appreciate you more every day.

To my friends: Georgia Noble, for your understanding, patience, and love. You are a wellspring of joy in my life. Celeste Fremon, for your belief in me as a writer, and your unflagging encouragement, and for the "retaliatory reading" sessions. Mary Ellen Strote, for your editorial expertise and steadfastness. They were a godsend. Maureen Murdock, a fellow writer, for understanding the ups and downs of the process. Jack Canfield, for your friendship and inspiration. Cathy and Dan Warren, for the stress-release walks and the case of Kleenex when I really needed it. Kate Driesen, for your friendship and New York humor. You helped to refuel me when I needed a boost. Johnathan Kirsch, for your counsel and compassion. You went well beyond the call of duty. Carol Trussel, for your friendship and good business sense.

To Beatrice Cooper, whose support in mining for the gold has paid off beyond what I thought was possible. I am deeply grateful for all I have learned from you.

To Sharon Shelbourne, program coordinator of Family Care at the Los Angeles Department of Water and Power, for your assistance in organizing support groups and circulating questionnaires. Hugh McIsaac, director of Los Angeles Conciliation Court, for your generosity of spirit, time, and knowledge.

To Lisa Bankoff, my agent, for her expertise, and to Liza Dawson for her editorial contribution.

Author's Note

Throughout this book I use case studies from my seminars, support groups, and private practice. I have changed all the names of the parents and children and anything that might identify them to protect their privacy.

Contents

Introduction

It is not in the still calm of life . . . that great challenges are formed. . . . Great necessities call out great virtues.

Abigail Adams, in a letter to her son John Quincy Adams

Twelve years ago my marriage ended. While the decision to divorce had come gradually, the experience was nonetheless traumatic. My life turned upside down. I was beset by conflicting emotions: relief and excitement, shame that I had failed at my marriage, guilt that my child wouldn't have the ideal childhood I had envisioned, and fury at my husband. I was faced with the new financial and emotional burdens of supporting my six-year-old daughter alone. I felt stigmatized, a failure, a disappointment to my family. I had spent the seven years of my marriage living a comfortable, middle-class lifestyle; now I imagined I would end up poor, isolated, and disgraced. To say the least, I was overwhelmed.

In the period immediately following my divorce, I became painfully aware that my emotional roller coaster was having a direct effect on my daughter, Ama. When I was depressed and despairing, Ama would act insecure and unhappy, and misbehave badly. When I could manage to feel hopeful, she would be calmer, more cooperative, and easier to handle. I had no way to buffer her from my feelings and she was forced to come along on a rough ride. I realized then that it was my responsibility to get myself back on my feet, not only for my own sake but for hers as well.

My ex and I divorced before joint custody became commonplace. We were uncertain about how we wanted to divide our time with our daughter, but we agreed that Ama's primary residence would be with me. On the advice of a therapist/lawyer friend, my ex and I decided to keep the visitation arrangement flexible and to amend it as our situations changed. Although I was still angry with him, I vowed silently to do nothing that would interfere with his relationship with our daughter. Little did I know that keeping that promise to myself would be one of my greatest challenges.

Over time, and with the help of friends, family, and therapists, I gradually began to rebuild my life and devise ways of functioning successfully in my newly single status. Learning how to deal with my ex-husband, however, was my hardest job. My initial instinct had been to go for the jugular. Contact with him continued to be extremely irritating, but in time I was able to separate my feelings toward him as a former marriage partner from what I felt for him as my daughter's father.

My interest in the process of divorce started as a desire to build a more satisfying life for myself while helping my daughter adjust. After devouring every book I could find on the subject I realized that if *I* needed help with these issues others also must be looking for guidance. *The Divorced Parent* grew out of my fourteen years of working with couples and families as well as from my own divorce experience. Regardless of your custody arrangement or the level of cooperation between you and your ex-spouse, it will provide you with effective tools to enjoy your family in its new form. Over the past twelve years, working as a family therapist and seminar leader and seeing hundreds of children, parents, and families in various phases of divorce, I have developed a set of "survival strategies"—concrete ways to help both parents and children cope with the stresses that arise from living in a divorced family.

Obviously, the optimal situation is to have two parents who are committed to cooperation. But if your ex is angry, provocative, and hostile—and especially if *you* are—the techniques I offer here will prevent any escalation of anger. You can't control your ex's behavior, but you can learn to deal with the situation in a way that fosters a working relationship.

THE NEW AMERICAN FAMILY

In recent years the shape of the American family has changed dramatically. According to the 1988 U.S. Census, half of all American marriages now end in divorce. Almost 25 percent of American households now are headed by a single parent. Sixty percent of all children under the age of eighteen are expected to spend three to five years in single-parent families. Nevertheless, the culture has been slow to come to terms with these enormous changes. We still refer to divorced families as "broken homes" with the underlying inference that they are inferior to the idealized two-parent traditional family. This myth needs to be shattered.

Children from divorced homes can grow up every bit as happy and healthy as those from intact families. But this will happen only if divorced parents recognize that the problems they face are different.

FOR YOUR KIDS' SAKE

Children are extremely resilient. Divorce does not necessarily leave them with permanent psychological scars. To ensure their healthy adjustment and development, however, five needs must be met: (1) children must be protected from their parents' disputes, (2) children must be free to love both parents, (3) parents must shift their roles from intimate partners to parenting partners, (4) children must have access to both parents without being placed in loyalty conflicts, and (5) parents must recover from the trauma of divorce and rebuild their lives.

When these needs are not met children are not well adjusted. They may do poorly in school. Many are aggressive with their peers, misbehave, and develop psychological problems that follow them into adulthood. They struggle with anxiety and fear of abandonment or rejection and are often unable to form and sustain significant adult relationships.

I believe that a family can be first-rate regardless of its configuration. Yes, two emotionally mature parents who work at resolving conflicts in a healthy manner are preferable to one parent raising a child without help. Unfortunately, this ideal is achieved less often than one might wish, even in so-called intact nuclear families. The fact that seems most critical in enabling children to grow up happy, successful, and well-adjusted is not the *number* of parents who live in the home, but how the people in and out of the home relate to each other.

THE FUNCTIONAL DIVORCE

In my workshops I ask participants to call out single words that pop into their minds when they think about divorce. Routinely, the responses are "failure," "shame," "loss," "anger," "pain," "guilt," "relief," "sadness," "revenge," and "escape." With the exception of "relief," all the words they use have negative meanings. Words such as "compassionate," "civilized," "friendly," "agreeable," or "cooperative" rarely, if ever, come up. People simply don't think of divorce in a positive context.

Yes, divorce is wrenching and tumultuous, but it is never a single event. It's a process that started long before you were aware of your decision to end your marriage and it extends well beyond the signing of the dissolution papers. Nor is divorce the culprit that damages children. The single most important factor affecting both your and your children's adjustment is how you handle your divorce and how you behave in the subsequent period.

The biggest mystery for most people is how to relate to an ex after divorce. Our instincts and reflexes are geared toward competition rather than cooperation. The last thing most of us want to think about in the midst of our divorce is how to maintain a working relationship with a former partner. The very idea of cooperating with the person who has caused us so much pain and unhappiness seems crazy.

Learning to cooperate after a marriage ends when you couldn't do it before requires a shift in attitude. Cooperation doesn't mean being friends with or even liking your ex-spouse, but it does require a commitment to protecting your children from open warfare. It asks that you lay down your weapons of destruction for their sake.

THE NEW PIONEER

Establishing a cooperative parenting partnership takes a tremendous amount of effort and dedication, especially if you haven't fully resolved the issues that hurt your marriage. Doing so while you are in the process of separating emotionally is one of the most difficult challenges you will face. Those who accept the challenge are modern-day pioneers, boldly going where few parents have gone before, exploring strange new forms of relating. There are no maps, no star charts, and precious few role models for navigating this uncharted territory.

SOMETIMES RESEARCH LIES[1]

From the hateful couple in the movie *The War of the Roses* to the highly publicized book *Second Chances: Men, Women, and Children a Decade After Divorce*[2] in which Judith Wallerstein describes a generation of children as permanently scarred, the media's portrayal of divorce has been negative. Many heard about Wallerstein's study. It was discussed in every medium from *People* to *The New York Times* to nightly news shows. Her alarming conclusions further fueled the turmoil and guilt felt by divorced parents. The children who learned about this study were also frightened and confused. According to parents and teachers, many kids who seemed successful and well-adjusted began to wonder if they were, in fact, carrying a hidden emotional time bomb. Would it go off in the future, they asked, leaving them crippled in their own intimate relationships?[3]

In my private practice and in groups of teens with whom I spoke the effects of the Wallerstein study came up frequently. "I always felt like I was doing pretty well," complained Lisa, the twenty-three-year-old daughter of one of my clients. "I had just graduated from Stanford with honors and was engaged to be married when my mom told me about this study. It was scary. I began to doubt myself. I started to think, 'Am I screwed up and just don't realize it?' " Young people like Lisa wonder if their sense of well-being is illusory. The reality is that most research has found few, if any, psychological differences between children of divorce and kids from intact families.[4]

Children do exhibit initial symptoms upon learning about their parents' divorce, but unless they are faced with additional stresses and adversity the majority recover within six months to two years.[5] Some children and adolescents have no adjustment problems. But Wallerstein's study, combined with parental fear and guilt, has convinced us that our kids are inevitably hurt by divorce. This is simply not the case. The picture painted in *Second Chances* is highly exaggerated, and the study upon which the book is based is unscientific and invalid.

Let me tell you why Wallerstein's research shouldn't have been generalized to represent all divorcing families: Her small sample was sixty recently divorced, white, middle-class families in a California suburb. There was no comparison group of families living in unsatisfactory marriages. Half of the men and almost half of the women in her study were "moderately disturbed or frequently incapacitated by disabling neuroses and addictions." Some were "chronically depressed" and "sometimes suicidal." An additional 15 percent of the men and 20 percent of the women were "severely disturbed," with long histories of mental illness and a chronic inability to cope with life's everyday demands. Only one third of the sample was deemed as passing "adequate psychological functioning" prior to the divorce. Briefly translated, the small group of people Wallerstein picked for her study were psychologically disturbed. They would have had problems in their families even if they stayed married. Given their psychological profiles, it seems evident that their children would have had difficulty after their divorce.

Despite Wallerstein's extremely negative, pathological portrayal of children in *Second Chances*, more than half of the kids in her study survived their parents' divorce with little or no lasting damage. Sixty-eight percent of the younger children and somewhat less than 40 percent of the older children were said to be doing well at the ten-year follow-up. Wallerstein, however, leads us to believe that most of the children were severely damaged by describing a disproportionate number of families that had "tragic" outcomes. Her own figures don't match her findings.

Wallerstein's study was strongly criticized in academic circles. The media attention it got obscured the facts: The majority of children, when assessed years after divorce, function normally.

Several British and American studies have indicated that most children who show academic and behavioral problems following their parents' divorce had the same difficulties prior to the divorce. Before-and-after studies of the effects of divorce on children suggest that the problems are not the result of the divorce itself, but could be predicted by the conditions that existed during the marriage. In other words, studies show that kids do fine if a parent can stay sane and provide a stable, noncombative postdivorce environment.[6]

Wallerstein's work may be the most frequently quoted study on children of divorce, but it obscures a fundamental truth: Children's responses vary widely. Some children do just fine, while others suffer deep psychological pain. They follow no set path.

The truth is that kids can thrive after divorce if their parents keep their welfare in the forefront of their minds. In this book I will take you through a step-by-step process that will help you prove for yourself that your family *can* make a healthy, constructive adjustment to your divorce and that your lives *will* be better.

HOW TO USE THIS BOOK

In my clinical practice as well as in my support groups the same issues are consistently raised: How do I let my kids know that they weren't the cause of the divorce? How can I relate to my ex in a constructive way when I'm still so angry? How can I help my child deal with his fears of abandonment and feelings of insecurity? How do I keep the children out of my own conflicts with my ex-spouse? What do I do when my child is upset? Why do I feel so guilty after all this time? And finally, Is there life after divorce?

This is the first generation in which divorce has been widespread. Divorcing parents are flying by the seats of their pants. They face a complex process, ending a marriage relationship while continuing a parenting relationship, and there are few signposts to mark their progress. This book provides a comprehensive map for you to follow. There may be parts of it that you're simply not ready to apply at this time. That's all right. In time you'll have the necessary emotional distance.

Not every technique or strategy I offer here is going to apply to your specific situation. There is no one right way to handle your divorce, but read this book with an open mind. Dare to imagine what your relationships with your former spouse and your children would be if you did implement my suggestions. Remember, there is no harm in trying something new. If one technique doesn't work for you, try the next. Allow yourself to experiment. Initially, you may have to "act as if" you and your ex are cooperative partners, but when you finally embrace that reality your effort will pay off a thousandfold.

Your children's ability to cope with your divorce depends on *your* ability to cope. The sooner you decide to heal and cooperate, the sooner your kids will begin to recover and go about the business of being children. But change doesn't happen overnight. There is a fine line between acceptance of where you are now and giving yourself a gentle nudge to move on to the next phase of your healing.

My own divorce was the most painful, difficult period of my life. But from the pain, confusion, and uncertainty came strength, clarity, and a motivation to change and grow. This can be true for you as well. You can use your divorce as a way to strengthen and transform yourself. In reading about the struggles and triumphs of the people in this book, you will be reassured that a functional, constructive divorce is possible, that there *are* new opportunities awaiting you, that you *can* raise healthy, responsible children, and that you are not alone in your struggle.

Chapter 1

Helping Your Kids Cope with Crazy Times

The world breaks everyone and afterwards many are stronger at the broken places.

Ernest Hemingway, A Farewell to Arms

Divorce is like an earthquake. It fractures and jars the foundation of your children's lives. Your family is all your kids have ever known. It is their only reality. Then, suddenly, their world is irrevocably changed. What they once took for granted, depended on, and trusted, now crumbles before their eyes.

Divorce affects children of every size, shape, and economic background. Some weather the storm and come out the other side well-adjusted, responsible, productive adults, while others remain scarred for life. What causes this difference? What determines how *your* children will adjust to your divorce? Research says that the age, sex, and natural resiliency of your child are significant factors. But equally important are three others: (1) how well you and your ex-spouse cope with the changes and stress, (2) how attentive you are to your children's needs while in the midst of your own grief, turmoil, and pain, and (3) how well your ex-spouse maintains a relationship with your kids.

There is no good time to get divorced, but there are good ways to help your kids cope with the stress. In this chapter you will learn how to talk to your children about your divorce, how children of different ages react differently, and what you can do to foster their sense of security.

The children who make the best adjustment after divorce are those who have a solid emotional foundation. They already feel loved, secure, and able to openly express their feelings. In a crisis you and your ex are the people they rely on to offer comfort and understanding. During this traumatic time your children need your reassurance and attention. The first step in helping your kids make a healthy adjustment is to talk with them about your decision to end your marriage.

TALKING WITH YOUR KIDS ABOUT DIVORCE

As startling as this statistic may be, 80 percent of parents do not discuss their divorce with their children.[1] The story of Rosalyn, 36, is a good example of the damage this can cause. Rosalyn had come to me for therapy because of low self-esteem. She had been married for eighteen years and she and her husband had two children. When her youngest was about to turn five, Rosalyn was suddenly flooded with memories from her own childhood.

Her parents had divorced when she was five but she hadn't remembered many details from that time. "I just remember my father packing his things and telling my older brother and me that we could visit him at his new apartment," she revealed during a therapy session. "I didn't know what was happening."

When her father left, Rosalyn's world fell apart. "One day we were living in a big house in Westchester and the next day we were moving into a small, dingy apartment in New York City," she said. "I lost my house, my friends, my yard, everything. I felt like I must have done something horrible for my father to leave. I kept thinking that if I had been a better girl my father wouldn't have left us."

Rosalyn's parents never told their children anything about their separation. "I only saw my mother cry once, but when I asked her what was wrong she wouldn't tell me," she remembered. After about a year and a half, Rosalyn and her brother figured out what had caused the breakup. "We spent a weekend at my dad's house and one morning at breakfast we noticed that he used salted butter. We knew that at my mother's house she used only unsalted butter." That afternoon, while she and her brother were sitting on the stoop outside their father's apartment, they discussed this earth-shattering revelation.

"We'd finally stumbled upon the reason for our parents' divorce," she said. "It finally made sense. You can't have two kinds of butter in the same house! My brother and I decided that that's why my parents split up and had to live in two separate houses. To this day I don't really know why they got divorced."

Rosalyn knows it sounds crazy, but she still feels the divorce was her fault. "I feel that if I had been a better little girl my father would have loved me more and he would have stayed," she told me. "I feel like I don't deserve to be loved." Many parents think that they are protecting their kids by not telling them what's happening. In reality, they are only protecting themselves from temporary discomfort. Children deserve to be told the truth, and Rosalyn's experience is unfortunately typical. After thirty-one years, she's still carrying the scars from her parents' divorce, in part because of their unwillingness to prepare her for their life-changing decisions.

I realize that you and your ex-spouse are struggling to cope with feelings of failure and shame about your past, as well as with fears and concerns about your future. You probably worry about how your children will react when you break the news. When parents in my support groups talk about this period, they inevitably report feeling frightened, vulnerable, and confused. Many parents admit to postponing "the talk" long past the point when they should have told their kids. They're reluctant to discuss divorce with their children for several reasons: They don't want to rehash the pain; they're afraid of their children's reactions; and they worry about losing emotional self-control.

Despite your natural reluctance, the question to be considered is not whether you should tell your kids, but how you should tell them. There is no way to avoid the pain your children will feel when you break the news, but the way you tell them can lessen that pain.

Before getting into the six steps for talking to kids about divorce, I'd like you to take a moment and put yourself in your children's shoes. Imagine that you're the age of one of your children and that your parents are getting divorced. What would you want to know? How would you like to be told? What do you need from your parents to help you cope with your pain, concerns, and fears? Once you put yourself in your children's place you will better understand how to talk to them and what kind of support they will need.

These are six steps for talking with your kids about your divorce.

1. If possible, tell your children with both parents present.
2. Present a clear, honest explanation.
3. Give your children time to digest the information.
4. Express your own feelings of regret and pain.
5. Keep communication open.
6. Prepare your children for what lies ahead.

Now let's look at each step in greater detail.

1. IF POSSIBLE, TELL YOUR CHILDREN WITH BOTH PARENTS PRESENT

Before you tell your kids about your decision to end your marriage, discuss with your spouse what you are going to say and how you will say it. This is one of the most serious conversations you will ever have with your children. What the two of you say and how you say it will leave a lasting impression.

There are several advantages to telling your children the news together. You let them know that your decision is mutual, mature, and rational, one that you both have considered carefully and to which you are committed. With both of you present, your children are less likely to feel abandoned or insecure. You convey the message that although one parent is leaving, that parent still will be available to hear and discuss their concerns. This paves the way for further contact and discussions.

When you tell your children together there is less impetus to assign blame. With both of you present, you're less likely to engage in mudslinging. A pitfall inherent in divorce is pressuring children to take sides. When both parents are involved in the initial discussion there is less chance for this to occur.

Life is far from ideal, and there will always be situations in which both parents simply cannot be present. These are examples where this is the case: A spouse has already left the family. He or she refuses to tell the children. He or she is unavailable because of a drug or alcohol problem or other illness. When a parent cannot or will not be present, children may interpret the absence as a lack of love and concern. If your family faces this situation, your children will need reassurance that they are still loved and that the decision to end your marriage had nothing to do with them. When children are truly abandoned by a parent they need extra support and reassurance from the parent who remains, as well as from other involved, concerned adults.

2. PRESENT A CLEAR, HONEST EXPLANATION

Your children deserve the truth. They are resilient and can cope with upsetting news, but when you withhold important information or are dishonest, you damage your children. Children who are lied to eventually discover the truth. Imagine a child who is told that her father took a job in another city, or children who are told that their mother has just gone to visit her sister. Soon enough they will begin to feel suspicious; they will wonder why Father doesn't call or visit or why Mother has been away for so long. In order to maintain these lies, parents have to fabricate more elaborate excuses. When children finally uncover the truth, they feel angry and betrayed, and their trust has been eroded.

This kind of deception only causes anxiety and confusion. Your children's sense of security depends on their trust in you. When that trust is betrayed, your relationship is in jeopardy. And your kids can't afford to be burdened with this additional anxiety.

Your Life Doesn't Have to Be an Open Book

Being truthful doesn't mean giving your kids the gory, intimate details of your personal life, but they do need to understand why you are getting a divorce so they don't blame themselves. For example, if a wife is leaving the marriage because she is having an affair with another man, the father can tell his children in very simple terms, "When your mother and I first married we loved each other very much. But we don't love each other anymore. Your mother loves someone else and wants to spend more of her time with him." If alcoholism or drug abuse is a contributing factor in the decision to separate, you can give your children a simple, honest explanation. "Your father has a problem with alcohol. It is an illness that he can't control, and I have decided to get a divorce because it is to hard to live with him while he has this problem." Most children know what's going on. They either have overheard conversations between you and your spouse, or have heard you talking with a friend, or have experienced the stress of your problems firsthand. Your honesty is an essential part of helping them to cope with the changes in their lives.

Children will sometimes ask questions that you don't feel comfortable answering or that may not be appropriate for discussion. (This is generally true of older children or those who are unusually more sophisticated.) When this happens, remember that you have every right to maintain your privacy. Your life doesn't have to be an open book. You need not, and in fact *should* not, reveal everything. You can always respond by saying, "There are some things that we consider private and not appropriate to discuss with you. As you get older you will have more and more things of your own that you want to keep private. And when that is the case we will respect your privacy as well. We still want you to feel free to ask us any questions you may have and we'll answer as many of them as we can."

Depending upon your situation and the ages of your children, you will modify your talk with them. Ideally, your goal is to present yourself as two mature adults who have come to a very difficult decision and are working at making the transition as tolerable as possible. By presenting your decision in this light you let your kids know that you are committed to their well-being despite your separation. Yes, the truth can be painful, but with the truth your children will have a better chance to start the healing process.

All Together Now

I also recommend that you have your initial discussion with all your kids present. When I suggest this idea in my seminars and support groups a parent will inevitably ask, "What if my children are dramatically different ages?" In this case, you can give separate explanations to each of them while they're together. Or you can talk in more depth with each child at a later time. The reasons I recommend that you tell your children together are twofold. First, when children are told separately they are often suspicious that information is being withheld and this creates an aura of secrecy and mistrust between them. When they compare notes the information is frequently miscommunicated, leading to greater confusion and misunderstanding. And second, when children are told together they experience a sense of comfort and closeness by being with their brothers and sisters. This feeling of closeness is even more important now that their parents are getting a divorce.

There is no magic formula or perfect script for telling your children about your decision to divorce, but this is an example of how one couple handled this very difficult situation. Todd had come to me for counseling on another issue, but during a session he described with great appreciation how his parents had told him about their divorce. "I was twelve at the time," he said as tears welled up, "and my sister Julie had turned eight a few weeks earlier. I knew something was wrong when I walked into the den and saw that my mother had been crying. My parents sat us down on the couch next to them. My dad started by saying that we needed to have a serious family talk. He said that when he and my mother first got married they were very much in love, but that they had been unhappy for some time now. He said, 'You've heard us arguing and we've finally realized that we just aren't happy with one another anymore.'

"My mother broke in and said that they had gone to a counselor and tried to work things out, but that it just wasn't working. She cried and said, 'Your father and I have decided to get a divorce. It's a very difficult decision, but we think that it's the best thing for all of us.' At first I was too shocked to say anything. I had friends whose parents were divorced, but I never dreamed that it would happen to my family.

"My father continued, 'We both want you to know that even though your mother and I have stopped loving one another we still love you both very much. We want you to know that you are the best gifts we've gained from our marriage and that we will both take care of you.' I remember Julie crying and my mother comforting her. I think I was too shocked to react. My dad said that he was going to move into an apartment near our house and that as soon as he got moved in we could come and see where he would be living. I felt sad and confused, but I knew we would be all right."

Todd's parents handled the discussion well. They broke the news together in a clear, supportive way. They reassured their children of their love and let them know how sad they felt. They were also definite that the decision had been made so the children wouldn't hope to change their parents' minds. Todd's parents told their children what to expect while they reaffirmed their commitment to them. Todd and Julie were saddened, but they also understood that they were safe. Your children need the same kind of reassurance. They need to know that their family has not been destroyed, but is being restructured.

When you break the news it's important to allow plenty of time not only for talking, but also for feelings, questions, comforting, and reassurance. It is essential that you make clear, especially to young children who are still very egocentric, that your decision to separate has nothing to do with them. You may need to stress this point several times during your initial conversation and again in the future.

3. GIVE YOUR CHILDREN TIME TO DIGEST THE INFORMATION

One of the most frequently asked questions is: When should we tell our children that we are getting divorced? There is no rule about timing, but I have a few guidelines. Children do best when they have some time to wrestle with their feelings while both parents are still present in the home. This gives them an opportunity to talk over their concerns with both of you. On the other hand, if there is too much time between breaking the news and a parent moving out, children may retreat into denial, pretending that nothing will ever change.

Giving kids short notice has both advantages and disadvantages. By telling them just before a parent leaves, the difficult waiting period is reduced, but they won't have as much time to express their reactions and feelings. Many parents chose to tell their children on the day of departure, primarily to avoid witnessing their children's pain. This is not in your children's best interest.

A good time frame is a few days to a week. This gives kids enough time to process their feelings with both parents' support, but not so long that they can ignore the painful reality.

Children need time to digest the information, ask questions, and begin to adjust to the change in lifestyle, *but only after you have come to a decision.* Don't talk with your children until you and your spouse are committed to a divorce. Most couples go through several rounds of deciding to separate and then trying to salvage their marriage. This is a natural process, but your children should be spared as much confusion and anxiety as possible while you wrestle with this important decision.

4. EXPRESS YOUR OWN FEELINGS OF REGRET AND PAIN

Many parents are afraid to express their feelings in front of their children. Take the case of Maureen and Brad. Several months ago they came to me for marriage counseling. Brad is a successful internist and Maureen has a career as a radiologist. They have two daughters. Brad had announced that he wanted a divorce. Maureen pleaded with him to see a marriage counselor. During the course of therapy, Brad confessed that for the past six months he had been having an affair with a nurse in his office. After much discussion, Maureen decided that she couldn't tolerate living with Brad while he was seeing another woman. She decided that she too wanted to end their marriage. But when we discussed how to break the news to their kids, Maureen panicked. "I don't think I can tell them," she said. "I know I'm going to cry. Seeing me fall apart will just make it worse for them." She turned to her husband. "Brad, you better tell them," she said. "You're much more rational." I explained to Maureen that talking about the decision to divorce is very much like talking about a death of a loved one. You wouldn't expect someone who is grieving to maintain a distant unemotional façade. Why should it be any different when you talk to your children about the death of your marriage? Hiding your emotions actually makes your children's adjustment *more difficult.* They get the mistaken message that feelings are wrong and should be disguised if they can't be avoided.

I can't emphasize enough how helpful it is for you to express your feelings in front of your children. This is one way to give your kids permission to mourn the loss of their family as they have known it. If you withhold your emotions, your children will probably repress theirs. This can lead to a number of psychological problems such as headaches, stomachaches, depression, and acting-out behavior.

Let me be clear, I am not advocating that you talk with your children while you are overwhelmed with intense feelings. I am not suggesting that you break down and sob uncontrollably. Wait until you have had some time to process your decision and feel more in control of your emotions. Nevertheless, it is normal and natural to feel sad and remorseful, and I recommend that you share these feelings with your children.

5. KEEP COMMUNICATION OPEN

Your children will be overwhelmed by the news of your divorce and the changes that will ensue. They won't be able to understand or absorb all that you have told them at one time. Fully grasping the impact that your divorce will have on their lives will take time. It is important that you be open to your children's questions as they struggle to digest and cope with the news. Your children need to feel that you are interested and available and that their questions are welcome. When you answer them honestly and patiently, they will gain a sense of safety, trust, and security which is essential during this chaotic period.

Your children, especially if they are very young, probably will ask the same questions over and over again trying to make sense of all the changes. During this time patience is in great demand, but in short supply. This will make you crazy, but remember that you have the power of choice and your children have none. Your divorce is tough on you, but it's even tougher on your kids. When your children repeat their questions, they do it less to get information than to engage you to get reassurance. Your kids are trying to make sense of the separation. If you can tolerate their questioning they will be better able to work through their feelings and refocus on school, their friends, and their own activities.

6. PREPARE YOUR CHILDREN FOR WHAT LIES AHEAD

Your kids need to understand what divorce means and what will happen to them. Of course, your explanation to a preschooler will be different from what you tell a teenager. But all children have the same basic questions. Children worry about what will happen to them. They want to know things like "Where will we live?" "Will I still get to see my dad or mom?" "Do you still love me?" "Will I be taken care of?" "Where is my dad going to live when he leaves our house?" "Do I have to change schools?" Give your children concrete information. If you know where the noncustodial parent is going to live, tell your kids in specific terms. "Dad is going to live in an apartment at 465 Bestor Street. He will have a room there for you so you can go and spend time with him at his new house." As soon as possible take your children to see where their other parent will be living. Knowing where that parent is lessens their anxiety, fear of abandonment, and feelings of insecurity. If you don't know specific details, give them as much information as possible. The unknown is frightening and the more information you can give, the more secure they will feel.

Admit honestly that things will change. And let your kids know that they will be told about any major changes that affect them. But keep in mind that your children can absorb and process only so much information. If their father has just moved out of the house and into an apartment and you are considering moving into a less expensive neighborhood, give your kids the information one piece at a time. Don't overwhelm them by telling them too much. How much you tell your children depends on their age and your knowledge of what they are capable of handling.

Talking to your children about divorce is an ongoing process. Your providing a safe space for honest, open communication helps your children navigate the rough seas created by the breakup of your marriage.

THE EFFECT OF AGE

Your children will react to the breakup of your family according to their age and stage of development. By understanding what to expect you will be better prepared to help each of your kids cope with the changes in their lives. This guide will help you understand how children of various ages react to divorce.

Preschool

Preschoolers are aware of their total dependence on their parents for their physical care and protection. They often become absorbed by fears of rejection and abandonment. Children this age won't understand completely the cause of the divorce or the implications for their own lives, but they will still feel the loss of their noncustodial parent.

What to Expect

They often exhibit separation anxiety. They may become clingy and have difficulty separating from you at school. They don't want to let you out of their sight.

They frequently regress to behavior they had previously moved beyond. They may return to thumb-sucking, the need for a security blanket or special stuffed animal, loss of bladder and bowel control, or the desire to have a bottle.

They may become angry and aggressive and hit other children or siblings. They may have more frequent temper tantrums and/or become more possessive of their belongings in an effort to regain a sense of control.

They may cry more often and have sleep problems.

Elementary School Age: Six to Eight

Early elementary school age children are frequently preoccupied with feelings of sadness, loss, rejection, and guilt. They are deeply concerned that they will lose their departed parent. One of the greatest fears these children have is of being replaced. "Will my daddy have a new little girl?" "Is my mommy getting a new daddy?" Children this age rely on their parents for stability; after divorce they tend to feel insecure and fearful. They are too old to escape into fantasy, and they are too young to understand fully that they aren't responsible for the divorce.

What to Expect

They may cry easily, act cranky, and be anxious.

They may be distracted and have difficulty concentrating. Their school performance may suffer.

They may get stress-related headaches or stomachaches.

They often take out their anger on the custodial parent who is a safer, more convenient target.

They have strong hopes of their parents' reconciliation and may actively seek to reunite you with your ex-spouse (sometimes by having problems that force parental involvement).

They may assume the role of the absent parent to support and comfort the custodial parent.

Preteens: Nine to Twelve

Children this age are prone to depression. They are in the midst of a major transition. They tend to feel alone and frightened, but because they are easily embarrassed they pretend to act cool and unaffected. Kids this age have a strong sense of loyalty and tend to side with the parent who they feel was "wronged." They are struggling to define their identity and may feel threatened by the possibility of losing their friends or changing schools. Theirs is the age of self-consciousness. They are afraid of standing out among their friends because of the divorce. Preteens may get angry at their parents for divorcing and be especially angry with the person who initiated the breakup.

What to Expect

They may get stress-related stomachaches, headaches, or nervous tics and may bite their nails.

They may take sides, choosing one parent over the other.

They may have a strong reaction to your divorce but are better able to hide their feelings

They may feel and/or express intense anger.

They may suffer from sadness, loneliness, insecurity, and feelings of helplessness.

They may worry about the "wronged" parent and jump in to rescue her or him by assuming an adult role.

They may engage in stealing, lying, or refusing to go to school.

Their friendships may suffer. There often is a drop in school performance.

They may become prematurely involved with dating and early sexual behavior.

Adolescents

Divorce can be especially disturbing to adolescents because they rely on their parents and family to provide structure and guidelines and to set limits on their sexual impulses. Teens are in the process of separating from their family and establishing a greater sense of independence. Divorce can interfere with the separation process. Several things can happen when divorce occurs during adolescence. Young adults can easily be pulled back into their families to assume a supportive, adult role. If there is a lot of stress at home they may escape by spending less time at home, using drugs or alcohol, or dropping out of school. And they may separate too fast by rejecting discipline, responsibility, and guidance.

Teens tends to be judgmental, taking the side of the parent they see as the victim. Their parents' breakup makes them worry about their own future and ability to establish and maintain a romantic relationship. Teens may also be anxious and disturbed by their parents' vulnerability. They are often upset by their parents' dating or overt sexuality because they are struggling to deal with their own emerging sexuality. Adolescents often feel abandoned and rejected by parents who are preoccupied with their own problems and adjustment. And they are resentful of their parents' lack of time and attention.

Teenagers are better able to understand divorce than are younger children, but they still experience pain, turmoil, and embarrassment.

What to Expect

They may become less communicative and withdraw temporarily to deal with their feelings.

They may become angry and rebellious.

They may become sexually active prematurely.

They may become involved with drugs and alcohol as a means of escape.

Their school performance may suffer.

They may become immersed in family life and assume a more responsible adult role.

While not all children react in the ways I have described, these are some of the common reactions children at these various ages have to divorce. If you would like more information on the effect divorce has on children of different ages, consult the Suggested Reading List at the back of the book for a list of resources.

FOSTERING A SENSE OF SECURITY

Now that you are aware of some of the reactions your kids may have, let's look at what you can do to help them make a healthy adjustment. While your divorce will add incredible complexity to your children's lives and cannot help but have a profound effect on them, several factors will ease their fears and foster a sense of safety and security. Of the utmost importance is *your* emotional stability and your capacity to maintain order in the midst of change. Your ability to establish a new family structure and provide a stable home environment will determine, to a large extent, whether the effects of your divorce will be short-lived or long-lasting.

Research shows us that divorce typically brings a diminished parental capacity in almost all areas, including discipline, emotional support, physical care, even in just having fun with their children. Newly divorced parents spend less time with their children and are less sensitive to their needs.[2] Many divorced parents are absorbed with financial concerns, their own emotional trauma, or a new love interest, leaving little time or energy for their children and *their* pressing needs.

Your kids desperately need your patience, understanding, and reassurance, and providing these while you're in the midst of your own emotional turmoil can be challenging. Take the case of Laura, 37, and her six-year-old daughter, Nicole. Laura was still riding the emotional roller coaster that is typical of the period following divorce. She needed time by herself to plan her new life, and she welcomed Nicole's entrance into school. But when Nicole started kindergarten she became insecure, clinging to her mother instead of going into her classroom. She would cry at breakfast and sob on the way to school, saying that she didn't want to go, that she just wanted to stay home with Mommy. Laura was feeling emotionally drained and short on patience, but she mustered up the strength to console and reassure Nicole.

After a week of Nicole's crying, Laura consulted the teacher for advice. With the teacher's guidance and support she was able to ease Nicole through this difficult adjustment. Nicole benefited from her mother's constancy and understanding and Laura emerged from the situation with increased self-esteem and a greater appreciation of her capability and strength. When we can rise to the occasion and put our own concerns aside, we discover new strength, coping abilities, and a depth of love we never knew existed. Focusing your attention on your children can help you through these difficult times. Laura established a special bond with Nicole that continues to blossom and develop. Helping Nicole through her rough times also nurtured Laura's own healing process.

Your kids need to know that they can count on you. You can best demonstrate your love and concern for your children by providing a stable, predictable home environment. Let's look at nine keys to raising healthy, secure children.

1. Encourage your children to express their feelings.
2. Discipline with love.
3. Create new family traditions.
4. Allow your children to love both parents.
5. Make time to be alone together.
6. Be generous with physical contact.
7. Foster outside relationships.
8. Give your kids the gift of self-reliance.
9. Keep in mind what is normal.

Now let's look at each key in more detail.

1. ENCOURAGE YOUR CHILDREN TO EXPRESS THEIR FEELINGS

When we are overwhelmed with our own emotions, we may deny those of our children. We may say things like "Cheer up. Don't cry. Everything's going to be just fine." Or "There's nothing to be so upset about. Be brave. Now, let me see a big smile." I know it's difficult to see your children struggling, especially when you feel guilty about having caused their distress. But ignoring their emotions or trying to talk them out of their feelings is only going to make them feel worse.

Children will often repress their feelings to avoid adding to their parents' distress. Their unconscious rationale is that they don't want to make things worse, but feelings that are repressed get bottled up inside and come out later either as headaches, stomachaches, or acting-out behavior.

What your children need during this traumatic time is a supportive, receptive listener, someone who can act as a sounding board and reflect back their feelings. When children are upset they need a safe place to vent their emotions. When you accept your children's feelings, you let them know that you understand them and that they are not alone in their pain and struggle. This kind of comfort and reassurance is crucial.

Take the case of Lauren, divorced for eight months and a participant in my parenting seminars. Her eight-year-old daughter, Jenny, was accustomed to seeing her father every other weekend. But he had recently moved to another city to take advantage of a new job opportunity. At first Jenny didn't seem bothered by her father's absence, but then Lauren noticed that Jenny was moping around the house. She wasn't playing with her friends and she seemed to cry over insignificant things. One evening Lauren walked into her daughter's room and found Jenny with her face buried in her pillow. Lauren sat down next to her. "Jenny," she asked, "what's the matter?"

J: Nothing. I'm just resting.

L: You seem really sad.

J: (With that, Jenny burst into tears) I miss my daddy. I don't get to see him anymore.

L: (Putting her arms around Jenny) I know it must be hard for you now that your father has moved away. I bet you really miss spending time with him.

J: I do. It was bad enough only seeing him on the weekends, but now I won't see him at all.

L: I know that this is a big change for you and you won't be able to see your father as often, but he loves you very much and you will get to see him soon.

J: When? He lives so far away now.

L: During summer vacation he wants you to come and spend part of your vacation with him. That's only eight weeks away. I know it's not the same as having your dad here and seeing him on the weekends. But what could we do to help you feel closer to him?

J: Eight weeks is a long time.

L: I know it is. Would you like to call and talk to him? I know it isn't the same as seeing him, but at least you can talk to him and tell him how much you miss him.

By identifying Jenny's feelings and reflecting them back to her, Lauren acted as a sounding board. Listening to your children when you have your hands full with your own problems is difficult.

An easy way to alleviate our own pain and guilt is to try to make things better for our kids either by denying their feelings or by immediately coming up with solutions. Better than trying to fix things is finding one word that identifies their feelings. Lauren, for example, realized that Jenny felt sad.

Feelings fall into four main categories: sad, mad, glad, and scared. Practice identifying your children's feelings by thinking of a word that describes the underlying emotion. For example, if your child runs into the kitchen and yells, "I hate Johnnie!" the underlying feeling is anger. If your daughter says, "My dad didn't send me a birthday card," she may be feeling disappointed and sad. By your identifying these feelings your children will feel relieved and be better able to cope with their problems.

Some children, especially those who are very young, find that talking about their feelings is too difficult. In this case, ask your child to draw a picture of your family now that you are divorced. Once he has finished ask him to talk about what he drew. Another valuable tool is play with puppets or action figures. These techniques allow your child to talk about his or her feelings in a less personal, indirect way.

How to Help an Angry Child

"My insecurity about being a good mother is worse since the divorce," Janet confessed during a support group meeting. "I'm dealing with the fact that my son is hurting. Even though I know intellectually that it's better for my husband and me to be apart, it's unbearable to see my child in pain. I know this is completely insane, but when he is upset I get angry at him. He reminds me of my choice to leave his father and the pain I have caused him. I know I'm hurting him more and I do it anyway."

It's difficult to deal with an angry child in the best of times, but when you're stressed-out and guilt-ridden it's even harder. Like Janet, many parents react to their children's anger with an angry response of their own. Not only is this counterproductive, it makes your children fear you will stop loving them. I am not suggesting that you allow your children to mistreat or abuse you, but I am recommending that you interpret your children's anger. Part of coping with an angry child is not to take his or her anger personally. For example, a child may yell "I hate you." Rather than taking this literally and reacting out of hurt, recognize what she is really saying is "I don't like what you did." Your acknowledgment of her anger will allow her to express the hurt and fear that is underneath. In this way you can continue to set appropriate limits for your children without undermining their sense of security.

Another approach to coping with an angry child is to redirect and refocus his anger. Physical activity is a wonderful outlet for feelings of rage. Your child's strong emotions shouldn't be repressed, but they must be channeled. Encourage your child to go for a run, pound on pillows, throw balls at the garage wall, stamp his feet, or tear up newspaper. These physical outlets will allow him to release pent-up emotions and redirect his anger in an acceptable way.

Our instinct is to rescue our kids from their distress and pain, in part to alleviate our own. But children whose emotions are denied feel discounted and misunderstood. One of the most loving and supportive things you can do for your children is to take the time to listen. When you do, give them the message "I care about you. You're important to me and I'm here to help."

2. DISCIPLINE WITH LOVE

Discipline is difficult for most parents, and during and after divorce the enforcement of house rules can be overwhelming. Both you and your children are in emotional turmoil, one minute up, the next minute down. Your children are probably more demanding, defiant, and irritable than ever before.

You and your ex-spouse probably had different styles of discipline while you were married. Usually one parent is stricter than the other. This may have caused some conflict, but at least you could call in your ex as a reserve when you were feeling overwhelmed or ineffective. Now you have to lay down the law and enforce it all by yourself. Finding the strength and conviction to be an effective disciplinarian is difficult when you're struggling with your own unmet needs and irritability.

Loving discipline is basic to creating a sense of safety and security. I realize that it's difficult to hold the line while you are under stress. But giving in to your children's demands, pleading, or manipulation only adds to their insecurity. What your children need most after a divorce is a parent who isn't afraid to be the boss, someone who is willing to set and maintain clearly defined limits.

A word of caution: All children misbehave even in the best of circumstances. When children's emotions are out of control and they're flooded with strong feelings, they'll have a more difficult time controlling their behavior. I think it is reasonable to expect and tolerate a certain amount of misbehavior during the period immediately following your divorce. (But not to the point where your values or limits are ignored or compromised. There is a fine line between tolerance and giving up out of exhaustion or guilt.)

When your children misbehave, they are saying subconsciously, "I'm frightened and I want to be loved and reassured. I'm upset and I don't know how to deal with my feelings. I want to belong and feel secure and I don't know a better way to get your attention." When your kids misbehave they are telling you that they don't feel valued or connected to you. Ask yourself what need is going unmet and how you can help them to get this need met in a more positive way. Remember, every action your children take is their best effort at getting their needs met. Here are five keys for implementing a method of effective, loving discipline.

1. Separate the deed from the doer.
2. Establish and maintain clearly defined limits and routines.
3. Be consistent.
4. Allow your children to live with the consequences of their actions.
5. Practice forgiveness.

Let me explain.

1. *Separate the deed from the doer.* When children misbehave, which they inevitably will, it is important not to criticize, ridicule, or belittle them. This is true for all children, but after your divorce your children are especially vulnerable, sensitive, and fragile. Their self-esteem needs to be strengthened, not undermined.

   I know you must be wondering how to correct misbehavior without criticizing. When you need to correct your children's behavior, focus on the behavior rather than on the child. In other words, separate the child from the behavior. For example, rather than saying "You're a real loser," you could say "I am furious that you left your homework to the last minute. From now on I want you to make your schoolwork a priority." Instead of saying "You're irresponsible just like your father," you could say "I hate it when you tell me you're going to meet me in front of the school and you don't show up." By focusing on your children's behavior you can make strong statements without undermining your relationship or damaging their self-esteem. When you do this, the message you give your child is "I love you, but I don't like what you did." You can focus on your children's misbehavior without attacking them personally, which is crucial in helping them to feel secure and connected.
2. *Establish and maintain clearly defined limits and routines.* Regardless of what form of discipline existed before your divorce, it is essential to define what you expect of your children

now that you are the only adult in the home. If you disciplined your children effectively before your divorce, the precedent will have been set and your job will be a lot easier. Still, your kids are bound to test you, your limits, and your rules. Sit down with them and discuss what you expect and what the daily routine will be. This emphasizes two things: (1) that you are still in charge and will continue to maintain order and control, and (2) that although your family has changed dramatically, your expectations and rules remain the same. Despite any protests you may hear, your children will be reassured by your authority and stability.

Children thrive on predictability. They are creatures of habit and divorce disrupts their much loved routines. Many recently divorced parents have to reinvent the wheel every day because they don't establish routines for dressing, getting ready for school, mealtimes, and bedtime. Once you establish a pattern and rules you won't have to deal with repeated crises. For example, in many families bedtime is a never-ending, bitter battle. When the nightly power struggle ensues, you get angry and the family ends the day on a sour, angry note. This is especially harmful to your kids; they need to feel connected and loved in order to have a restful night's sleep.

Instead of battling your way through bedtime every night, why not establish a pleasant bedtime ritual? Sound good? First you let your children know ahead of time what you have in mind and involve them in your strategy. "I'm tired of nagging, yelling, and screaming when it comes time for you to go to bed," you might say. "I bet you're tired of hearing me yell. From now on this is what I expect. Bedtime will be at eight. We're going to start getting ready at seven-forty. First you're to go up and get your pj's on, then go into the bathroom and wash your face, brush your teeth, and go to the toilet. Once you've finished, I'll read you each a story. If you dawdle, argue, or fight there won't be any bedtime story that night. I am only going to ask you twice to get ready. If you don't cooperate with these rules, you'll lose your bedtime story." Once you establish routines and set up consequences, your children will gradually stop testing your limits. This will make it easier for all of you.

A word of warning: Things usually get worse before they get better. When you first implement new rules your children may not take you seriously. They may challenge you to see how serious you are. If you stick to your guns they will take you seriously. It's a matter of establishing credibility. As a rule, you are better off if you talk less and act more!

3. *Be consistent.* Don't get me wrong, no one is asking you to be 100 percent consistent; that's not humanly possible. But all too often newly divorced parents let their emotions dictate how and when they discipline their children.

Martha, one of my clients, fell into the trap of being a wishy-washy parent. One of her house rules was that her eleven-year-old son, Josh, could watch a half hour of TV each day. When his half hour was up, she would ask him to turn off the TV. Josh would plead, "Mom, can't I watch just one more show?" Her initial response would be no, but he would persist, as will any strong-willed child, "Mom, please. Can't I just watch *3-2-1 Contact*? I finished all my homework." Martha would feel herself weaken but would still say no, this time with less conviction. Josh would sense her ambivalence and persist, knowing that victory was only moments away. "But, Mom, it's a really good show. Can't I watch it? Just today. I won't ask you again." At that point she was so frazzled and worn down that she would shout, "Okay! Go watch your damn show; just leave me alone." Josh would learn several things from Martha's reaction. First, that if he asked long enough and pushed hard enough he could wear her down and she would change her mind. Second, that she didn't mean what she said. And third, that he could get his desires met through manipulation. She didn't want to convey any of these messages, but her actions were clear.

Martha's discipline also fluctuated based on her moods. One day she was firm and the next day she acted as if rules didn't exist. When you enforce a rule one day and then, based on your mood or physical stamina, change it the next, you confuse your kids. Don't make any rule you're not prepared to enforce. When you consistently set limits and back up words with actions, your children will benefit. Only you can provide predictability and stability. I have never met a child who will thank you when you tell her to turn off the TV or when you remind him to do his homework, but in the long run your children benefit immeasurably from your commitment to providing a family structure.

As If It Weren't Hard Enough!

Discipline can be compromised when children go back and forth between two homes with two different sets of rules and expectations (or, in some cases, the lack thereof). If your children travel back and forth between your home and their other parent's, you can expect some confusion and attempt at manipulation when they return. This is the time you have to reaffirm your house rules. Remind your children that while they may not have chores at their other parent's house, they do have responsibilities when they are with you. This can be difficult, but your children are counting on you to set and maintain order.

4. *Allow your children to live with the consequences of their actions.* One effective way to help your children learn to cooperate with your house rules is to use consequences. This technique teaches your children about cause-and-effect thinking, and it helps you avoid power struggles.

   Let me give you an example. Eleven-year-old Nathan lives with his mother, Jessica, who has been divorced for a year. One of his friends from Boy Scouts invited Nathan to go with him and his dad to the car races on a Saturday. They planned to leave on Saturday, spend the evening at the racetrack, and come home the following afternoon. Nathan came charging into the house after his Boy Scout meeting and asked his mother for permission to go. "It sounds like a wonderful weekend," Jessica agreed. "I'm happy for you to go, with one condition. You have a social studies report due on Monday. Since you're going to be away all weekend, you have to finish it before you leave on Saturday afternoon. If the report is done you can go. If not, no trip!" "Okay, Mom, no problem," Nathan shouted as he ran to call his friend and tell him he could go.

Jessica mentioned the report to Nathan once more during the week and he told her to stop bugging him. Jessica took her son at his word and didn't mention his project until Friday evening when the other boy's father called to confirm their plans. When Jessica checked with Nathan he said his report hadn't been completed. She told the father that unless Nathan finished his report he wouldn't be able to go. Nathan was furious and started to scream and cry. "That's not fair. I never get to do special things. You're mean. You don't want me to have any fun." Jessica reminded Nathan of their agreement. Whether or not he went was totally up to him. Nathan stormed into his room and thrashed around for a while, slamming down books and pounding the walls until he realized that no amount of fussing was going to change his mother's mind. "Mom," he said, "what if I work on my report until nine and then finish it in the morning. Could I go then?" Jessica agreed that as long as he finished his report and it was done properly he would be able to go. Nathan got busy writing his report and Jessica hadn't had to scream or threaten. Nathan realized that his mother meant what she said. He had to cooperate with the rules or live with the consequences of his decisions.

The consequences you impose for your children should be (1) reasonable, (2) related to the behavior so that your children can avoid them the next time, and (3) carried out matter-of-factly, in a way that respects your children's dignity.

5. *Practice forgiveness.* As I have mentioned, children are especially vulnerable during and after divorce. They are also particularly susceptible to feelings of rejection and disapproval. Make clear to your children that no matter what they do, you will continue to love and care for them. Sometimes we get so caught up in our children's misbehavior that we forget that they are far more important than anything they could ever do. Unconditional love is at the foundation of effective discipline.

Once the misbehavior is done and the consequence carried

out, let it go and affirm your love for your children. After you have disciplined your child put your arms around him, give him a big hug, and tell him that you love him. No matter what he's done, that hug of reassurance tells your child, "While I don't like your behavior, I still love you." All kids need to be reminded of a parent's love, but your children need some extra TLC during this period of adjustment.

Effective discipline equals dedication and commitment. The message you give your children when you discipline with love is "I care too much about you to let you misbehave. I care enough about you that I'm willing to spend the time and effort to help you learn what is appropriate." All children need the security and stability of food, shelter, love, and protection, but unless they also receive effective and appropriate discipline, they won't feel secure. This is especially true of children living with divorce.

3. CREATE NEW FAMILY TRADITIONS

Children's basic need is to belong. A sense of belonging enhances their emotional and psychological health. One way to foster this sense of belonging is to establish family traditions. When parents divorce, family traditions often change. This gives you a chance to examine what's important to you and to create new family traditions that will provide your kids with a sense of continuity.

One of the holiday traditions that my ex-husband and I had established was cutting down our own Christmas tree. But after we divorced I wanted to establish a new tradition, one that validated my new family form. My daughter, Ama, was seven at the time and we were living in a cozy adobe house in Santa Fe, New Mexico. Shortly before Christmas, we discussed the idea of creating a new holiday tradition. We decided that rather than cut down a tree we would buy a live Christmas tree and watch it grow from year to year. The next afternoon we went to our local nursery and bought a small Norfolk pine tree in a brightly decorated clay pot. Then each Christmas after that we would bring it into the living room, measure its growth, then decorate it with our assortment of memory-laden ornaments.

When we moved to California we brought our tree with us. Since December was too warm there to keep our tree in the house, we planted it in our backyard—nine years later the tree is fourteen feet tall. We still had to continue our tradition, so again we bought a living tree, a beautiful three-foot fir in a forty-five-gallon pot, which lives on our brick patio until Christmas. Then Ama and I go through the drudgery of dragging the tree from the patio into our living room. We unearth Ama's ancient skateboard, which has rarely been used for its proper purpose, and wrestle the tree onto it. With great care and a lot of laughter, we slowly roll the tree around to the front of our house. Thoroughly enjoying the comic aspect of our awkwardness, we heft the tree up the front steps and into our living room. Friends always offer to help us get this heavy, prickly, cumbersome object into the house, but the fun and hilarity of hauling it by ourselves is an essential part of our Christmas ritual.

Traditions don't need to be elaborate. They can be as simple as having a special waffle breakfast together on Sunday mornings, playing softball with other families in your single parent's support group, or reading a special story every Thanksgiving. Be creative and think of some new traditions for your family.

4. ALLOW YOUR CHILDREN TO LOVE BOTH PARENTS

Children need permission to love both their parents. During the initial phase of divorce emotions run hot. You may be furious with your ex-spouse, but your kids need to know that they can have a separate relationship with their other parent. You must learn to respect your children's thoughts and feelings toward their other parent. You must never ask them to take sides. Children shouldn't have to choose one parent over the other. Make it safe for your children to love both of you.

Throughout this book I will continue to stress this point. All the research confirms that children who have the active involvement of both parents make a healthier adjustment after divorce. Believe me, I realize that it can be tempting to criticize your ex-spouse in front of your kids, especially in a moment of utter frustration. But your children will suffer every time you bad-mouth their other parent. Kids pick up on subtle signals about what you want from them. Their survival depends on you and they will often do and say what they think you want in order to maintain the relationship or to protect you.

Children who believe that to love one parent requires that they betray the other are trapped in a no-win situation. You may feel bad when you see your children's love for their other parent, but it is crucial that they maintain a separate, independent relationship with each of you. Your kids need to know that there is plenty of love to go around and that they don't have to sacrifice an important relationship in order to be cared for. Children who can freely love both parents will remain focused on their own lives, interests, and developmental tasks. They can go about the business of being kids. Isn't this what you want for your children?

5. MAKE TIME TO BE ALONE TOGETHER

This concept is important to all children, but it is especially critical to children who have just experienced a divorce. I frequently suggest to parents that they make time to be with each of their children alone on a regular basis. I realize that for single parents time is a precious commodity. Your demanding schedule may feel so overwhelming that you can't squeeze in one more thing. But spending focused time with your children can foster a sense of security that prevents behavioral and psychological problems. I am not suggesting that you enroll in the Martyr School of Parenting and sacrifice yourself or your career. But you can carve out some time every day to connect with each of your children. When spending focused time with your children, take care to avoid interruptions: Turn on the answering machine; put a DO NOT DISTURB sign on your door. Your time together can be spent playing games, reading, talking about their day and any successes or disappointments they had, discussing what you each did while you were apart, baking cookies, or working on a model. When you give your children this kind of attention, they can say to themselves, "I must be important to my mom or dad for them to spend this time just with me." By spending time alone with each of your kids you strengthen the bond between you and foster a sense of love, caring, and empathy. If you are the custodial parent, carve out some time every day to connect with each of your kids. If you're a noncustodial parent make time every day that your kids are with you.

6. BE GENEROUS WITH PHYSICAL CONTACT

Telling your children that you love them is important, but your loving touch is an even more fundamental way to communicate. Children often feel lonely and disconnected after a divorce. A simple pat on the back, a squeeze, or a cuddle is a wonderful way to convey your love to your children. As I have said, children of divorce often begin to doubt their "love-ability." There is no greater reassurance than to be lovingly held or touched.

Children are never too old for a hug, but their comfort with physical contact may vary based on their temperament and age. If your children haven't been used to a lot of physical contact in the past, they may find this new form of communication awkward. But you can always give your child a high-five (hand slapping), stroke her face, or gently touch her hand when you put her cereal in front of her.

You have a wonderful opportunity, literally at your fingertips, to promote your kids' sense of emotional security. The message you convey through loving physical contact is "I'm glad you're here." Your children need and deserve this tangible reassurance.

7. FOSTER OUTSIDE RELATIONSHIPS

In the Maori culture of New Zealand, the idea of family, the *whanau,* includes the extended family. Children do not belong to individual parents but rather to the *hapu,* or tribe. All the adults in that *whanau* are responsible for the children, their upbringing, and their care.[3] The child is seen as a cultural treasure. Uncles, aunts, grandparents, all help to support the child financially and/or emotionally. Maori children are not cut off from half of their heritage when their mothers and fathers separate; the *whanau* remains responsible for their care.

In our culture, this is seldom the case. When parents divorce, children often lose half of their families and, consequently, half their support system. This doesn't have to be the case. You divorced your spouse, but you don't have to eliminate your in-laws from your children's lives. Remember, your ex-spouse's parents will continue to be your children's grandparents, and they can offer stability and comfort in an uncertain time. Whenever possible, it is important to keep the door open for involvement.

If you had a good relationship with your in-laws while you were married, then continuing the relationship will be much easier. But despite how you may feel about them, your children should not be deprived of this relationship. Of course there will always be exceptions. Some children's grandparents are abusive or have problems with drugs or alcohol. But aside from these cases, your children will benefit immensely from an ongoing relationship with their grandparents.

Another Caring Adult

It is often helpful for your children to have a relationship with a caring adult outside your family. This person can be a teacher, coach, neighbor, or grandparent. There will inevitably be times when you are too involved in your own problems to devote your full attention to your children. When you can't fully meet your children's needs, it is essential that they have another caring adult to whom they can turn, someone who will listen, encourage, comfort, and act as a role model. I believe, as the Maori people do, that children should have more adults in their lives than just their mothers and fathers. Children need more than one or two positive role models. It is in your children's best interest that you help them cultivate a support system that extends beyond their immediate family.

After my divorce I was consumed both with my own emotional pain and with the stress of supporting my daughter and myself. There were days when my daughter would come home from school only to find me completely self-absorbed and unavailable. Ama and I had developed a friendship with an older woman, Bea Miera, who had been hired to care for the aging gentleman who lived across the street. After school, Ama would run across to Mr. Shea's house; Bea would open the door and scoop her up into her warm loving arms. Ama would spend hours with Bea, reading stories, making tortillas, shelling piñon nuts, coloring, and just enjoying her company.

My parents lived in New Jersey and we saw them only a few times a year, so Bea became Ama's Santa Fe grandmother. Bea was a godsend. She filled in for me during those times when I just didn't have the energy to give to my daughter. She spent time with Ama out of love and the generosity of her heart. Even after we moved to Los Angeles we maintained our friendship with Bea. Whenever we visit Santa Fe we stop by to see her and reminisce about the old days. She was a saving grace during a difficult period.

8. GIVE YOUR KIDS THE GIFT OF SELF-RELIANCE

Divorce is an opportunity for your children to learn that when life has difficult periods and hardships, they have the strength to face these challenges and not only survive, but thrive. Children's natural tendency is to become stronger and more self-reliant. One way to foster self-reliance in children is to allow them to do more for themselves.

I don't have to remind you that as a divorced person you have at least two full-time jobs and less emotional and physical support. When I discuss this issue with parents in my seminars or support groups they are always quick to offer, "I feel like I am juggling ten balls at once. I'm afraid of what will happen if I slow down." "Being a single parent is like being a rubber band stretched to the max and ready to snap at any moment." "There's just not enough time in the day to keep my career going and take care of my children. I have no backup and sometimes I just want to scream at everyone: Leave me alone!" Does any of these statements sound familiar? Most single custodial parents feel overwhelmed by the increased responsibilities and resulting stress.

Many single parents feel so guilty about disrupting their children's lives that they overcompensate by doing everything themselves. The truth is that when you don't ask your children to pitch in with household responsibilities you're not only making your life more difficult, you're also robbing your kids of feeling like valuable, contributing family members.

Children need to feel competent and capable. This is true in all families, but is especially important in single-parent families. I recommend that you make a list of everything you are currently doing for your children. Then go down that list and check off those things that they can do for themselves: for example, dressing themselves, making their lunch, picking up their toys, etc. Start this week and choose one thing from your list that you are going to allow your children to do for themselves. Don't do for your kids what they can do for themselves.

I also recommend that you have a family meeting to discuss setting up a chore system. Explain to your kids that you're a team and to be a winning team everyone needs to do his or her share. Then make a list of all of the household responsibilities such as grocery shopping, unloading the groceries, setting the table, emptying the dishwasher, taking out the garbage, etc. If your children are old enough, you can give them a choice as to which chores they will be responsible for during the next month. (With younger children you will need to delegate.) Then make a chore chart listing what is expected of each child. Not only will this lighten your load, but your children will feel needed. Your kids will feel that they are members of a team to which they make a valuable contribution. Don't allow your guilt about being a single parent get in the way of fostering a sense of responsibility and self-sufficiency in your children. The message you want to convey is "You are safe and secure, not only because I'm here to care for you and support you but also because you are capable and competent and are growing into a responsible, self-reliant person."

9. KEEP IN MIND WHAT IS NORMAL

Divorced parents often attribute all of their children's difficulties to their divorce. It's important for you to distinguish between normal *kid behavior* and divorce-related problems. In one of my parenting classes the topic was discipline. Elizabeth, the mother of six-year-old Justin, confessed, "Since my divorce I feel like the mother and the father. It's very hard. I'm not a good disciplinarian.

I let things go too far and then I become a screaming maniac. Whenever Justin does something wrong or has a problem I immediately blame it on the divorce. When someone else's kid does something she attributes it to a developmental stage. I never know what is fallout from divorce and what is just normal behavior. I assume that any acting out or anger is due to Justin's dreadful pain." Like many divorced parents, Elizabeth didn't know what was normal; her judgment was clouded by her guilt.

There are several ways to find out what is typical behavior of similar-aged children. You can ask other parents, you can read one of the many books on child development, or you can consult your child's teacher or school counselor for information. Parents are often too quick to attribute the normal struggles and craziness of growing up to the trauma of divorce.

On the other hand, there are stressful periods that require professional intervention. Most parents realize that their children will have some dramatic reactions to their divorce. Your children may be clingy, cry more often, have more frequent temper tantrums, sleep difficulties, or other disruptive behaviors. These intense reactions are natural during the initial stress and adjustment to your divorce, but they should diminish within a month or two as your children settle into their new family routine. If disruptive behavior persists and your child's normal activities are hampered, consider consulting a mental health professional. Don't allow chronic divorce-related stress to interfere in your children's lives. If you suspect that your children need professional help, I recommend that you contact the school psychologist, your pediatrician, or a local social service agency for a referral. If they are having trouble coping with your divorce, taking them in for an evaluation can't hurt.

Your divorce doesn't end your parenting responsibilities. In most cases it intensifies them. But once you understand how divorce affects your children, their needs, and how to fulfill them your job will be a lot easier.

Parents are in the driver's seat when it comes to children and divorce. They make all of the decisions and set the tone for their home life. If you are constantly angry, depressed, and overwhelmed, this will have an impact on your kids. But so too will your love, care, and concern for their needs. Don't misunderstand; I am not suggesting that you ignore your own valid needs. But I am asking that you not get so caught up in your new life, whether excruciating or exciting, that you overlook the people you love and who depend on you. Your divorce may be the single most disruptive event that your family has to overcome. But children are survivors. And parents can provide the survival skills necessary to weather the storm.

Chapter 2

Games Parents Play

It's easy to lose a good friend. It's harder to lose a good enemy.

Truman Capote

As they shuttle between their parents' homes children often carry far more than just their backpacks. Sometimes they carry messages, other times they act as spies, go-betweens, and allies. "Tell your father I don't have enough money for your art lessons." "Tell your mother that I give her plenty of money and if she learned how to manage it she'd have enough for your lessons." "Tell your father that he'll have to have you back two hours early on Sunday because we have a party to go to." "Tell your mother that I don't have enough time with you as it is." "Tell your mother . . ." "Tell your father . . ." And it goes on and on until they feel more like Ping-Pong balls than children who are loved, protected, and cared for by two divorced parents.

It is not uncommon for parents to enlist their children's support in the battle with their ex-spouses. Children assume these roles for several reasons: out of loyalty to a parent, a desire to restore the marriage, a wish to protect an injured parent, or attempts to placate the parent they worry about losing or of whose anger they are most frightened. Kids will often do and say what they think their parent needs to see and hear. Their most basic need is for belonging and children will do almost anything to ensure that they are loved and cared for, even at their own expense. If they could express their fear in one sentence it would be: My dad left my mom, so how can I make sure that I won't be abandoned too?

Several games that parents play are extremely damaging to their children. Most parents are unaware that they have recruited their kids as participants in their war games, but when I ask, they frequently realize that at one time or another they *have* put their children in the middle by drafting them into their ranks.

As you read through this chapter, see if you identify with any of the parents who have engaged in these damaging games. If you do, take heart. There is a wealth of information in the next several chapters that will help you stop this destructive behavior. But here let's look at the most common games that parents play.

1. The Put-Down Game
2. The 007 Game
3. The Messenger Game
4. The Revenge Game
5. The Surrogate Game

Now let's look at each game in greater detail.

1. THE PUT-DOWN GAME

"Your mother's a slut. She's running around with a guy eight years younger than she is. Someone should tell her to stop."

"I don't know how you kids put up with your father. He's completely irresponsible. I can't believe he forgot to pick you up from school. What a teenager."

"Order whatever you'd like. I know how tough it is to eat your mother's cooking. Her food is barely fit for the dog, let alone you kids. I always had to drown everything in catsup. How do you survive on that garbage?"

Angry parents frequently disparage their ex-spouses in front of their children. They feel victimized and wronged. They want to vindicate themselves or vent their frustration by complaining, so they trash the other parent. But as an old adage states, "You can't kick the crap out of one another without also kicking the crap out of your kids."

Valerie, 35, walked into a counseling session clearly upset. She described a recent incident that involved her five-year-old son and his father. "Adrian spent the weekend at his father's house," she said. "His daddy usually takes him straight to school on Mondays. This Monday morning he called to say that he had an early meeting and asked if I could take Adrian to school. I said fine.

"Adrian ran into the house at seven-fifty A.M., frantic. He's supposed to be at school by eight and there was no way he was going to make it on time. It was apparent that he had just gotten up. He hadn't washed and his clothes were all wrinkled. He threw his lunch box on the kitchen counter as he ran into the bathroom to brush his teeth.

" 'Mom, I'm hungry,' he yelled. 'Didn't your dad give you breakfast?' I asked as I grabbed a piece of toast and a glass of milk for him. I picked up his lunch box to put by the door, and it felt awfully light. I opened it and all that was in it was one lone jelly sandwich. No drink. Nothing. Not even peanut butter, just a plain jelly sandwich. 'What's with your dad?' I yelled. 'This isn't enough lunch for you.' I started ranting and raving, 'He only thinks about himself. How could he let you go to school with nothing to eat? I don't think he takes good enough care of you when you're at his house. What an idiot!'

"Adrian got very upset and immediately began to defend his father. 'My dad is not an idiot. He just didn't have much food in the house. I don't get very hungry anyway.' "

As soon as she had spoken, Valerie regretted what she had said. Not because she didn't believe every word, but because she could see how hurtful it was for Adrian to have her attack his father. "The guy was a flake during our marriage and he's a flake now," she said. "But Adrian really loves him and counts on seeing him.

"I feel so frustrated at times, but I don't want Adrian to hear me bad-mouth his father. What can I do to keep from spewing criticism about his dad in front of him?"

I empathized with Valerie's frustration. And then I suggested that she call a friend to vent her anger rather than express it to her son. I further recommended that once she had calmed down she could speak with her ex directly about her concerns. I cautioned Valerie to use a neutral, nonemotional style so as not to provoke a confrontation. I reminded her that the point was not to criticize but to come to an understanding that would benefit her son.

When you discredit your ex-spouse in front of your kids, it is your children who suffer. Your comments may contain a kernel or even a whole bushel of truth, but any criticism inevitably causes your children pain. The negative messages intended to hurt the other parent instead get lodged in your children's hearts. When someone your children loves is attacked, their natural tendency is to defend, but they are in a terrible dilemma because the attacker is also someone they love. Criticism puts your children in a confusing and frightening bind.

From a Child's Perspective

Sarah, 11, had been coming to me for counseling. She was fighting with kids at school and was generally argumentative and uncooperative on the playground and at home. Sarah and I were playing cards, a technique I use with children to create a relaxed atmosphere in which they can talk. I asked Sarah how her weekend with her dad had been. "It started out all right," Sarah explained as she continued playing cards. "But when I got home my mom got really mad."

I prompted Sarah to continue. "What happened?" I asked. "Well, when I'm at my dad's house we just hang out and have a good time," she replied. "I don't have to go to bed at a special time. He lets me stay up and watch videos. A lot of times we go to the mall. My dad bought me a pair of Rollerblades and the new R.E.M. tape.

"When I got home I wanted to try out my new skates, so I went outside and skated for a while. Then I went up to my room to listen to my new tape. My mom asked me to help her get dinner ready, but I was really tired and just didn't feel like helping. When I didn't come down and help, she started yelling. 'Your father spoils you,' she screamed at me. 'You always come back from his house tired and with a bad attitude. He doesn't even make you go to bed at a reasonable hour. It's just one big party over there. He's just a selfish pig.' " Tears ran down Sarah's face as she recounted her mother's reaction to her lack of cooperation.

Sarah was both upset and confused. I empathized with Sarah about how painful it must be for her to hear her mother criticize her father. When I questioned Sarah about her feelings she responded, "My mom seems to be mad all the time. I hate that she's mean to my dad. Sometimes I just want to go and live with him so I don't have to hear her picking on him all the time." Sarah was used to her parents' fighting before the divorce, but she had thought that would change once they stopped living together. "I just want my mom to stop saying bad things about my dad," she cried. I pointed out to Sarah that she was caught in a painful bind. I asked if it would be helpful for her to come see me together with her mom so I could help them talk things out. Sarah agreed.

In the next session it became clear that Sarah's mother, Carol, had a hidden agenda. She felt put upon and enraged at Sarah's father. She resented that he was the fun parent and she had to be the disciplinarian. Not only did she want a nonconfrontational release for her anger, but unconsciously Carol was trying to convert Sarah to her way of thinking. She was vying for Sarah's loyalty and in effect asking her to take sides. Unfortunately, her rage at her ex-husband was alienating her daughter.

With my support Sarah was able to tell her mother how hard it was to hear her father criticized. I gave Carol several suggestions about how to relieve her anger in ways that wouldn't hurt her daughter. First, I empathized with her frustration at being the one who does the major share of parenting. But I also pointed out to her that Sarah's father had a right to spend his time with her as he saw fit, as long as she was safe. I suggested that Carol talk with Sarah's father in a nonaccusatory way about Sarah's difficult transition between such radically different parenting styles. But I cautioned that she shouldn't expect him to change. Most likely she would have to accept the differences and anticipate the period of adjustment when Sarah returned home.

I also suggested that she and Sarah talk openly about the differences between the two households. Her father had a different set of rules at his house, but Carol expected Sarah to respect her rules when she was with her. I recommended that Carol be clear with Sarah about the consequences should she chose not to cooperate.

I helped Carol understand the negative effect her words were having and asked if she were willing to allow Sarah to point out when she was dumping on her father and ask her to stop. Carol and Sarah devised a signal that Sarah could use if she needed reminding.

Over the next several months Carol worked at controlling her anger and stopped bad-mouthing her ex-husband in front of her daughter. From her greater sense of acceptance of the situation and a more realistic expectation of her ex-husband Carol's anger began to dissipate and the overall tone in her home improved. Carol expected Sarah's transition difficulties when she returned from her father's, and she was much more matter-of-fact about Sarah's resistance to rules. Gradually, Sarah's behavior changed and the fighting at school stopped.

Speak No Evil

Many mental health professionals advise parents *never* to criticize the other parent to their children. For the most part I agree, but some parents carry this advice to the extreme. If your children hear nothing but positive, admirable comments about that wonderful, sterling human being, they will begin to wonder why the two of you divorced. If you think so much of him or her, they will wonder why you can't be a family again. It should be no secret to them that you have differences with your ex-spouse.

I suggest that you reflect back to your children a realistic picture of what you think their other parent is, including both attributes and deficits. Children need information whether they live in an intact, single-parent, or stepfamily. Your former spouse has some negative qualities, as we all do. There is nothing wrong with pointing these out, especially when they affect your kids. But there is an immense difference between a belittling remark and an honest statement about someone's behavior.

You can express your opinion about the other parent's actions without attacking character. A good way to do this is to discuss a fault when your child is experiencing its effects. For example, if your ex-spouse is consistently late it is perfectly appropriate to talk about the fact that the other parent has difficulty being on time. For example: "I can see that you're upset that your mom is late picking you up. Promptness is something she has trouble with, not just with you, but in other areas of her life as well."

The fine line between criticism and stating the facts is difficult to find when you are newly divorced and caught up in the heat of emotions. But helping your children form an accurate picture of who their other parent is will also help promote their healthy adjustment.

Differences Create Richness

Your children need to realize that you and your ex-spouse have differences and that disagreement on issues is normal. Neil, the father of Randy, 5, and Anna, 9, handled this situation well. Neil had cooked a dinner of hamburgers, salad, and frozen shoestring potatoes for his children. They were sitting at the kitchen table and both kids had just scarfed down most of their hamburgers when Randy proclaimed, "My mom says that it's not good for you to eat meat. She says it clogs your body." Anna chimed in, "Yeah, she told us that it's bad for the environment too, because they burn down the rain forests to make room for the cows."

Neil was taken aback by his children's comments, but he responded matter-of-factly. "Your mom has her opinion about what she thinks is healthy," he said. "And when you're at her house you can eat what she feels is best for you. But I think eating meat makes you strong. Your mom and I have different opinions about health. You can decide what *you* think." Without criticizing his ex-wife, Neil demonstrated to his kids that each person is entitled to a point of view.

Put-down Inventory Exercise

Awareness is the first step in changing behavior, so take an inventory of yours. First you must examine your actions honestly in order to evaluate what you have done and identify any changes you want to make.

1. List five times when you realize that you criticized your child's other parent in front of him or her. ______________________

   ____

2. How do you think your child felt when you criticized the other parent?______________________________________

   ____

3. What was your child's reaction?______________________

   ____

4. How did you feel about yourself after you put your former spouse down?______________________________________

   ____

5. What things can you do to give your child permission to let you know you are criticizing the other parent and ask you to stop?[1]

   ____

   ____

2. THE 007 GAME

"Is your mother still seeing that guy? Does he sleep over at her house? Is he nice to you? What kinds of things do you do when he's there?"

"Did your father buy that new car he was talking about? What kind did he buy?"

"How often does your mother take you out to dinner? Does she buy a lot of new clothes for herself? Do you still have a cleaning lady every week?"

It is natural to be curious about what your ex-spouse is doing, especially in terms of finances and new relationships. And children are a veritable gold mine of information, especially when they return from the other parent's house. We may seem to be asking our kids innocent questions, but this type of interrogation is far from innocent: "Does Daddy have a new girlfriend?" "Did Mommy buy that new furniture?" Our curiosity blinds us to the harm quizzing does to our children.

Playing Twenty Questions with kids puts them in the position of informers. They inevitably feel disloyal to the parent on whom they report. They also feel ashamed because they know they are doing wrong. They are torn between disloyalty to one parent and not wanting to alienate the other.

Alice and Ray are a good example. They have two children, Tina, 9, and James, 11. Alice came into a support group meeting and confessed, "I try really hard not to ask my kids about what goes on at their father's house, but it's a huge temptation. When I do question them, I try to be subtle. But this week I found myself playing private detective.

"Since Ray married his receptionist, a woman ten years younger than he is, I haven't been able to contain my curiosity," she said. "I knew her while Ray and I were married and we were pretty close. So I was really shocked when I got stabbed in the back."

Alice admitted that when Tina and James come back from the weekends at their father's house she quizes them. "What did you do?" she asks. "What is their house like?" "Is she nice?" "Does he hug and kiss her?" Alice felt threatened by this new wife. She worried that the younger woman would take her place as mother.

"My kids get very upset," Alice acknowledged. "I see them look guilty. They hesitate to answer because I cry when they tell me."

When money issues come up, Alice uses the information the kids give her against Ray. "Whatever the kids tell me always comes out when I talk to their father," Alice admitted. "I have an inside track on his life. He's not going to get away with pleading poverty anymore." Then she reported that Tina said her father questioned her about who her mother is dating and what the men are like.

Tina and James are, in effect, double agents. They carry information in both directions. They are debriefed at both homes. The children are uneasy with their roles as informants, but neither Tina nor James wants to alienate either parent by refusing to cooperate.

Children who act as spies are motivated by several concerns: They worry about their injured parent; they fear punishment or rejection if they don't comply with their parent's request; they want to keep the peace; and at times they feel a sense of power and excitement in passing on secrets. Whatever their reasons, children can't help but feel ashamed of their actions.

Nor can any parent feel good about using a child as a spy or informer. When you put your own needs ahead of your children's welfare, youngsters lose respect for you. This adds further stress. Kids shouldn't have to report on their parents' private lives. Doing so forces them to betray one or both of their parents' trust.

Keeping Secrets

Parents frequently say or do things they don't want the other parent to know about. Children who are privy to these things are in an awkward position. Take the case of Florence and Ralph and their six-year-old son, Brandon. Two years after their divorce, Florence and Ralph were still arguing about money. One night, when Brandon was spending the weekend at his father's house, as Ralph was tucking him into bed he said, "I want to take you to Disneyland tomorrow, but I can't if you tell your mother. She's always hassling me about money and if she finds out, she's going to get mad at both of us." Brandon looked puzzled but promised his father that he'd keep their trip a secret.

When Ralph dropped Brandon off at his mother's after their weekend, Florence asked innocently, "What did you and your dad do this weekend?" Brandon became very quiet and said, "Nothing." Then he ran to his room. That night, and for the next several nights, Brandon woke with bad dreams. When his mother asked what was bothering him, he blurted out, "My daddy will be mad at me if I tell you." Florence reassured Brandon that it was all right to talk about what was bothering him, and finally he told her about the trip to Disneyland. The pressure of keeping a secret was too great for Brandon. He wanted to protect his father from his mother's anger, but doing so left him feeling disloyal to his mother. When parents war, the only prisoners taken are their children.

Here is another example of what happens when you ask children to keep secrets. Lilly, 7, spent the weekend with her father. When she came home she was clearly upset but adamantly refused to talk with her mother, Kate. For days Lilly was irritable. She refused to do her chores, picked a fight with her best friend in Brownies, and wanted to sleep in her mother's bed. Finally, while driving in the car together Kate asked Lilly yet again what was bothering her. After staring out the window for a short time, Lilly finally admitted, "My dad told me how much money he makes, but he told me not to tell you or you would try to take it all away from him." Kate wanted to say, "I've always made *much* more money than your father. In fact, I've paid off his credit card debts and bailed him out of his bad investments. Why is he worried about my taking what he doesn't have?" She thought these things, but she knew saying them would only upset Lilly further.

Instead, she empathized, acknowledging how hard it must be for Lilly to keep such an important secret. She coached Lilly to tell her father that she didn't want to be told things that she had to keep from her mother. "Tell your dad that it's just too hard for you to have to keep secrets," Kate reassured Lilly. "I'm sure he'll understand." Lilly's relief was obvious. Asking your kids to keep information from their other parent is too much of a burden to place on them. Parents are often unaware of how stressful secrets can be.

Exercise

1. Recall between three and five situations in which you asked your children questions that violated their other parent's privacy._____

   ____

2. What was your children's reactions to such quizzing?__________

   ____

3. How did you feel afterward?____________________________

   ____

4. What can you do when you catch yourself playing Twenty Questions with your kids?____

5. Can you give your children permission not to participate in your quizzing?____

3. THE MESSENGER GAME

"Ask your father if he's going to pick you up after Little League practice tomorrow."

"Tell your father that if he doesn't get me this month's support check he won't see you next weekend."

"You look like street urchins. Can't your mother send you to my house in decent clothes? I can't take you out looking like this. Tell your mother that if she doesn't buy you some decent clothes I'm going to stop sending her the child support."

Many divorced parents don't like to talk to each other. Instead they use their children to carry messages back and forth. These messages can be as benign as "Ask your mother if she is going to be at the parent-teacher conference," or as emotionally charged as "Tell your father to stop calling here every fifteen minutes." No matter the nature of the information, using your children to carry messages has several harmful repercussions. First, secondhand information delivered by a child is rarely accurate. When you ask your kids to relay messages you leave yourself open to misunderstandings and miscommunication. Second, children, especially young children, are notorious for having poor memories. If you rely on your ex-spouse to act on the communication conveyed by your child and it doesn't get there, you leave yourself open to frustration, inconvenience, and unnecessary arguments. Third, and most important, using your children as message bearers puts them in a position of receiving a negative reaction from their other parent when they deliver provocative information.

Let's look at what can happen when you depend on your child to deliver a simple message. Robert, 7, was on the phone with his father making plans for the weekend. His mother, Ellen, walked into the room, realized that he was talking with his dad, and said, "Please remind your father to get you a haircut while you're with him this weekend. You're starting to look like one of the Mötley Crüe." Robert forgot to convey the message. When he returned from the weekend with his dad his mother was angry at both of them for not complying with her request. Ellen, and for that matter everyone involved, would have been better off had she communicated directly with Robert's dad. When you ask your children to carry messages, no matter how benign their information, you put them in the stressful position of go-between.

The Ping-Pong Effect

Sometimes children are asked to act as couriers passing a string of messages between two warring parents. Peter, 10, was caught in this situation. He regularly was asked to carry messages back and forth as he shuttled between his two homes. Peter and his father were supposed to go to Cincinnati over his spring break to visit both sets of grandparents. As Peter was getting ready to go to his father's house his mother reminded him, "Ask your father to make sure he makes plans for your trip over spring break. Tell him if he doesn't make arrangements soon, the flights will get sold out and you won't be able to go." Peter's father picked him up and they drove back to his house, stopping to get a few groceries on the way. When they got home Peter nervously delivered his mother's message to his dad. His father became furious with his son. "Why the hell doesn't she stop hassling me about the vacation? What does she think I am, a moron? I'll take care of it." Peter didn't know how to respond to his father's rhetorical questions or his anger. Because he was the bearer of irritating news, their time together started out on a bad note.

On the drive back to his mother's house Peter's father said, "Ask your mother why she's such a worrier and a nag. Tell her I'll make the reservations and to keep her nose out of my business."

During the week, while Peter was on the phone with his father, his mother asked him to pass on yet another message. "Tell your father that he'll have to pick you up at my office on Wednesday," she said. When Peter relayed this his father shouted, "You tell your mother that I will not drive all the way downtown to get you and that she'd better have you home by six as usual." Peter suffered tremendous strain from being the instrument of communication between his bickering parents. Each time he was asked to pass a message to one of his parents he felt nervous and hesitant, but he wanted to do what was asked of him. Then he resented getting the static when he delivered the charged information. Children who must carry hurtful information become shell-shocked and battle-weary. You are asking them to serve on the front lines of the parental war.

Subtle Messages

Messages can be far more subtle than a blatant request for money or a threat to deny visitation. Many parents feel that because the other parent loves and cares about the child the child is more likely to get additional financial support than if the custodial ex-spouse asked directly. For example, Joanne's ex had provided the major share of the income during their marriage. He was an engineer while she worked as a receptionist in a dentist's office. Since their divorce Joanne had struggled financially. Over the years, her ex faithfully paid child support, but he had refused to contribute to any additional expenses, such as summer camp, braces, or dance classes.

When their daughter, Nina, 16, needed a prom dress, Joanne coached her to ask her father. "Honey, I'd love to buy you a dress, but I just can't afford to," she said. "You know that if I ask your dad for extra money he'll turn me down. But if *you* ask him, he'll spring for it." Both Joanne and her ex were unaware of how well they had worked together to teach their daughter the fine art of manipulation.

Mothers usually suffer financial stress after divorce, but fathers are faced with a different issue. Many find their time with their children severely curtailed; some ex-wives refuse any flexibility in schedules. Jerome and Evelyn had been divorced for a year and a half. In the past she had been rigid when it came to changes in visitation with their son, Jesse. Evelyn was still angry that Jerome had left her for another woman, but she had few outlets to express her fury. Jesse was her one sure way to make her ex pay for the pain he had caused. Jerome had an unexpected day off coming up and wanted to spend extra time with his son. He was hesitant to ask his ex-wife, so instead of talking with her directly he called Jesse. "I'm not working on Wednesday," Jerome explained to his son. "How about I pick you up after school and we go to the driving range and hit some balls together?" Jesse was excited. Then his father went on. "Jesse, you know how your mother is about my seeing you," he said. "If you ask her, she may be more reasonable."

In both these cases, one parent played on the other's bond with the child to get cooperation. This kind of subtle control is emotional blackmail.

The situation between my client, Larry, and his ex-wife illustrates the danger of alienating the children from the parent who receives the unwelcome messages. Larry, a pediatrician, had been divorced for three years. When he and his wife separated, she moved east to be close to her family. From the beginning of the separation Larry traveled monthly from his home in California to see his children, Alex, 6, and Pam, 8. In those three years his children never telephoned him. One evening, much to Larry's amazement, Alex called. Larry was shocked to hear his son say, "Hi, Daddy. It's getting really cold here. It just snowed and we didn't have to go to school today. The floor in my room is really cold and I want you to buy me a rug for my floor to keep my feet warm."

It was clear to Larry that his ex-wife had put their son up to making the call. "When I go out to see my kids they're always dressed in rags," Larry fumed. "I'm embarrassed to be seen with them. I resent having my kids look like paupers when I send plenty of money for their care. But I don't want them to go without, so we go to the mall and I end up buying them shoes and clothes.

"Last time Pam told me, 'Mommy said that you're the richest person she knows. She told me to ask you to buy us boots and winter clothes while you're here.' What the hell does she do with all the money I send her?"

Using children as messengers is always inappropriate. When they bear bad news, it is worse. They are afraid that the information they bring will anger the receiver, and they know that if they forget to relay the message their other parent will get mad. It is especially hard for children to relay information that is a complaint about that parent. When they are put in the position of go-between, kids feel they must take sides. Keep your children out of the middle. Don't use them to deliver messages, no matter how benign. When you need to communicate with your ex-spouse, speak directly and leave your kids out of it.

Exercise

These are some common messages that children are asked to carry. Notice if any sound familiar or remind you of things you've asked your children to tell your ex.

"Tell your father the check is late."

"Tell your mother I won't be able to take you to school tomorrow."

"Ask your father why he never picks you up on time."

"Tell your mother that my social life is none of her business."

"You tell your father that I'll spend my money any way I like."

"Ask your mother not to call my house so often."

"Ask your father to get you a new pair of shoes."

"Find out if your mother got a raise at her job."

1. What are some messages you have asked your children to carry to their other parent?________________________

2. What are your children's reactions when you ask them to be message bearers?________________________

3. How do you feel when you are the recipient of messages delivered by your children?____________________

4. How do you think your kids feel?____________________

5. What can you do to help get your children out of the middle?

____

4. THE REVENGE GAME

Ernie forgets that he is supposed to pick up his children at 5:00 P.M. and shows up at 7:00 P.M. instead. He ruins his ex-wife's dinner plans.

Claudia ignores the fact that her children are supposed to be with their father. She takes them out to dinner and a movie on the night he is supposed to pick them up. When Rob arrives at their house no one is home.

Roberta wants to change the day she sees the children so they can go to a family function. Frank refuses to cooperate and won't allow her to change the date.

An easy way for the custodial parent to get revenge is to threaten the noncustodial parent with denial of access to the children. All parents are aware of the powerful emotional attachment between parents and children. Keeping children from the other parent threatens this bond. This threat is easy to make good because taking legal action to enforce visitation privileges is time-consuming and costly.

Sally and Ron had been divorced for three years, but their battle raged on. They fought at almost every opportunity over money, visitation, and their different styles of parenting their daughters, Megan, 6, and Naomi, 9. Ron called to talk to his kids and during the course of the conversation he told Naomi that he had a business meeting on Friday. He asked her to tell her mother that he'd be late picking them up. "Tell your mother that on Friday I'll be there at eight P.M. instead of at six P.M."

When Naomi told her mother, Sally lost her temper. "No way," she screamed. "He can't change plans at the last minute and expect me to accommodate his every whim. Tell your father that he picks you up on time or he doesn't see you at all." Naomi relayed this information to her dad and he became furious. "What's she talking about?" Ron snapped. "I rarely change plans. What's the big deal? This is only Tuesday. I'm giving her plenty of notice. Ask her to give me one good reason why I can't be a bit late." Naomi was getting more and more upset. Tears welled up in her eyes as she relayed her dad's words.

Sally grabbed the phone. "What do you think you're doing?" she yelled. "You have no idea how upsetting this kind of scene is for the girls. They're counting on seeing you at the regular time. You louse everything up by trying to change things at the last minute."

"Sally, this is only Tuesday," Ron countered. "I'm giving you plenty of warning." "Well, buddy, it's just not going to happen," Sally shrieked back. "I'm sick and tired of having to accommodate you. Either pick up the girls at your regular time or don't bother coming at all."

"I have a right to see my children and if you don't cooperate, you'll hear from my lawyer," he said. Sally screamed back, "Listen, buddy, don't try this lawyer crap with me. If you threaten me, you won't see the girls at all, ever."

The threats terrified Naomi and Megan. They worried that they wouldn't see their daddy and were angry at their mother for putting them in a pressure cooker. These kinds of incidents create stress and anxiety in kids. Continued over time they can cause long-term psychological damage.

Exercise

1. Have you ever used your children as weapons of revenge against your ex-spouse? ______________________________
2. How do you think your children felt when they thought they wouldn't be able to see their other parent? ______________
3. How did you feel after you made the threat? ______________

4. Did your threat or vengeful actions improve the situation in any way?____________________________________

5. What can you do to prevent putting your children in the middle of a war zone?________________________________

5. THE SURROGATE GAME

"Now that your father is gone, you're the man of the house. I'm counting on you."

"I want you to look after your sister and brother tonight while I'm at my class. Make sure they behave and get them to bed on time."

"You're my little company. I'd be really lonely without you. Why don't you stay home with me this weekend and we can do something fun together?"

"I just don't know how I'm going to pay this month's bills plus insurance and taxes. We may have to move to a cheaper apartment."

Divorce destroys children's sense of safety and security. Many are forced to fill the vacuum left by their missing parent. They're asked to assume greater responsibility and provide emotional support, comfort, and companionship for their custodial parent.

Since divorce is devastating for most people, in the period directly following, parents who are overwhelmed with changes often become preoccupied with their own needs. Their children may be both neglected and thrust into the role of surrogate spouse.

Patty, 35, and Nick, 38, had been married for fourteen years and had two children, Amanda, 13, and David, 7. Nick was a successful architect and Patty had worked briefly as an elementary school teacher before she had children. But when Amanda was born she stayed home to be a full-time mother. In the last year of their marriage Nick began to spend longer and longer hours at his office. He complained that their relationship had deteriorated into a convenient living arrangement. He asked for a trial separation and Patty reluctantly agreed.

At first she was optimistic about their future together, but after eight months of living apart Nick filed for a divorce. Patty panicked. It had been thirteen years since she had worked; she was unsure of her ability to reenter the work force.

Although Nick sent monthly child support, Patty worried about his continuing to do so once the divorce was final. She worried about how she would manage to keep and run the house on a limited income. Even when she had worked she never earned enough to maintain her current lifestyle. She visualized moving into a less comfortable house in a bad neighborhood. She obsessed about her inability to get back into teaching after such a long absence.

Patty couldn't contain her anxiety. She talked to her children about her fears. "I'm not sure we'll be able to stay in our house," Patty confided. "I don't know how I'm going to keep up with the payments and buy food and clothes now that Daddy's gone. Who will hire me? I haven't worked since you were born." David was too young to respond, but Amanda was sympathetic. "Mommy, don't worry," she reassured. "We'll be all right. Davie and I don't need many new things. You can keep my allowance. It's going to be okay." Amanda gave her mother a big hug.

These kinds of soul-baring discussions continued, and Amanda became more and more cooperative around the house. She took over household chores, helping to cook dinner, look after her brother, and unload the dishwasher without prompting from her mother. Amanda became Patty's buddy. She abandoned her friends to become her mother's confidante. They did errands, went shopping, and had special lunch dates. Amanda was filling the void left by her father's absence, but while the close companionship filled a very real need for Patty, it interfered with Amanda's normal development.

Patty was vaguely aware that Amanda was acting overly responsible, but she desperately needed her daughter's comfort and support. One day when David had nagged her to buy him a new toy, Patty overheard Amanda telling him, "David, Mommy's too poor for us to buy toys now. We have to be grown up and help Mommy. If we spend too much money we will have to move. Now stop asking."

A few days later Patty received a call from Amanda's teacher. Amanda had always been one of the brighter and most popular children in her class, she said, but recently she had fallen behind in her studies. "She seems to think the rules don't apply to her," the teacher complained. "When I asked Amanda about why she didn't do her homework, she gave me the impression that she had more important things to do at home. The other kids don't seem to want to include her in their games and when I ask why they exclude Amanda, they say she bosses them around and won't play by the rules. I'm really puzzled by this dramatic change."

Patty told Amanda's teacher about her divorce and the teacher suggested that Amanda see the school psychologist to help her to cope with the stress. Patty agreed. The psychologist soon recommended that Patty see me.

After several sessions Patty realized that she was imposing responsibilities on Amanda that were far beyond her age or ability. I helped her to see that Amanda was feeling overwhelmed and that this was clearly taking its toll.

Amanda's more adultlike role at home was confusing to her. It was interfering with the normal developmental task of moving beyond the emotional ties of her family to enter the larger world and cultivate peer relationships. Although Amanda felt powerful, she was burdened with concerns and pressures far beyond what her age could bear.

Comfort at a High Price

A major deprivation after divorce is the loss of a partner to share the bed. For many divorced parents night is when they are confronted with the most intense feelings of abandonment, isolation, and despair. Lonely, distraught parents often make excuses to have their children sleep in the same bed or in the same room with them.

When I discuss this point in my seminars or support groups, I am struck by how sensitive this issue is for parents. They'll say "My child is lonely and she feels safer when she sleeps with me." Or "We only have one bed at my house and so he has to sleep with me." Or "He wakes up with nightmares, so I let him climb into bed with me. I don't think it hurts anything. Besides, I like the company." In each case the parents are rationalizing their own unconscious wish to have their child close to them and to get some relief from *their* feelings of abandonment, loneliness, and isolation.

I understand this issue all too well. I, too, fell into this pattern shortly after my divorce. I can remember numerous nights when I would lie there wide awake and feeling completely alone. I hated being by myself in such a big bed. During this period my daughter, then six years old, would often wake up crying. She would tiptoe into my room and ask to sleep with me. It was so much easier to let her get into my bed than to get up, put her back to bed, and comfort her. Night after night, she would crawl into my bed, snuggle under the covers, cozy up, and fall back asleep. Having her in bed with me was a great comfort. I was soothed by the sound of her breathing and the reassurance that someone still loved and needed me.

This went on for several months until Ama began to get clingy and had difficulty separating from me when I took her to school. This was a radical change for her. The kindergarten teacher called me in for a conference and reported that Ama had started to suck her thumb during class. Though she had once been gregarious and outgoing, she now seemed shy and withdrawn. I listened to the teacher describe this dramatic change and I knew that her sharing my bed was contributing to this regressive behavior. I had to put a stop to it.

That night at bedtime I talked with Ama about how nice it had been for her to be able to sleep with me, but that it was time for her to stay in her own bed. I reassured her that if she got scared in the night she could call me and I would come in and check on her, but that she had to stay in her own bed. Ama cried and said she felt more comfortable being with me. I empathized but was firm about my decision. That first night was tough for both of us. Ama woke up as usual and came into my room, but this time I calmly walked her back to bed and sat with her for a few minutes until she settled down and fell back to sleep. Then I climbed back into my own bed and cried. I knew I was doing what was best for my daughter, but I hated being alone.

Most children enjoy sleeping with their parents, but the emotional price can be high. The establishment of a sense of autonomy is a developmental milestone for children. Sleeping alone is one way of asserting independence. When you take your child into your bed, you are in effect expressing your lack of confidence in her ability to manage separation and successfully cope with feelings. This kind of message can have a detrimental effect on your child at school, with friends, and at home. As innocent and as comforting as sleeping together may seem, it is important for your child to sleep in a separate room or at least in her own bed, if that's what your circumstances permit.

Another negative effect of having children sleep with you is that children of the opposite sex can find it sexually stimulating. Children are confused by these unknown feelings. They often feel guilty and ashamed about the closeness they feel and will act uncooperative during the day to create some distance between themselves and their parent. For all these reasons it is important to insist that your child sleep apart from you. Of course there will be the occasional exception, but for the most part, this should be the rule.

From the Child's Perspective

Brady, now 24, has unhappy memories of being the "man of the house" when his parents divorced. "I was fourteen and I felt so scared," he told me. "My mom seemed to be completely overwhelmed with having to work full-time and take care of my younger sister and me. I was really worried about her and started to take over some of the household chores. I got into the habit of making her tea when she got home. We would sit and talk about my sister and our concerns about her. It was such a relief to feel in charge.

"We lived in kind of a bad neighborhood," Brady continued. "I used to lie awake at night thinking about what I would do if someone broke into our house. I can remember listening to every sound, the wind blowing a can down the alley, a branch hitting a window, or the cat door slamming shut as our cat went out for the night. I think I was terrified that I was the only man in the house and would have to protect my mother and sister if anything happened. I realize now that I carried a very heavy burden. Looking back on that period of my life, I think it was too much for me. I smoked dope to escape all the pressure and responsibility. I just needed to get away."

Brady, like many children who are thrust into adult roles, put his own needs on hold and became overly somber. He wanted to fill the vacuum made by his father's absence, but he was scared of the responsibility and incapable of living up to the challenge. When I asked how assuming an adult role at such an early age had affected him, he responded, "It's hard for me to let go and just have fun. I'm always thinking about what I *should* be doing. I still find myself filling in the gaps whether it's at work, with friends, or in my relationship with my girlfriend. I put other people's needs way before my own. Sometimes I just want to chuck it all, take off, and be free, but I know I can't."

Many parents who are faced with the trauma of divorce use their children to ward off depression and to keep themselves from falling apart. Children often feel frightened and helpless. By assuming the role of caretaker children at least have a purpose and a sense of power. In the midst of chaos, they feel in control.

However, when kids step into this pseudo-adult role their developmental needs get put on hold. They become serious little adults who focus on others and never achieve a strong sense of themselves. These children are prime candidates for the affliction of our time, codependency.

Psychologist and best-selling author John Bradshaw defines codependency as "the most common family illness." In every dysfunctional family, Bradshaw says, there is a primary stressor, perhaps Father's drinking or workaholism, Mother's hysteria, one parent's physical or verbal violence, even the divorce itself. According to Bradshaw, each member of the family adapts to this stress in a desperate attempt to control it; each becomes, in his or her own way, dependent on the stressor. "Co-dependence is a loss of one's inner reality and an addiction to outer reality," he says.[2] I think that this accurately describes what happens to children who are burdened with adult responsibilities.

Children should take some responsibility for household chores, especially if the custodial parent has to work. But there is a great difference between teaching children about responsibility and demanding that they assume adult roles. E. Mavis Hetherington of the University of Virginia found that children who were required to assume responsibility that was beyond their capabilities and that interfered with normal childhood activities exhibited resentment, rebellion, and behavior problems.

Children must be permitted to remain children, and even to regress for a time, after divorce. They may accept the greater responsibility and welcome what they see as increased closeness with their custodial parent, but in the long run they feel robbed of their childhood.

THE EFFECT OF GAME PLAYING

The pain of divorce is heightened when kids are used as agents of revenge against their other parent. An estimated 10 to 12 percent of divorcing families engage in ongoing conflicts and bitter litigation over the children. Kids who are used as weapons of their parents' anger carry the effects of their parents' behavior into their adult lives. Many grow up learning to manipulate people, others have a tremendous amount of rage, while still others suffer from depression, guilt, and low self-esteem. When parents enlist children into parental game playing it is not out of love or concern for the children's welfare but rather out of their own selfish need for retaliation and revenge. These children feel that no one really recognizes or attends to *their* needs, but that they are simply extensions of their parents' rage and anger. Children who are used as pawns in their parents' games are psychologically less stable than children who are not caught up in parental conflicts.[3]

A study by Kathleen A. Camara and Gary Resnick of Tufts University found that the social behavior of children from both divorced and intact families seems to be related to how the parents cope with conflict and whether they can cooperate as parents. When parents can move beyond their anger, resentment, and blame, their children are in a much better position to come through a divorce well-adjusted. Two years after the divorce, researchers found these children were less aggressive, had higher self-esteem, and formed better peer relationships.[4]

Put Yourself in Your Kids' Shoes

Your kids love both their parents. Putting yourself in their shoes may help you understand why your fights are so frightening. Take a moment and recall someone from your childhood whom you loved. Imagine how you would have felt if someone else had asked you to do something you knew would hurt that person. You probably would have been confused and upset. Your children will have a similar reaction if you ask them to take sides or carry hurtful messages or if they hear you say negative things about someone they love.

Parents at war make anger an ongoing presence in their children's lives. They, in turn, carry the residue of these unresolved conflicts into their adult lives. If you continue to attack your ex-spouse, your children are likely to grow up handicapped in their ability to form and sustain personal relationships. It is essential that you gain control of your emotions and put an end to the game playing. In the following chapters, I will take you through a step-by-step process in which you will learn how to (1) get an emotional divorce from your ex-spouse, (2) shift from an intimate relationship to a parenting partnership, and (3) communicate in a way that fosters cooperation.

Games Inventory Exercise

It's difficult to admit that you have put your children in the middle of conflicts with your ex-spouse, used them as go-betweens, or become overly dependent on them. But almost every divorced parent I have worked with has fallen into game playing at one time or another. Only when you recognize what you have done and the impact it has had on your children can you begin to change your behavior.

By answering yes or no to the following questions you will be able to identify which games you have played and which you may still be playing.

1. Have you ever criticized, trashed, or demeaned your children's other parent in front of them?____________________

2. Have you ever quizzed your children about their other parent's social, sexual, or financial affairs?____________________

3. Have you ever asked your children to carry messages to your ex-spouse?____________________

4. Have you ever threatened to forbid them contact with their other parent out of your own anger or frustration?____________________

5. Have you ever invited your children to discuss adult issues such as financial, personal, or legal problems?____________________

6. Have you ever relied on your children to comfort you, to provide companionship, or to fill your social and emotional needs?_____

Chapter 3

Getting an Emotional Divorce

How to Stop the Battle with Your Ex

> *A time to weep, and a time to laugh; a time to kill, and a time to heal; a time to break down, and a time to build up.*
>
> *Ecclesiastes 3:3*

You may have thought your relationship with your spouse was over when you signed the final decree, but cutting the legal ties is a small part of the divorce process. Your marriage is finished and you have divvied up the CD collection, stereo, espresso maker, salad spinner, maybe even your friends, but your emotional divorce may not yet have started. Until you recognize and resolve negative emotions left over from your marriage, you are going to be stuck in the past, unable to move on.

Completing a divorce means that you have to separate psychologically as well as financially and legally. Early in the process your feelings seem to have a life of their own; you are likely surprised by their contradictory nature. One minute you are ecstatic with newfound freedom; the next moment you are angry and resentful or sad and nostalgic. The emotions of divorce are like being tossed and tumbled by a huge wave. Ultimately you find your footing, but you emerge scraped and bruised, frightened and disoriented. There is no such thing as a painless divorce.

DEATH OF A MARRIAGE

The end of your marriage is similar to the death of a loved one. There is, unfortunately, no formal ritual to mark this major life transition, but the process of grieving is the same. The person who leaves and the person who is left experience different kinds of grief. The one who is left tends to suffer excruciating pain: He or she is not only dealing with the loss of a marriage but also with feelings of rejection and abandonment. The partner who initiated the divorce usually has similar but less intense feelings, and some amount of guilt.

Both parties will inevitably replay old tapes from the marriage, trying to understand what went wrong. The tapes elicit a myriad of emotions, including denial, anger, sadness, regret, loss, and eventually, one hopes, acceptance. All these emotions are valid parts of the grieving process, but you don't want to get stuck in any phase before you get to acceptance. If you are still consumed with intense feelings after eighteen months or two years, you are carrying around excess emotional baggage. It is essential to keep moving through the grieving process even if you do it in fits and starts.

BINDS THAT TIE

Sometimes it's difficult to recognize when you are caught in a rut. Following are five common ways people get stuck. The people in these examples thought they had gotten an emotional divorce, but when they came to me for therapy we found they were stuck in depression, self-pity, dependence, jealousy, or guilt. When you read these profiles, take note of similarities to your situation.

- Diane, 35, had been married for twelve years. She had a successful career as a legal secretary, took good care of her two children, and earned enough to live comfortably. Her divorce was three years ago and her ex had since remarried, but when Diane first came to see me she still kept some of his clothes hanging in her closet. She also carried a dog-eared photo of their fly-fishing trip to Maine tucked away in her wallet.

Diane hadn't dated since her divorce. She spent most of her free time at home, listening to oldies on the radio and watching Katharine Hepburn and Spencer Tracy movies. "I feel like half a person," Diane confessed one day. "My life feels like it's on hold, but I'm not sure what I'm waiting for."

Diane was living in a fantasy, clinging to memories of how things used to be. She was unconsciously holding on to the hope that maybe she and her ex-husband would be reunited. By staying in the past, Diane could play it safe, warding off the temporary fear of being single and avoiding the frightening challenge of rebuilding her life.

- Paul and Heather had been married for nine years. One night Paul called from work and announced that he had been seeing another woman and that he wanted a divorce. Paul moved out and eventually remarried. "I feel ugly, horrible, and lost, like a complete failure," Heather said at her first session. "All I ever wanted was to be a wife and a mother to our son. I devoted my life to him. He made me give up my career when we first got married and now I'm left with nothing. I'm useless. How could he do this to me? I hate him for it."

  Heather felt like a victim. She was stuck in self-pity and her self-esteem was at an all-time low. She avoided taking responsibility for her future by blaming Paul for her unhappiness.
- Susan had been married to a lawyer. Her ex-husband, Gavin, kept their financial records and prepared their taxes. Divorced for a year and a half, Susan was now living with another man, but Gavin still called her regularly to offer financial advice and occasionally they got together to go over her financial statements. Susan liked Gavin's attention and rationalized their involvement by saying she needed the advice. She enjoyed knowing that even though she was in-

volved with someone else Gavin was still attracted to her.

Gavin, on the other hand, was trying desperately to maintain a thread of his bond with Susan by offering advice she could easily have gotten from an accountant. Her dependency gave him a false sense of security and kept him emotionally entangled. Gavin ignored Susan's new relationship and clung to a remnant of her attention.

- Alan and Inez had been divorced for two years and they shared custody of their two children. Alan had remarried and he and his new wife had a three-month-old baby, and yet when he went to pick up his kids and saw Inez's new boyfriend, he was consumed with jealousy. In one of our early therapy sessions he reported thinking, "They really look good together. She seems really happy. I hate seeing her happy." When the children came to his house he would quiz them. "What kind of a car does he drive?" "How long has your mom been seeing him?" "Does he sleep over?" "Do you like him?"

  Alan was overly interested in Inez's new relationship. His jealousy arose from feeling that someone had taken his place. Despite his happy new marriage, Alan maintained the old emotional connection by prying into Inez's private life.
- When Roger called Regina about seeing their ten-year-old daughter, he would inevitably want to chat about his personal life. Regina's gut reaction was to cut him off. She didn't want any intimate involvement with him anymore, but then her guilt would click in. "He is your child's father," she told herself. "You really did hurt him by getting the divorce. He lost his home and family. The least you can do is to listen. What does it cost, anyway." She gave in and let Roger talk about his new girlfriend and the problems they were having. Each time she got off the phone she was a nervous wreck. She didn't want to be his best friend, but again she had allowed herself to connect with him in an intimate way.

  Regina was acting out of guilt for having left her marriage and causing Roger pain. "I feel like a criminal," she confessed. "I am depriving him of a full-time relationship with

> his daughter." By making herself available to Roger, Regina repeatedly compromised her need for privacy and distance. By allowing her guilt to override her judgment, Regina maintained their emotional bond.

When these people came to me for counseling they thought they had completed the painful business of divorce. It was only in the course of therapy that they acknowledged their attachment to their ex-spouses. They were unaware of how these emotional bonds prevented them from being fully involved in their new lives. These people's emotional divorces were not yet final.

The first step in completing this unfinished business, getting an emotional divorce, is to recognize your emotional attachment to your ex-spouse. Although each of the people in the previous examples played out their attachment differently, they were all nonetheless hooked. Only by recognizing the connection and facing the toll it takes on your life and the lives of your children can you heal and let go. But how do you do this? There are a series of eight steps that you must take in order to complete an emotional divorce. These steps, which are tools to help you, can be divided into a two-phase process. In the first phase, you allow yourself to recognize, identify, and, at times, experience your emotions, which is done by using the first three steps.

1. Take stock of your losses.
2. Identify constructive anger versus destructive anger.
3. Allow yourself time to be depressed.

Now let's look at each of these steps.

TAKE STOCK OF YOUR LOSSES

Whether or not you initiated the breakup of your marriage, divorce shatters your life and your dreams. You may well be faced with loss of your family, many of your friends, your home, your belongings, your self-esteem, your sense of security, and even your identity. You may be left with only the stark reality of your fear and guilt and the overwhelming challenge of rebuilding your life.

Very few things remain the same. The changes range from increased financial responsibilities to an empty bed. Perhaps not all of the changes caused by divorce are negative, but human beings resist change; we prefer the familiar no matter how uncomfortable or destructive it may have been. When we are forced to change, even the slightest reminder of our old life can trigger feelings of loss—his missing razor in the bathroom, the bare hook that used to hold her nightgown, the blank space on the wall where our wedding picture once hung. The reminders are everywhere.

"Those first few months, so many things made me sad," said Gail, a thirty-eight-year-old real estate agent, during a counseling session in which she described driving cross-country with her oldest son on his way to Vassar. "Mile after mile I watched families drive by in their cars," she remembered. "I noticed mothers and fathers in the front seat and their kids in the back. Intact families. I was just devastated. We were different. We no longer had an intact family. Even if I remarried, we would never be the original family. There will always be this father who belongs with my kids, but who doesn't belong with me, and vice versa." Gail's sadness came from the loss of her dreams. She was forced to accept that there was no turning back, that nothing would ever be the way it once was.

It is natural to want to regain your sense of order and to make things the way they used to be. In many cases, however, that is as impossible as it is inappropriate. So what *can* you do? First, you must take time to mourn. Allow yourself to cry and to experience the pain for what was or what could have been. You may want to set aside some time to be alone so you can really let yourself experience your feelings. In my practice I occasionally see people who are afraid to cry. They fear the pain will be unbearable, that if they start to cry they won't be able to stop. I reassure them that I've never had any client dissolve into a puddle and be unable to function. Crying is an important part of divorce. It's a cleansing of your old self and a baptism of the new. If you are having difficulty getting in touch with your feelings, listen to a moving piece of music or read some poetry that touches your soul or ask yourself,

"What will help me to release my feelings of pain and loss?" Then do what works for you.

In one of my seminars I asked the participants to share what they had done to help themselves grieve. "I let myself cry and sob," one participant responded. "I was traveling alone in Greece and I felt completely bereft. In one place where I had a room to myself, for three days I lay on my bed and cried, wrote, and plumbed the depth of my feelings. I normally keep myself so busy my feelings are kept at bay, but I realized that it was taking a tremendous amount of my energy to hold back the torrent of feelings I was keeping bottled up inside. It was such a relief to just let them flood over me. I felt like I had been washed clean."

Another participant admitted that he would go running in the hills alone and listen to sad country music on his Walkman. "When I would feel the pain well up in my chest I would run faster and let the tears stream down my face," he said. "Sometimes I would let out a yell to release the pain. It helped to be physically active." Men in our culture have been taught that expressing sadness or pain is taboo, but they need to break this rule and allow themselves to grieve.

Taking Stock of Your Losses Exercise

In my seminars I ask participants to recall the dream they had for their marriage. Some people say they wanted the traditional two kids and a house with a white picket fence, others wanted to incorporate a family into their common career. Take a moment to recall what you wanted for your family. In order to make room for a new dream you have to recall the old one in as much detail as possible and then grieve your loss. If writing it down is helpful, do that. The second part of this exercise is to make a list of the things that have changed since your divorce, and how you feel about these changes. For example:

I had to assume financial responsibility for myself and my daughter. I'm scared.

I lost my sexual partner. I'm lonely.

I have a greater sense of freedom. I'm excited.

I lost some of my friends. I resent their staying friends with my ex.

I'm not in close contact with my in-laws. I miss them.

Take the time you need to mourn these losses. Think about the new opportunities available to you and what you would like to do to fill the space. Then make a wish list.

IDENTIFY CONSTRUCTIVE ANGER VERSUS DESTRUCTIVE ANGER

Anger is a natural reaction to the pain of divorce. Feeling this emotion is appropriate because anger is an impulse for self-preservation; it comes from feelings of loss, and something you once had is indeed being taken away; and it arises from the perception that you have been treated unfairly, if only by life. Whatever the circumstances of your divorce, anger is necessary to propel you toward change. In many ways it is a positive step, but there is a fine line between constructive and destructive anger.

Constructive anger helps you make better choices for yourself and your children. It motivates you to set and maintain new boundaries and forces you to redefine your identity. Disconnecting from your ex-spouse and defining yourself as a separate person are hard work and healthy anger pushes you to take the first step in this process.

While you were married you were a couple. You based your decisions and plans on what was best for two people. Now your anger helps you think and act as an individual; it reminds you that you are no longer Mr. and Mrs. ________ .

A political revolution that establishes a nation's independence is fueled by the healthy anger of its citizens. The same feeling incites you to break the patterns of the past and establish a new way of relating in the future. It also allows you to establish new boundaries for your old relationship. An excellent example of anger used constructively is the case of my client, Patricia, the mother of six-year-old Nate. Nate routinely spends the weekends with his father, Greg, and one Sunday night Greg called Patricia to say that he might need to stop by her house to pick up the permission slip for the field trip on the way to Nate's school in the morning. She said that that would be fine but asked him to please be especially quiet if he came into the house so he wouldn't wake her. "I knew I'd be staying up late completing some reports and I didn't want to be disturbed," an enraged Patricia later complained in a therapy session.

"Greg came into my house in the pitch dark and yelled, 'Pat, are you awake?' He woke me out of a sound sleep! Then he yelled louder, 'Pat!' " At this point Patricia was ready to kill. Nate straggled in from the car and curled up on the couch in the living room. Then Greg went into the kitchen and ground coffee beans to make himself a cup of coffee. At which point, Patricia said, she jumped out of bed and flew into the kitchen and screamed, "Greg, you're such an inconsiderate asshole. I asked you not to wake me. You not only barge into my house, but you have the nerve to act like you still live here and fix yourself coffee. From now on, ask me before you make yourself at home. You don't live here anymore. I'm perfectly happy for you to pick up Nate or drop him off, but I don't want to be pals with you."

Patricia's anger motivated her to set clear boundaries for her relationship with Greg. This was her way of informing him that their intimate relationship had changed to a more formal parenting arrangement. Anger can help you identify the areas in your life that need to change. Use it, but don't abuse it.

Constructive anger can be a powerful tool for positive change, but destructive anger is something else entirely. If you find yourself crippled by rage or rousing your anger to hide from the world, you are caught in a destructive cycle. Raving fury and constant bickering serve no purpose other than retaliation or self-protection. Take a moment and ask yourself, "Am I in control of my anger or does my anger control me?" Then take a look at who is being hurt by your outrage; in most cases the unfortunate answer is yourself and your children. Destructive anger prevents you from discovering your strengths and seeing your opportunities. It also keeps you from learning from your mistakes and prevents you from healing.

Alison, a thirty-eight-year-old dental hygienist and the mother of two children, was still consumed with anger three years after her divorce. Her long dark hair and striking blue eyes could have made her attractive, but her tension overrode any observable beauty. During the first three months of her therapy she didn't smile once. Alison was overwhelmed with keeping a full-time job, running a household on a shoestring budget, and caring for her children. She did the lion's share of the parenting as the children's father, Bill, took them only one weekend a month.

Alison came to therapy with complaints of uncontrolled rage. She was lashing out at her kids, at people at work, and even at strangers. She had a constant knot in her stomach. She spent her free time on the phone with her female friends bemoaning her rotten life and repeating the list of Bill's sins. Her sessions with me were more of the same.

"I was at back-to-school night at the children's school when Bill walked in with his new wife," Alison said through clenched teeth. "She was wearing an eight-hundred-dollar designer suit. This guy was the ultimate tightwad; he would never spend a penny on our house. Now the kids tell me he's remodeled his new house. When I ask him to cover some of the kids' extra expenses he pleads poverty, but he has the nerve to lavish his new wife with expensive things and parade her in front of me. Here I am wearing bargains that I find at K mart specials. He's going to pay for this!"

Her toxic anger also was taking its toll on her well-being. Her rage sapped her energy and kept her stuck in a self-destructive emotional bind. Her friends were starting to avoid her. Alison's vitriol was depriving her of happiness, self-esteem, and future relationships. I helped her to see that she had made Bill the focus of her life. Her bitterness bound her to him as tightly as her love once had.

Alison's anger was caused by her state of mind. Whatever Bill had done to her was over, but continually replaying her chorus of complaints enabled her to keep fueling the flames of rage. Through anger she could maintain a connection, albeit a negative one. Alison's anger was a detour from facing her fears and insecurity, a diversion from healing.

After several sessions it came out that Alison, the youngest of three children, had always been babied. A decade and more younger than her siblings, she had been coddled to the point where she felt inadequate. Alison had never lived alone. She chose strong, domineering men as partners. With them she felt protected, as she had in her childhood, and she could avoid the terror of living alone and caring for herself. Alison's anger masked her feelings of low self-esteem and inadequacy and prevented her from grieving. Her rage gave her a false sense of power, but it kept her from growing up. As she confronted these deeper issues in therapy her rage began to dissipate.

Many people would rather feel the force of rage than acknowledge vulnerability. Without their anger, many fear they won't know who they are. The irony is that remaining stuck in destructive anger prevents them from discovering their true strength.

Anger Inventory Exercise

At some point you have to assess the impact your anger has both on your life and the lives of your children. Take a few minutes to answer the following questions. Your responses will determine the nature of your anger and whether you are using your anger constructively or are caught in a self-destructive cycle.

1. Are you angry at your ex on a regular basis?_______
2. Do you ever fantasize about terrible things happening to him or her?_______
3. Do you find yourself bad-mouthing your ex to anyone who will listen?_______
4. Do you ever transfer your anger at your ex-spouse to other people you care about?_______
5. Does your rage ever feel out of control?_______
6. Do you ever criticize your ex-spouse to your children?_______

If you answered yes to two or more of these questions you are caught up in your anger. Read through your answers, then consider the nature of your anger. Ask yourself: Is my anger moving me forward and helping me to make better choices or is it crippling me? And what effect is my anger having on my life and the lives of my children? Focusing on the nature and effect of your anger gives you the opportunity to release it and move on.

ALLOW YOURSELF TIME TO BE DEPRESSED

You feel terrible. You can hardly drag yourself out of bed. You get your kids ready for school and then you feel paralyzed. You wonder how you are going to make it through the day. All you want to do is crawl back in bed and pull the covers over your head. You either sleep all the time or your sleepless nights are plagued by guilt and anxiety. You ask yourself: How can I put my children through this pain? How am I going to pay the mortgage and all the bills? How can I go on? Your house is a mess, you have two weeks' worth of laundry piled up in the kitchen, dishes are overflowing in the sink, and brown mold is growing in the half-empty cartons of take-out food stacked on your stove. If your life were a movie it would be called *My Life Is a Dog.*

Take heart. You are suffering from divorce depression and in time this too shall pass. Divorce depression is different from other forms of depression in that it is caused by a specific event and is a natural part of the healing process. At the root of divorce depression are feelings of loss, helplessness, and low self-esteem. You feel like a failure; you don't like who you've become or the way your life has turned out. You recognize that you are in pain, you know you are causing your children pain, and you feel that it's your fault.

The depression itself finally arrives when you realize that there is no going back. "For a long time I pretended that things were still status quo," explained my client Frieda, a young mother whose usually clear brown eyes were rimmed with red. "At least now I feel my pain. Before, I walked around in a numb daze. All my feelings were just stuffed down. I felt like a zombie, going through the motions but not really alive. Now everything is pretty much out there and yeah, it hurts, but at least I know why I hurt and can cope better with the situation. I feel very grateful for that." You are no longer who you were and yet you aren't quite sure of who you are. One door has slammed closed and a new one hasn't yet opened. You are overwhelmed with feelings and you need time to assimilate the changes. Depression gives you this time to crawl into your shell and integrate all that has happened.

I'm a Failure

The most common reason for divorce depression is feeling like a failure. It is all too easy to make the jump from "My marriage has failed" to "I have failed" to "I am a failure." The case of Sharon is a good example. "I'm the oddball in my family," confessed the thirty-eight-year-old lawyer who came to me for counseling. "There has never been a divorce in my entire family. I have the distinguished honor of being the first. I'm the only one who couldn't make marriage work."

These feelings of low self-esteem and guilt lead to a sense of hopelessness that makes it next to impossible to take action. This in turn leads to a greater sense of despondency. While it is important to take the necessary time to integrate the changes, it is also essential that you eventually take the risks necessary to rebuild your life. When you feel depressed, taking action becomes almost unimaginable. Negative feelings interfere with any effort to improve your situation. I remember days when I felt as if I was sinking into a swamp of despair. All I wanted was to go to bed to escape my pain and anxiety. Most of the time I would resist the temptation. Doing even the smallest tasks such as cleaning the kitchen, making the beds, or going for a walk with a friend helped me know that I could still function. Once you take action and are feeling better you can focus on underlying problems

The up side of depression is that it forces you to face the sadness and loss created by the end of your marriage. It's time to accept the regret not so much for what was but for what could have been. Depression signals that you are accepting your losses, that you are saying good-bye to your past and your dreams. It is a sign that you are on the road to recovery.

This part of the divorce process is when you begin to learn about yourself and discover strengths, abilities, and resources you never knew existed. Use your pain to transform yourself into the person you want to be. Theologian Paul Tillich said, "The courage to be as oneself is the courage to make of oneself what one wants to be." I know it can be a difficult time, but you are like the mythical phoenix. A new you is being born out of the ashes of your divorce.

If you find yourself stuck in despair for a long period, you must seek professional help. A trained therapist or a support group can help you navigate this stage of the grieving process. This is the time to reach out. Call your local church or temple for referrals to a single parents' support group, contact Parents Without Partners, or make an appointment with a trained psychotherapist. You will find this additional support invaluable.

Emotional Ties Inventory Exercise

Take a few minutes to answer the following questions. No one else needs to know your answers, but if you hide the truth from yourself, you and your children are the ones who pay the price. Remember, this isn't the time to act stoic or to deceive yourself. This is a time to be completely honest about your situation. This is only for you.

1. Do you still have strong feelings and reactions to your ex? If you answer yes, note which emotions apply: anger, jealousy, guilt, self-pity, resentment, sadness.______________________________

   ____

2. Do you find yourself frequently compromising your boundaries and needs out of feelings of guilt?_______
3. Do you feel that your ex is to blame for making your life difficult? Do you often feel powerless and hopeless?_______
4. Are you angry at your ex on a daily basis? Do you ever fantasize about terrible things happening to him or her?_______
5. Do you try to get as much information about your ex as possible? Do you ever question your children about your ex's personal life?_______
6. Do you find yourself talking about him or her frequently?_______
7. Do you call or meet with your ex unnecessarily?_______

8. When you walk around your house do you find special mementos or reminders from your marriage?______

If you answered yes to two or more of the questions, you are still emotionally involved with your ex-spouse. Ask yourself, What is the cost of this emotional bond, both for you and your children? Your answer will help you to evaluate the impact of your attachment on your life.

Identify the emotion in which you are stuck, perhaps guilt, blame, anger, regret, etc. The most common place people get stuck is in feelings of anger and resentment. The following section will help you disengage from your ex-spouse and begin to rebuild your life.

In the first half of this chapter you learned how to recognize, accept, and deal with your emotions. In this second section, phase two of the emotionally divorcing process, you will focus on attaining control of your emotions, taking charge of your life, and gaining a sense of direction. As the comedian Jack Parr once said, "My life seems like one long obstacle course, with me as the chief obstacle." These next five steps will help you get out of your own way. So take this opportunity to discover who you want to be and what you want in your life. This is your second chance.

4. Gain control of your emotions.
5. Give up being a victim and take responsibility for your life.
6. Face your fears.
7. Set goals and take action.
8. Practice forgiveness.

Let's look at each of these steps.

GAIN CONTROL OF YOUR EMOTIONS

You must give yourself a mourning period, *but* after you have mourned it is time to stop letting your emotions rule your life. There is a natural period in which your feelings have a life of their own, and for the first year or two, that's as it should be. But at a certain point you have to pull yourself out of your emotional tailspin, grab hold of the rudder, and start steering yourself in a more rational direction. Here is a three-step process you can use to rein in your emotions.

1. Monitor your internal dialogue.
2. Shift from reacting emotionally to a more rational, logical way of responding.
3. Take stock of what's working and the positive things in your life.

Let me explain.

1. Monitor Your Internal Dialogue

The first step in gaining control of your emotions is to monitor your internal dialogue. In my seminars I ask participants, "How many of you talk to yourselves?" The majority raise their hands. Then I say, "And the rest of you are sitting there saying to yourself, 'I don't know. Do I talk to myself? I don't think I talk to myself, but then again, maybe I do talk to myself.' " We all keep a running commentary going inside our heads, but most of us aren't aware of it. Listen to what you say to yourself when you drive in your car alone. Notice the first thing you hear in your head when you wake up in the morning. What do you say to yourself about your ex-spouse on a daily basis? What do you tell yourself as you drift off to sleep at night?

When you listen to the little voice inside your head, you will probably hear a monologue that sounds like this: "You're a complete failure. Your life is ruined. Look how you've made your kids suffer. You're never going to get your life together. He never really loved you anyway. How do you think you're going to support yourself and your kids? You don't have any salable skills. You think you're miserable now, it's only going to get worse." Chances are this doom and gloom makes you feel depressed and angry, like the slug of the universe. Maybe your situation *is* unfair, maybe you have been deeply hurt and rejected, but rehearsing self-critical, hostile dialogue is not going to improve your situation. It only keeps you wallowing in your emotions.

Spend some time acquainting yourself with your Doomsday voice. Take a 8½″ × 11″ sheet of paper and fold it down the middle. Make two columns, one for your Doomsday voice and the other for your Realist voice, the more optimistic you. Then, without censoring, give yourself permission to write in one column the messages of doom and gloom you most commonly hear. In the other column use your Realist voice to combat the Doomsday chatter. For example:

Doomsday:	You're a failure.
Realist:	I'm not a failure. My marriage failed, but that doesn't make me a failure.
Doomsday:	You've been rejected and you're unlovable. No one wants to be with you.
Realist:	Because my marriage ended doesn't mean that I am unlovable; it simply means that we weren't able to work out our differences. I know several people who divorced and are now remarried.
Doomsday:	You're going to end up on the street, destitute and alone.
Realist:	Give me a break. I have talents that I can hone into salable skills. I have enough savings in the bank to tide us over until I can find a job. It's going to take some work, but we're going to be just fine.

Your Doomsday voice may carry a kernel of truth, even in the most negative statements. Ask yourself, "Is there some information that may be helpful as I adopt a more realistic perspective?"

Once you begin to recognize your pessimistic internal voice you will understand why you feel as bad as you do. Talking critically to yourself has a major impact on how you feel and act. When you hear your negative Doomsday voice, fight back. Tell it to stop.

2. Shift from Reacting Emotionally to a More Rational, Logical Way of Responding

The second step in gaining control of your emotions is to shift from unthinking reaction to a more rational, logical coping strategy. When you take time to stop and think you have more distance from your problems and can be more objective in solving them. You will still have feelings, but you won't be ruled by them.

One technique that seems simplistic but actually works is taking a few deep breaths and relaxing before you react. This helps clear your mind and allows you to consider a more rational response.

Take charge of your emotions by first identifying them. Ask yourself what you are feeling. "I'm always going to be alone. I'll never meet anyone to be in a relationship with. I'm afraid to go out by myself. Oh well, I guess I'll just settle in for another lonely weekend with a bag of popcorn and some videos." These are feelings of a person who is feeling lonely, discouraged, and helpless.

Connie, 39, the mother of three, told in one of my seminars how she had used this technique with miraculous results. "I got the kids up and put their breakfast out on the kitchen table. When I walked back upstairs to get dressed, I could feel my emotions starting to well up inside of me. At first I decided to ignore them. I rushed to get dressed and was in the bathroom putting on my makeup when my nine-year-old walked in and asked if I could drive her to the library after school. I lost it. That was the final straw. I started to scream at Angela and then burst out crying. Poor Angela, she didn't know what hit her. I quickly told her that my upset had nothing to do with her and I just needed a few minutes to pull myself together. I asked myself what I was feeling and the answer came to me loud and clear. I was exhausted and overwhelmed. I realized that I was completely overextended. I was starting to feel more like the maid than a mom. I needed to find some time to recharge my batteries. I also realized that I needed to enroll my kids in assuming some of the household responsibilities. I pulled myself together, finished putting on my makeup, and went down and explained to the kids that I needed them to pitch in and help out more around the house. That night after dinner we came up with a new chore plan in which they would pick up some of the slack. I felt so relieved."

Another key to emotional control is to shift from a feeling mode to a more rational, problem-solving mind-set. This is especially important when dealing with your former spouse. Pay attention to what I call "yellow alerts." Those early warning signals tell you you're starting to get upset. If they are left unheeded, you can easily escalate into a full-scale attack.

Tracy, a mother of two, was fuming when she came to see me. "I can't believe what a selfish bastard Eric is," she said. "I took my son to the dentist and I gave the receptionist my insurance card. A couple of days later she called to say that I was no longer covered. Eric had taken us off his policy. I just want to kill him."

I encouraged Tracy to imagine that Eric was in the room with us. She was to hurl at him all the angry, accusatory things she was feeling. Her list started with "irresponsible bastard" and went on to "You're so unreliable. I can't count on you for anything, you selfish creep." She vented her rage for about five minutes.

Once she had released her pent-up emotions we discussed how she could talk to Eric in a way that would promote cooperation rather than escalating to a fight. The next week Tracy reported that she had taken a few deep breaths and prepared herself to talk calmly with Eric. "I was amazed at how apologetic he was," she said. "He explained that he was changing to another company and that there shouldn't have been a lapse in coverage. I was glad that I didn't jump on his case before he had a chance to explain. It was a good lesson for me."

Don't expect yourself to be completely unemotional. We all react irrationally from time to time, but the best way to repress your impulse to react is to acknowledge your feelings and allow yourself to feel them, but *don't* allow them to dictate your behavior. It's perfectly fine to think and feel your angry feelings, but before you take action, call in your rational side to consider the situation objectively.

3. Take Stock of What's Working and the Positive Things in Your Life

Jennifer, the harried, disheveled mother of two teenage boys, came to me feeling discouraged. "I have nothing going for me and nothing to offer. Yes, I'm a good mom, but that's not enough. I cry a lot, especially when I'm alone in my car. I spend a lot of time looking at all that I've lost and feeling sorry for myself. I feel like I'm worthless and incapable."

Jennifer and I worked to discover where she had gotten the message that she was incompetent. She realized that one of the most destructive aspects of her marriage had been her husband's extreme criticism. Nothing she had done was ever good enough for him. After fifteen years of being told that she wasn't good enough, pretty enough, smart enough, etc., Jennifer had integrated these negative messages. Now she believed them. We worked to uncover the negative beliefs she had about herself. Jennifer began to realize that a lot of what her husband had accused her of was simply untrue.

Once she had confronted her inner critic, I asked Jennifer to describe her strengths and positive qualities. At first she felt awkward and uncomfortable, but as I reminded her of strong qualities I had seen in the time she had been coming to see me, her face began to light up. She realized the truth of what I was saying. She was willing to take credit for the parts of her life that worked. I asked her to write down ten of her strengths and bring the list to our next session.

She returned the next week with this: "I am reliable, honest, trustworthy. I am a good mother. I have a good sense of humor. I am a great cook. I am creative, a good friend, persevering, willing to try new things." In this way, we began to change her perspective. When I asked how it felt to discover her wealth of resources, she replied with pride, "I really do have a lot going for me. I have two beautiful kids, a well-paying, satisfying career, a few good friends, and a supportive family." She also reminded herself of what she had gained in her sense of self and feelings of independence. "Focusing on my assets has helped me to get hold of my emotions and turn things around." Start to recognize your strengths and positive qualities and appreciate the opportunities available to you.

The Total Truth Process Exercise

An essential part of gaining control of your emotions is finding a way to release pent-up feelings. Most people think that if they ignore feelings they will simply go away. But when you find yourself screaming at your kids for a minor infraction or weeping when you hear the song that you and your ex both loved, you may realize that is not the case.

The total truth process helps free you of excess emotional baggage. The idea is to write a letter to your ex-spouse expressing the full range of your emotions, starting with anger and ending with forgiveness. If you get to the section on forgiveness but still have feelings of anger or sadness, go back to the angry part of your letter and keep writing until you feel free of that particular emotion. Don't fake it. The point of the letter is to express anything that needs to be said.

You don't have to send this letter to your ex. It is simply a structured activity to help you release unexpressed emotions. The letter should be written so that each section is approximately the same length. Follow this format:

Anger and Resentment

I'm angry that . . .

I hate it when . . .

I'm fed up with . . .

I resent it when . . .

I can't stand it when . . .

Hurt

I feel hurt when . . .

I feel rejected when . . .

I feel sad when . . .

I feel jealous about . . .

I feel disappointed about . . .

Fear

I feel scared when you . . .

I feel scared that you don't . . .

I'm afraid that . . .

I feel insecure about . . .

I'm afraid that I . . .

Remorse and Regret

I'm sorry that . . .

I regret that I . . .

Please forgive me for . . .

I didn't mean to . . .

I feel sad that . . .

Wants

All I ever want(ed) . . .

I want you to . . .

I wish that . . .

I deserve . . .

I want us to . . .

What I really want is . . .

Love and Forgiveness

I forgive you for . . . and I forgive myself for . . .

What I love most about you is . . .

I understand that . . .

I appreciate you for . . .

Thank you for . . .

This letter exercise can be used any time you feel yourself getting stuck in your emotions. Feelings need to be expressed in order to be released and this is a safe and highly effective method for releasing them.[1]

GIVE UP BEING A VICTIM AND TAKE RESPONSIBILITY FOR YOUR LIFE

"He ruined my life."

"I'll never find another relationship."

"She's depriving me of my family."

"He robbed me of my youth. Now I'm damaged goods."

"If she hadn't held me back I would have been doing much better now."

It is natural to feel sorry for yourself after your divorce, especially if you were the one who was left. You may have felt taken advantage of, wronged, and victimized, but whatever the case you don't have to remain a victim. If you hang on to feeling like a victim you will remain frozen in time, bound to your past, and powerless. No amount of blame or complaint is going to make your life better. No one is going to come to your rescue. You have to save yourself. And the best way to do this is to recognize that you are not helpless and powerless, that you *can* take action and change your life. Easier said than done, you may be thinking.

For some people, the idea of being in charge of your own life, no longer dependent on someone else to fill in the gaps, is frightening. After being married and allowing yourself to depend on another person, you may doubt your ability to make it on your own. One way to avoid facing this fear is to blame your ex-spouse for misfortune or difficulty, but the "if-only syndrome" allows another person to have power over you. It keeps you locked into remorse, regret, and self-pity. You remain the victim of wishful thinking. "If only he paid his child support on time." "If only she didn't hassle me so much about the kids." "If only we were still together the kids wouldn't be so uncontrollable." Each time the focus is on another person who holds all the power. Most people try to change the other person in order to make their life better or to improve their situation. But most likely that won't happen. You can't change someone else. You really have power and control only over yourself.

Ted, 42, was married for fifteen years. One night he returned from work to find a note from his wife announcing that she had taken the children and moved home with her parents in another state. There was no explanation.

During their marriage she had assumed all the responsibility for their entire social life. Ted was introverted and shy and had relied on her to make up for his lack of social poise. If it had been up to him, Ted never would have left the house. He was perfectly content to spend his evenings glued to the TV or sitting with his nose in a book. Now that he was on his own, Ted felt isolated. The one time he did venture out to a friend's dinner party he felt so awkward that he left before dessert.

Ted came to me for therapy almost two years after his divorce. He was still saying things like "She ruined my life. She left me stranded. I can't manage without her. I'm going to be alone for the rest of my life." Ted had dropped contact with his children and he blamed his ex-wife for this loss too. He still believed she held the key to his happiness. He was terrified to enter the social world alone, and as long as he continued to play the blame game, he could avoid the real issue, his fear.

I pointed out that it was time to stop spending so much energy blaming her for the breakup of his marriage. To undo his emotional bind, he had to deal with his insecurity. I asked Ted what would happen if he accepted that his marriage was over and that what he would make of his future was up to him. Ted balked at first but gradually began to wrestle with his fear of being alone and responsible for himself. I asked what was his worst fear. "My wife and I married while we were still in college. I have never been on my own," Ted confessed while holding back his tears. "I just don't know if I can go out there in the dating world. I'm not sure I know how to make polite conversation." I empathized with Ted's fears and asked what was the worst thing was that could happen. "I just won't have anything to say and I'll look like a fool. I guess I'm afraid of being rejected again." Now Ted was in touch with his feelings.

In the course of therapy I encouraged Ted to take low-risk actions. He attended sporting events with friends from the office. I recommended that he sign up for a class at a local college so he could interact with people in a nonthreatening environment. With enough positive experiences, Ted gained confidence in his social skills. Within six months he began to date a woman from his office.

Once Ted felt more secure, he contacted his ex and arranged to have his children come and stay with him during their Christmas and summer vacations. Ted also began to call his kids weekly to stay in touch with the details of their lives.

Ted needed to shift his focus away from feeling rejected and deal with his underlying anxiety. Once he recognized his fears he was able to confront and conquer them. Remaining in a blaming, self-pitying, victim stance is ultimately counterproductive.

Many people get lost in the maze figuring out who was to blame; but who was right or wrong doesn't really matter. All that matters is building a future for yourself and your children. We often blame our ex-spouse for how we feel and for what has happened to us, but blame distracts us from finding solutions. The only things that we can control is our response. Regardless of who was at fault, we are responsible for how we feel now. We can't change or control another person, but we can control our response to an event and, in turn, affect its outcome.

This formula will help you understand this concept. E+R=O. An Event plus your Response equals an Outcome. An outcome is produced by the combination of an external event and your response to it. By changing your response you can alter the outcome. For example, two people may be at a crowded party. One person feels lonely and isolated while the other feels welcome and connected. Though they're both at the same event, they have very different responses to the event. One person says to herself, "These people are stuck-up, cold, and aloof. I can't relate to anyone!" She has created an outcome of loneliness and isolation. The other person thinks, "What wonderful, warm people. I feel welcome and connected here. What a great crowd." This person has responded to the situation differently; he has created an outcome of connectedness and joy. You will often be able to alter the outcome by changing your response.

The Power of Words

Many people don't realize that the very language they use keeps them stuck in a victim position. Simply shifting your speech from victim-focused words to language in which you assume responsibility can help change the way you think. Victim language grants power to someone outside yourself. A particularly insidious belief is that other people can make us feel. "*He* makes me miserable." "*She* makes me nuts." This kind of language makes someone else responsible for your state of mind. I suggest you assume responsibility for your feelings. The reality is that short of inflicting physical pain, no one can make you feel something. Other people say or do something, you interpret what they said or did, and your interpretation produces emotions. More accurately, we make ourselves feel a certain way by what we tell ourselves. A more useful response would be to ask yourself what part you played in that situation. When you look at your life from this perspective you get a greater sense of personal power. Rather than blaming someone else by saying "He makes me furious," a more honest response would be "When he is late picking up the kids, I feel furious." In the second statement you own your feelings.

Here is another way that language can help to empower you. This chart shows you how to shift from using victim language to thinking and speaking in a more empowered, self-responsible way. Each statement in the victim language column is either disempowering or negative. By saying "I can't," you imply that you are either incapable or helpless. For example, you may say "I can't find time to call the children's father," when a more honest statement would be "I won't take the time to call the children's father." With the second statement you take responsibility for your actions.

VICTIM LANGUAGE	RESPONSIBLE LANGUAGE
I CAN'T	I WON'T
I SHOULD	I COULD
I HAVE TO	I CHOOSE TO
THIS IS A PROBLEM	THIS IS AN OPPORTUNITY
THIS IS HORRIBLE	THIS IS A LEARNING EXPERIENCE.

The word "should" conjures up images of being forced to do something. Many people live their lives ruled by the "tyranny of the should." "I should volunteer at my children's school," "I should eat healthier food," "I should have a social life." These statements make you feel as if you are being forced or pushed to do something. When your actions are dictated by what you should do, you don't think about what you want or even consider alternatives. By shifting from "should" to "could," you allow yourself a choice. "I should cook nutritious meals for my kids" may inspire feelings of guilt or obligation. Saying "I could cook more nutritious meals for my kids" focuses on a choice you have made and assumes responsibility for your decision. The same concept applies to the difference between "I have to" and "I choose to." "I have to send my ex-wife the child support check" puts you in the position of victim, which always generates feelings of resistance. Choosing to send the check empowers you. The problem is never the problem; the problem is how you cope with it.

You always have a choice about how you deal with even the most negative situation. That's one of the gifts of being human. We can choose how we perceive even the most disastrous events. Many people think that negative things have to be dealt with negatively, but what usually results is more negativity. You have the power to deal with negative events positively and to use them for your own growth and transformation.

The last two victim statements on the chart, "This is a problem" and "This is horrible," produce feelings of helplessness. Only when you shift your focus to what you can learn from the situation does it become an opportunity for change. You can make an attitudinal shift and begin seeing events as stepping-stones rather than as stumbling blocks. The choice is yours.

Victim Recall Exercise

This exercise may help you clarify the difference between thinking of yourself as a victim and taking charge. Remember a situation in which you felt victimized. Write a description of the incident or talk about it into a tape recorder in as much detail as possible. Then read it over or replay the tape and notice how you feel.

Now take the same situation and this time write it or say it as if you have power and control. Notice how different you feel when you go over the new interpretation. When you assume responsibility for yourself, you operate differently. You act as though you have choices and certain power. This frees you.

FACE YOUR FEARS

When you want to ignore the void of being alone, an ex-spouse comes in handy. To truly finalize your emotional divorce you have to make a leap of faith and jump across the abyss. That means you have to let go of who you were and what you had. There is no way to straddle an abyss. You have to let go of the old in order to experience the new. You have to jump from safety and security (or perhaps false security) to find yourself on the other side. You have to get to know yourself in an entirely new way.

Madeline, a stylishly dressed woman whose gnawed-down fingernails belied her superficial self-confidence, had been divorced for almost two years, yet she was still paralyzed with fear. "I'm really scared," she said in her first counseling session. I encouraged her to look at what she was afraid of, no matter how irrational or unfounded her fears might seem. I asked her to complete the sentence "I'm afraid that ______." She began with "I'm afraid that I'll start to cry and never stop," and continued "I'm afraid that no one will want to be with me. I'm afraid that without my marriage, I'm nothing. I'm afraid that no one will want me or find me attractive. I'm afraid I'm boring and only know how to be a wife and a mother. I'm afraid that I'll always be alone." By the end Madeline had unearthed many of her fears.

We then began to confront them one by one and introduce some reality into the picture. Even she could see that many of her fears were ludicrous. I pointed out that her worst fears had already been realized. Despite her memories, she really was alone now. And while being alone wasn't her preference, she was coping just fine. Madeleine was shocked by this revelation. In her imagination being alone was something far worse than what she was actually doing. I encouraged her to do things on her own as well as with friends, to take this opportunity to rediscover interests and activities she may have put aside during her marriage. I gave her two assignments. She was to think back to the things she was interested in before her marriage and to write them down. Then she was to do at least one thing on her list before the next session, either by herself or with a friend. I wanted her to reconnect with herself and her passions.

"I started to think about what I used to do before I married Bob," Madeline reported at our next session. "There are things I haven't done for years because my ex-husband didn't want to do them. I used to love opera, browsing through galleries. I was a foreign film buff, but I stopped going because he always made such a fuss when I asked him to come along." Madeline was beginning to realize how much of herself she had given up. Now she had the freedom to do the things she loved to do and it excited her. "I went to the movies by myself and saw *Cyrano* with Gérard Depardieu," she said with delight. "It reminded me of when I lived in Greenwich Village and spent afternoons at the Bleecker Street Cinema with my friends and having intense intellectual discussions. I'm rekindling my old interests and learning to like my own company."

When you recall what once made you happy, facing the void will feel more like an adventure than a frightening journey. What you resist persists. The feeling of being neither here nor there, of being caught between two worlds, is what most people resist, but trying to avoid your fears prolongs the inevitable. If you feel shaky, get the support you need to handle the changes in your life.

Getting to Know You

Most fears are much worse than reality. One way to deal with them is to use a personal journal. Recently I dug up some old journals from the period during my divorce and reread them. I realized that I had used my journal as if it were a wise, old friend to whom I could tell anything.

Start by listing your fears. They may not be rational. Most fears aren't. One of my postdivorce fears was that I would end up destitute, unable to support myself and my daughter. I would have dreams of Ama and me walking down the street, penniless and homeless, with our possessions crammed into a shopping cart. Once I wrote out my fear I saw how loony and out of proportion it was. But I also realized that my overblown fear was masking a genuine concern.

During my marriage I had relied on my husband to provide for us. I was twenty-eight but I didn't have a career or much formal training. I needed to earn a living, but I also wanted to stay home with my five-year-old daughter. I listed my salable skills, and at the top of the list was cooking. At the time we were living in Santa Fe, New Mexico. I took a survey of the local health food stores and found that healthy lunchtime food was limited and in some cases nonexistent. I decided to start a lunch service in my home. Three days a week I cooked egg rolls and vegetarian sushi. To my amazement, they sold out. Within a month I expanded to five days a week.

By confronting my fear and learning from it I was able to change my situation. Writing in a journal made a big difference. I recommend that you get in the habit of using it every day, even if it's for only ten minutes. The journal will help you release your anxiety and fears. When fears are brought out into the light of day they lose some of their power and can be put into perspective.

Crossing the abyss sounds frightening, but this is the bridge to your future. You may not have a clear picture of what lies ahead, but as long as you put one foot in front of the other you will reach the other side. Every time you make a major change in your life you are confronted with the unknown, and I don't know anyone who loves uncertainty. A journey of a thousand miles starts with one step. The same is true of facing your fears and designing your future. Most people have no idea of their own strength and resourcefulness. As you leave your past behind you will discover new interests, new abilities, new skills, and new ideas. You don't have to face your fears all at once. You can move at a pace that is right for you. This is an opportunity for you to look inside and discover who you are and what your deepest hopes, dreams, and aspirations are. Use your journal to chronicle your journey.

Victory Log Exercise

Create a section in your journal called Victory Log, a list of your personal triumphs and achievements. These can be anything from getting your kids to bed on time or giving your first dinner party since your divorce, to avoiding an argument with your ex or going out to the movies alone. Start by writing down every victory you can remember. Don't put them in any order, simply write them down. Keep your Victory Log handy and consult it when you are facing a difficult situation. It will remind you of your strengths and capabilities and act as your own personal cheerleading squad. Research has shown that losers relive past defeats while winners review past successes.

Each time you take a risk or try out a new behavior, write it down in your Victory Log. For example: "I asked my boss for a raise." "I told the PTA chairman that I wouldn't be available to be a room mother." "I went to a dinner party alone." This will give you a record to look back on when you need courage to take another risk.

SET GOALS AND TAKE ACTION

During this transition period it is especially important to consider how to bring your dreams and aspirations into reality. On the other hand, you may be feeling completely overwhelmed with the multitude of challenges in your life. Regardless of your situation, goal setting is essential to gaining emotional freedom. It is a vehicle to move you forward.

Many of us set goals, but we aren't conscious of the process we use. Goal setting has four steps. The first is to determine what you want; the second, to state those goals in specific terms; the third, to decide what steps are necessary to achieve your goals; and finally, to take action. Let's look at each step in more detail.

1. Determine What You Want

Be specific. Many of us have been taught since childhood to consider what others want, but not to focus on ourselves. This is especially true of marriage; we spend the majority of our time considering our partner's needs and taking into account his or her preferences and dreams as we plan for the future. Now it is time to think about what *you* want. What changes would enhance your life?

Think in terms of the various areas of your life. I suggest that people in my seminars use a journal to make a wish list. On the top of successive pages you write categories such as mental, emotional, physical/health, relationships, spiritual, financial, etc. Be sure to include all the areas that are important to you. Then list the changes you want to make in each area. This may take you an hour, a day, or a week. Allow yourself the luxury of dreaming about what is really important to you. Once you have listed your wishes in the categories, ask yourself what is most important to you right now. When you have chosen an area you want to improve, visualize the changes you want to make. Close your eyes and imagine what your life will be once your goal has become reality. If you are unhappy with your job, picture a career you would like or visualize where you want to work. That will become your goal.

2. State Those Goals in Specific Terms

Many people have good ideas but are too wishy-washy to state them. I'll try to find a new job, they say, or I'll get in shape. But these statements aren't specific and don't indicate any necessary steps for self-direction. When you have determined your goal, it is important to state it as a specific, positive objective. Rather than saying "I'll try to find a new job," state "I will be doing interior design and earning thirty thousand dollars a year by next February 3." Instead of saying "I need to lose weight," state a clearer objective: "I will weigh 157 pounds by October 12." Defining your goal in specific terms helps you see what you need to do to accomplish it.

3. Decide What Steps Are Necessary to Achieve Your Goals

Once you have seen your goal clearly, picture the specific steps needed to reach that goal. This is the equivalent of coming up with a strategy. You know what you want; how are you going to get there? It's important to break the process down into small achievable steps that will move you in the right direction. Make sure your goal is realistic. Ask yourself, "If I take the steps to achieve my goal, do I have a reasonable chance of succeeding?" If the answer is yes and you are willing to take the steps, you are ready to write down your goal. For example, "I want to be seriously involved with someone by the spring of next year." Ask yourself what steps you need to take to achieve that goal. Some of the steps might be: leave my house so I can meet available people; find two interesting activities and get involved; and tell my friends that I want to date and ask them to set me up with a blind date. Picture yourself taking the necessary steps. For another example, instead of putting down "I want a better job," write "I will start immediately to update my résumé," or "I will begin to explore new places of employment and I'll mail out a dozen résumés by March 1." This gives you a blueprint for achieving your goal.

4. Take Action

No matter how small your effort, it is essential that you take steps that will move you toward your goal. Almost everything we do in life requires a number of small steps from beginning to final goal, including writing a report, cooking dinner, losing weight, or redecorating your living room.

A woman in one of my support groups used the goal-setting process to overcome a frightening obstacle in her life. Cathy, a ponytailed blonde in too youthful clothing, had worked as a physician's assistant before she met her husband, but had given up her career when her first child was born.

Cathy came to the group in a panic. "I feel so stupid and dependent," she admitted through her tears. "Here I am, thirty-two years old, and I've moved back in with my mother. It's been so long since I worked that I've lost all my contacts." She had found a job at a furniture manufacturing company, but it didn't pay enough to cover her expenses. "I go to the market but I can only buy the basics," she complained. "I can't afford desserts, fruit drinks, pizzas, or sodas. I can only buy things we absolutely need. I hate having to watch my money so tightly. I don't even have enough to pay my taxes and the thought of not having health insurance gives me anxiety attacks. I just don't know what to do."

Over the next eight meetings I worked with Cathy to identify her priorities. After setting some goals and discussing her ideas with the group, Cathy realized that finding a satisfying, well-paying career was her number one priority. We encouraged her to come up with a clearly defined, specific objective. "I want to be working in the health care industry by November 4," she said. We began to explore what steps she needed to take to move in the direction of meeting her goal.

Once Cathy had a clear goal, she moved quickly. She contacted several doctors' offices and realized that in order to break into a competitive profession she would have to go back to school. Cathy had gotten her prior job without full credentials; because of her personal connection with the doctor she had provided services that only registered nurses can administer. She interviewed at several schools and qualified for financial aid at a local community college. Cathy arranged to take classes two nights a week and continued to work during the day.

One of the group members suggested that Cathy explore her options within the health care industry while she was working at the furniture job. Cathy contacted several hospitals and health product firms. Within a month she had a new job as a sales representative for a hospital bed company. Her income increased significantly. This was another step toward pursuing a new career and improving her financial situation.

Clearly defined goals can help you take action to improve your present situation. As you take the necessary steps you will feel a greater sense of competence. This, in turn, will boost your self-confidence.

PRACTICE FORGIVENESS

You can't change what happened between you and your ex-spouse, but you can change your attitude about it. Forgiveness doesn't mean that what your ex did was right or that you condone what he or she did; it simply means that you no longer want to hold a grudge. Forgiveness is not a gift for the other person; it is a purely selfish act that allows you to put the past behind you.

"For a long time I held my ex-wife responsible for all the pain in my life," said Michael, a balding assistant principal of a large middle school. "Visualizing her driving off a cliff in a fiery car about five hundred times finally got to be an old movie. I realized that she really didn't divorce me to hurt me. She ended our marriage because that's what she needed to do. Now I can see her as a separate, vulnerable person who has her own pain, issues, unfulfilled needs and dreams. What a relief."

Forgiveness is the ultimate healer. Forgiveness doesn't require you to remarry your ex-spouse; it simply means that you let go of your anger. Forgiveness is an inner attitude that lightens your heart. Once you have gone through the grieving process, allowed yourself to mourn your losses, and cut the emotional ties with your ex, forgiveness is the natural next step.

Eileen, a petite woman whose physical delicacy masked a hard-nosed attitude, had been divorced for three years. "I'm finally making headway," she reported with great pride at one of my support group meetings. "I used to prevent my ex from seeing his kids if he didn't pay the child support on time, but then the kids suffered. After a year of fruitless arguments I realized they were getting me nowhere and only causing my kids pain. So I let go and started to reason with him. Using the kids to get back at him wasn't working anyway."

Eileen had felt that she did all the hard work and her ex got all the goodies. Their kids adored him, even though he wasn't around for them. "I really despise this man, but I had my son call and invite his dad to his birthday party. My ex was amazed but he came. He saw that I had dropped my bitterness. I'm so relieved. It's like a weight has been lifted off me. You should have seen how happy my kids were to have their dad at the party. They really missed him."

Forgiveness helps create an atmosphere of cooperation between you and your ex-spouse. Robert Muller, former Secretary General of the United Nations, said it very eloquently:

> *Decide to forgive, for resentment is negative, resentment is poisonous, resentment diminishes and devours self. Be the first to forgive, to smile, and to take the first step, and you will see happiness bloom on the face of your human brother or sister. Be always the first; do not wait for the others to forgive. For by forgiving you become the master of fate, the fashioner of life, the doer of miracles. To forgive is the highest, most beautiful form of love. In return you will receive untold peace and happiness. Only the brave know how to forgive. A coward never forgives. It is not in his nature.*[2]

THE GIFTS OF YOUR DIVORCE

Tanya, a forty-three-year-old paralegal, had resented her ex-husband's cavalier attitude toward child support. She had jumped through hoops to collect the little bit the court had ordered him to pay. As a result she had little appreciation for the role he had played in her life. One day he dropped by her house to pick up their six-year-old son. While there, he overheard a message being left on her answering machine. A national television news program was planning an exposé based on an article she had written. The next day when he brought the boy home, he congratulated her. She was so surprised that she blurted out, "George, you would have been proud of me! They offered me some money to act as a consultant for the show. I said it wasn't enough and held my ground. Eventually they doubled their offer. I realized that I've gotten so much stronger as a result of having to deal with you."

"All the people that I have loved," Tanya said during a session,

"I hold in a special place in my heart. Each relationship has given me a gift. With George it's different; I mostly wish he would disappear. Yet George is probably the largest gift of all, except he is a gift in black wrapping paper. Still, he's much of the reason I am who I am today. Because of him I had to deal with issues that were deeply difficult. Because of him I am more understanding. I can't believe I'm saying this, but I'm really grateful for our relationship and all the growing it forced me to do. I would never have pushed myself like this. George was a real catalyst in my life."

Every relationship touches us in ways we are not always aware of. We are changed by the experience of interacting with another human being so intimately. Sometimes the experience may feel more like sandpapering than growth, but nevertheless, our lives are enriched. At some point you will want to look at the gifts you received from your ex-spouse and even from your divorce. Yes, I realize this means making a major shift in your thinking, but I think you will find the results of your exploration worth the effort.

"My ex-wife blamed me for not being in touch with my feelings and she was right," said Steve, the twice-married, middle-aged father of an eighteen-month-old son. He came to me for counseling in conjunction with his new involvement in a support group. "My support group has seven women and only one other man," he said. "They have seen me in pain and encouraged me to share it. Now I can express my feelings to women without feeling like I am going to repel them. Expressing myself actually draws people closer. It has been a terrific gift. I didn't choose to get divorced, but as difficult as it is, it's been a wonderful opportunity to learn. If nothing else, I'm a much better parent."

You have many choices. You can choose forgiveness over revenge, joy over despair. You can choose action over apathy. You hold the power. You make the choices that mold your life and the lives of your children. Make choices for life. Make choices for growth. Make choices for cooperation. You hold the key to how well you make the emotional adjustment to your divorce and consequently how well your children will adapt. Think carefully about the choices you make, the actions you take, and the impact they will have on those you love. Remember, because of your children you will have a relationship with your ex-spouse for the rest of your lives.

The Gifts of My Marriage and Divorce Exercise

Ask yourself in what ways you benefited from your marriage. Perhaps you have been so caught up in emotional turmoil that you have forgotten the good things that resulted from your marriage. Perhaps, like Tanya, your ex-spouse forced you to grow stronger; maybe you have made friends you wouldn't have known if it weren't for your marriage; perhaps you have new interests as a result of your ex's influence. List the gifts you received from your marriage. Yes, there are some. If you are having trouble getting started, list your children. Write down at least five.____

____

Next, consider how you have benefited from your divorce. Maybe you have discovered talents and abilities you never knew you had. You may have made changes in your career. Perhaps you have felt more alive or a greater sense of freedom. You may have deepened your relationship with your children or discovered a new sense of inner strength. List at least five ways you have benefited from your divorce.

____

____

The process of emotional divorce doesn't happen overnight. The ties you have woven with your former spouse are strong and complex. I hope the tools in this chapter will help you identify the bonds you maintain with your past and will support you in changing the feelings and behavior that are keeping you bound. As you use these tools you will cut the cord, one thread at a time. Honor your own pace in this process. We all have our Achilles' heels, our private weaknesses, particular buttons that when pushed send us into a fit. But the more work you do to rewire your circuits, the less reactive you will be.

The next step in this process is to shift your perspective of your relationship from intimacy to a more detached businesslike way of relating. It is important that the foundation of your new parenting relationship be based on the fact that the two of you still have children to raise. It's time to shift the focus of your relationship from marriage to parenting. Letting go of excess emotional baggage will help you take this next step more easily.

DIVORCE CEREMONY

I recently read an article in *Life* magazine on the importance of rituals. As I flipped through the pages I saw brief descriptions and photographs of the various rites of passage celebrated around the world. They include christenings, weddings, confirmations, bas and bar mitzvahs, school graduations, funerals, and so on. But there was a very telling gap when it came to the dissolution of a marriage.

Take a few minutes and think about what would help you to feel a sense of closure. A man in one of my seminars decided to symbolize the letting go of his marriage by buying a bunch of brightly colored helium balloons, going to the beach, and releasing them. As he watched the balloons float off on the breeze, getting smaller and smaller until they disappeared, he visualized releasing himself and his ex-wife from the ties of marriage. A woman I know took strips of paper and wrote memories, appreciations, and regrets she had from her marriage on each piece of paper. Then she built a fire in her fireplace and as she read each one she balled it up and, one by one, threw them into the fire to symbolize the end of her dreams. Then she took some Indian sweet grass and sprinkled it into the fire to clear the air. A friend of mine took the seashells that she and her ex had collected on their honeymoon in Tahiti and dug a hole in her backyard. She gently placed the shells in the hole and buried them to symbolize the death of her marriage. She then sprinkled a packet of wildflower seeds on top of the patch of dirt as a way of representing the new direction her life was taking. In all of these cases the ritual helped each person to gain a sense of closure.

Think about what would help you to honor the place your marriage played in your life. Allow yourself to be creative; invent whatever would suit you. I recently read about a woman who made a divorce quilt. She had quilted professionally and she made the quilt during the end of her ten-year marriage. She used quilt making as a form of therapy, sewing various panels that signified her marriage and her feelings toward her ex-husband.

One technique that I use frequently is drawing on a large pad of paper with crayons. Trust me when I tell you that I'm not an artist, but I find it very effective and satisfying to create pictures that symbolize the changes in my life. Create a space that evokes creativity. Put your kids to bed, turn on the answering machine, find a beautiful piece of music. Then take a few minutes and close your eyes and ask yourself for an image or a symbol that represents your past, your old life, or whatever you're letting go of. Then draw a representation of that image on a piece of paper. It may be something recognizable or it may be an abstract form. You're not in an art contest. Give yourself permission to play and let what's inside you come out. Once you have made that image, close your eyes again and this time ask for an image that represents the new you. When I did this I saw a doe in a lush green woods. Once again, put your image or the feeling you had on paper. Finally, close your eyes one last time and ask yourself for an image that represents your new life, what you have to look forward to. Draw that on a third sheet of paper. You may want to write on the back of each sheet what the images mean to you and how you are feeling as you see them. Then take the image of your past and either burn or bury it to release the energy. Take the other two drawings and put them up in your bedroom as a reminder of your journey.

Rituals and ceremonies are ways of honoring a phase of your life that you have passed through. They help you usher in the next. They give validity and closure to important transitions. Of our life's important transitions, the only one our culture does not mark with ritual is divorce. Divorce, the closing of one door and the opening of another, deserves to be recognized as a significant passage; it needs to be ritualized. You began your married life with a ceremony and you should end it with another ceremony.

The following words of François Mauriac sum up the concept of appreciating the gifts your marriage gave you as well as the riches you are mining from your divorce.

We are, all of us, molded by those by who have loved us, and though that love may pass, we remain nonetheless their work . . . A work that very likely they do not recognize, and which is never exactly what they intended.

No love, no friendship can ever cross the path of our destiny without leaving some mark upon it forever.

Chapter 4

They Said It Couldn't Be Done

Building a Parenting Partnership

People can alter their lives by altering their attitudes.

William James

Imagine that you have been told the wiring in your house is corroded. If it isn't replaced immediately your house could go up in smoke. You live in a small town and the only electrician is someone you dislike, but if you don't find a way to work with him your house and family will be in danger. The electrician isn't particularly fond of you either, but he needs the business. After trying to find a way around working with him, you realize that your choices are limited. Despite your feelings, you hire the electrician. To minimize misunderstandings, you spell out the job in as much detail as possible: total cost, deadline, and the work hours. You don't have to like him to get the job done, but you do have to be courteous and clear about your expectations.

The same concept applies to your dealings with your former spouse. This person is your children's other parent. Despite how you feel about him or her, you must learn how to shift from a marriage relationship to a less intimate way of relating.

In the 1970s, family counselor Isolina Ricci came up with the ingenious idea of using business principles as a model to redefine relationships. I use a variation on this model with clients and have found that it works exceptionally well.[1] There is a wide range of child custody relationships. Some noncustodial parents choose to have a great deal of involvement with their children and set up a joint custody plan. Some have limited contact and see their children perhaps once a month. Some move away and decide that visits with their kids will be infrequent, if they happen at all. Regardless of the type of custody arrangement you have, or the frequency of contact you have with your ex-spouse, using certain guidelines can make your parenting partnership work more effectively.

BELIEVE IT OR NOT

When I introduce the concept of parenting partnerships in my seminars, I inevitably hear from the naysayers. "Such a partnership is impossible," they insist. "If we couldn't get along in our marriage what makes you think we can cooperate now?" The truth is that for many parents, the end of the emotional involvement makes communication in a detached, civilized manner much easier.

"My husband is a real jerk as a husband," confessed a participant in one of my seminars. "But I'm not his wife anymore. And he's a terrific father." As she described it, their divorce was like World War III, but over time the anger dissipated. They untangled their ties as a couple and concentrated on their kids. "I'm surprised that we could do it, but I think it's the power of having children that you both adore," she said. "I still feel frustrated with him from time to time, but it's so much easier to be civil to him now that we're not together."

Your obligation as a parent requires that you separate how you feel about your ex-spouse as a marriage partner from how you feel about him or her as a parent. A successful parenting partnership depends on your ability to do this.

Businesspeople don't have to like each other to have a successful business relationship, but certain conditions are basic: You have to communicate clearly, act courteously, offer a minimum of self-disclosure, and take responsibility for your actions.

Think about your everyday business dealings. When you are in the grocery store check-out line and the clerk asks, "How are you today?" you reply, "Fine, thanks." You may be having a terrible day, but you don't go into the intimate details. He totals up your purchases, hands you the bill, and you pay. As you leave, you exchange more politeness. "Have a nice day" and "You too," then you take your groceries and go home. To maintain a pleasant working relationship you are courteous and respectful while disclosing very little of your personal life. The same principles hold true in building a parenting partnership with your ex-spouse.

LEARNING TO DO BUSINESS

Any business relationship needs time to establish trust. A good reputation is earned over the long haul. And for both parties to continue an association, the relationship must be mutually beneficial.

You may recognize these basic principles from your work life, but now is the time to apply them in your relationship with your children's other parent. Good business principles can help you redefine your relationship and reorganize your family. These are the keys to a sound business relationship:

Privacy/minimum self-disclosure

Courtesy

Explicit rules for relating

Clear boundaries

In the following section you will learn concrete, practical methods for applying these principles in your interactions with your ex-spouse. Regardless of the custody arrangement you may have with your former spouse, these six steps for building, and maintaining, a successful parenting partnership can be applied.

1. How you feel about the other parent is less important than how you act toward him or her.
2. Respect your own need for privacy and the other parent's too.
3. Each parent's time with the children is sacred.
4. Each parent has the right to develop his or her own parenting style even though it differs from yours.
5. Acknowledge what the other parent has to offer to your children.
6. Expect to feel awkward and uncomfortable about this new way of relating.

Let's look at each step in more detail.

1. HOW YOU FEEL ABOUT THE OTHER PARENT IS LESS IMPORTANT THAN HOW YOU ACT TOWARD HIM OR HER

"My ex-husband is probably one of the lowest people I know," said Jane, a woman in one of my support groups. "If I saw him on the street I'd say, 'What a jerk.' I don't want to be one of those women who puts her kid's father down, but frankly I would rather be a single mother without a father in the picture. Then I could choose my son's male role model. That would be easier for me, but not for my son. So all my life I'll have to have a relationship with a man who I don't like or respect. I have to try to find a way to get along with him for my boy's sake. I say to him, 'I disagree with your daddy, but that's the way your dad is and that's okay, but it's still very hard.' " Jane is applying one of the basic principles of successful business. Despite her dislike of her former husband she's willing to relate to him in a way that benefits her son.

Putting aside your negative feelings toward your ex-spouse is in your children's best interest, as my client Jean found out. "I hate Jeff's father," Jean, a thirty-year-old bank teller, said for maybe the twentieth time during counseling. "I hate him as a human being." Jean saves her hateful words for my professional ears. She consciously reminds herself to say positive things about his father in front of her son, Jeff. "Whatever my ex's problems are, he's still Jeff's father and they adore each other," she told me. "I will do anything I can to support their relationship. I buy baseball tickets so they can go to games together. My goal is to have Jeff feel secure and loved, so I put my personal stuff aside as much as I can." Your goal is to go about the business of raising your children. A big step in doing this is to find a way to treat your ex-spouse with respect and courtesy.

Calling a Truce

Yvette came to see me at the recommendation of her son's preschool teacher. For the past three months, four-year-old Chris had been hitting other children, wetting his pants at school, and biting his nails.

Yvette acknowledged that she was involved in an intense, ongoing conflict with her ex-husband, Dan. "Every time I have contact with Dan he attacks me verbally," she cried. "Then I fight back. Before you know it, we're screaming at each other."

Children of Chris's age resonate with their parents' emotional state. They may be angry at their parents for causing them distress. It was also likely that Chris blamed himself for the fighting between the two. Preschool-age children develop frightening fantasies when they see their parents fight. When the parents finally divorce, the children may develop fears of abandonment.

I recommended a two-pronged approach to decrease Chris's anxiety. First, Yvette was to do everything possible to reduce the conflict with her ex-husband. She had to restrain herself from responding to Dan's attacks and minimize the amount of contact she had with him. I suggested that when he came to get Chris or drop him off that she insist that he wait in the car rather than coming to the house. This would diminish the opportunities for bickering and verbal assaults. I also asked her to have Dan call me for an appointment.

When I met with Dan, I conveyed how difficult it was for Chris to witness his parents at war. I emphasized the importance of limiting his son's exposure to their conflict. I noted, too, that Dan was struggling with the loss of his family and the stress of adjusting to a new life. "I'm constantly on edge," he acknowledged. "I feel like a time bomb waiting to explode. One word from Yvette and I blow up." It was clear that Dan felt relieved by the necessity to withdraw from the battlefield. After a series of meetings with each parent they were able, for their son's sake, to call a truce.

The second part of the plan was for Yvette to set aside a part of each day for Chris. They could simply sit together, read a story, play, or talk, thus providing Chris with a dependable opportunity to feel connected and reassured. This also gave him a safe place to discharge any worries.

At my suggestion Yvette gave Chris large sheets of newsprint and some stubby crayons and encouraged him to draw out his feelings. The combination of these approaches began to alleviate some of Chris's distress. After six weeks he stopped fighting with the other kids and no longer wet his pants. His nail biting lessened. His mother continued with the special time and incorporated the therapeutic play once a week. Within four months Chris made a healthy adjustment to a situation that had threatened his fundamental well-being.

It is always possible to find some way to cooperate for the sake of your children. The first step is to redefine your relationship with your former spouse. You may have divorced, but you aren't divorcing your kids. You are in the business of being parents together, albeit separately, for the rest of your lives. Many parents are better moms and dads after the divorce than they were during their marriage. Freed of the discord and tension of marriage, they can concentrate on being parents.

2. RESPECT YOUR OWN NEED FOR PRIVACY AND THE OTHER PARENT'S TOO

Marital intimacy includes sharing the personal details of your life with your mate. Communication tends to be spontaneous. The end of marriage signals the end of this intimacy. To coexist in a successful parenting relationship you have to relate with greater formality and less personal disclosure.

Lorraine and Phil have two children, eleven and thirteen. Lorraine has primary custody of the children and Phil sees the kids every other weekend. Lorraine had been under great strain and needed an evening off. She went out on a date with a man from her office. While she was out, Phil called and the kids told him that their mom wouldn't be home until bedtime. Livid, Phil called Lorraine later to complain about her leaving the children alone.

"Where were you?" Phil snapped. "You know I don't think the kids should be home alone." Lorraine was used to this kind of pressure and usually gave in to Phil's demands, but this time she defended her right to privacy. "Phil, the kids were perfectly fine," she said. "You know I'd never do anything to jeopardize their safety." But Phil persisted. "Where the hell were you anyway?" "That's none of your business," Lorraine replied calmly. By asserting her right to a life that was not under her ex-husband's scrutiny Lorraine set the standard for a more formal relationship with her ex-spouse.

Think about what your ex-spouse really needs to know. Does he need to hear about the argument you had with your co-worker? Does she need to hear the details of your trip to the dentist? Does he need to know about the problems you are having with your accountant? Does she really want to listen to you describe the gift you bought your new girlfriend? The answers are clearly no. The only information that needs to be communicated with your ex-spouse is that pertaining to your children. The intimate details of your personal, sexual, and social life have no place in your new partnership. Keep them to yourself and do not allow your ex to share the details of his or her personal life with you. This will help to facilitate your newly defined partnership.

Curiosity Killed the Cat

Of course we're curious about our former partner's new life, even when the result is pain. A woman feels hurt when she hears about her ex's one-night stands with young women from his office. A man is angry to know a new boyfriend has spent the night at his old house. But as counterproductive as this information is, we often pursue it. We want to know who they're with and what goes on in their beds. We ask friends and use our children as spies.

When I first divorced, I would drive by my ex-husband's house several times a day to see if his car was there. After my daughter had spent the weekend at her father's house I asked her out of the blue, "Does your daddy have a girlfriend?" To my surprise she said yes. My heart sank. I had been replaced. Obsessed, I wanted to find out everything I could about her. I watched for her car around town and pressured mutual friends for information.

Details, however, would only increase my pain and torment. I finally realized that this was adding to my agony and forced myself to stop quizzing people about my ex-husband. I made a pledge to ask no more questions. When people volunteered information I would ask them please not to tell me about him. I realized that his private life was no longer any of my business.

By rooting around for information about your ex's private life you are maintaining an illusion of intimacy. This will make establishment of a parenting partnership more difficult. Leave the personal details alone. Stick strictly to business.

Free Advice Can Be Costly

Another way that ex-spouses cross the boundary from business to a more personal relationship is by asking for advice or professional guidance. Bonnie was divorced from Ed, a pediatrician. She kept asking Ed questions about the children's health despite the fact that they had their own doctor. By asking her ex-husband's advice she set up a dynamic in which he had power in the relationship and she was still dependent. If your ex is a CPA, lawyer, carpenter, nurse, or expert of any kind, and you've been relying on your ex for expertise, stop. Finding another professional to help you will put your parenting relationship on a more businesslike footing.

Act Like a Guest

Whether your former spouse has a new house or lives in the house you once shared, it is important to respect his or her right to privacy. Tom and Julie have a six-year-old daughter, Mia. Tom picks Mia up from school every Friday and Julie isn't supposed to be involved in her care until Sunday evening at 5:00 P.M. One Saturday morning, she was lying on the couch listening to music and reading her favorite escapist magazine when Tom and Mia showed up at her front door, unannounced.

"I could hear Mia's little voice calling, 'Mommy, Mommy, where are you?' or I wouldn't have answered the door," Mia said through clenched teeth. " 'We came by to pick up some of Mia's clothes,' Tom said. I was furious. What if my boyfriend had been over? Besides, Mia has a closetful of clothes at his house."

Julie helped her daughter to get some of her things and told her ex not to show up unannounced again. He reacted with a threat. "Maybe I just won't pick her up at all if you're going to be so uptight about your space. Remember, I used to live here too," he said. Julie admitted that she could have been more diplomatic about setting boundaries with Tom, but she really resented his barging into her house as if he still lived there.

Her resentment makes sense in the context of a business relationship. Would you think of barging into an office unannounced? Of course not. You would go through the proper channels of making an appointment and following the prescribed business decorum. When establishing a new business relationship with your former spouse you have to extend the same courtesies to your parenting partner.

Respecting your ex's privacy and space is essential. Don't just waltz in, help yourself to some chips and dip, and make yourself at home around the kitchen table. It is no longer your home. You must act as a guest would. It may be difficult to shift to such a formal way of relating when you were so used to being casual and spontaneous, but there have to be clear boundaries or this newly defined relationship won't work.

The rule of thumb is not to enter the other parent's house without invitation or permission. Your kids may encourage you to come in and make yourself at home, but to be safe I'd suggest that you check with your ex-spouse before you let yourself in. This may seem like an unnecessary formality, but what you communicate is that you respect the other parent and your newly defined relationship. Your children witness your respect for their other parent and this sends a powerful message.

3. EACH PARENT'S TIME WITH THE CHILDREN IS SACRED

Don't make other plans or change plans on your ex's time. When there is a regular schedule for your children to be with each parent, you need to honor it. All too often a child will convince one parent that he or she doesn't want to go to the other parent's house or that something more important has come up. The first parent frequently will give in without consulting the other one. To avoid arguments, misunderstandings, or hurt feelings, make it a house rule that no plans be changed without the other parent's consent.

Richard, a computer programmer, has primary custody of his two children, Skip, 7, and Dennis, 9. Carolyn sees the boys every other weekend. She picks them up from school on Friday afternoon and returns them to their father's house Sunday evening at 6:00 P.M. Richard had been given three tickets to a special gymnastics event for a Saturday when the boys were scheduled to be with their mother. Rather than consult Carolyn, he told the boys about the special event. Naturally they wanted to go to the gymnastics competition instead of seeing their mother.

When Carolyn called to talk with the boys, Dennis blurted out, "Daddy's taking us to a gymnastics program on Saturday, Mom. Hope you don't mind." Carolyn asked Dennis to put his father on the phone. "Richard!" she exclaimed. "I really resent your making plans for the boys when they're supposed be with me. I don't want to be informed after the fact. In the future talk to me before you tell them of any change in plans." Richard realized his error and offered the tickets to Carolyn so the boys could see her and still go to the competition.

If you don't respect the other parent's time with the children or if you think of his or her time with the kids as baby-sitting, you undermine their connection. This is detrimental to both parents and children.

Situations will come up when you have to change the schedule or you have a special request. When this happens, it's important to ask the other parent about the desired change before you tell your kids. That way you avoid misunderstandings and one parent won't be made to look like the bad guy. "If my ex has something he wants to do with our little girl on my weekend, he respectfully calls me in advance and asks me if he can change the plans," Sukey, the mother of a three-year-old, explained. "We're very flexible about that. We've found a way to cooperate that works for all of us."

Adopt a Noninterference Policy

There will be times, especially with teenagers, when your kids don't want to interrupt their social life to go to their other parent's house. Eve was supposed to go to her father's house for the weekend. She ran into her mother's room after school on Thursday complaining, "Mom, I can't go to Dad's this weekend. There's a play at school Saturday night and everyone is going to be there. Do I have to go to Dad's?" Rather than get caught in the middle, Leslie advised her daughter, "You have to work it out with your father. It's his time and it's between the two of you. If you want to change your plans you'll have to call him and talk to him about it. It's really none of my business." Eve argued for a few minutes until she realized that her mother meant business. Then she called her father to see if she could work out the plans.

Leslie has adopted a noninterference policy in the relationship between Eve and her father. This serves to strengthen her child's relationship with her dad as well as fostering greater cooperation between the parents. When you have your children deal with their other parent directly, you put an end to the manipulation of playing one parent against the other. You also show your children that you value and respect their relationship with their other parent. Seeing two parents continue to share parental authority and responsibilities provides your children with a sense of security and consistency.

4. EACH PARENT HAS THE RIGHT TO DEVELOP HIS OR HER OWN PARENTING STYLE EVEN THOUGH IT DIFFERS FROM YOURS

Essential in any parenting partnership is each parent's right to a personal parenting style. What Mom does at her house is her business. You may disagree with the other's lack of structure, rules about TV or homework, eating habits, bedtime or sleeping arrangements, but you no longer have the right to criticize the other parent's choices. As long as no harm is being done to your children, as long as there is no neglect, no emotional, physical, or sexual abuse, the other parent can relate to the children as he or she sees fit.

When your children are with you, you have the authority. How you relate to them and what kind of rules you enforce are your business and the same holds true when your kids are with their other parent. "Matthew knows that there are different rules in each of his homes and he tells me that," said Andrea, a mother of a five-year-old and a participant in one of my support groups. "Matt will say, 'At my dad's house I can go to bed anytime I want.' I tell him that these are the rules we have here and you have different rules at your dad's house." In the past Andrea tried to change the way her ex did things. "But I just came off as critical." She shrugged. "I never got anywhere."

His father sometimes didn't change Matt's clothes for three days and when he would bring him home Andrea used to blow up. "Look how filthy he is," she would yell. His dad would get defensive and Andrea could see that Matt was really upset. "Now if he's dirty I give him a bath," she said. "I decided that it wasn't the end of the world. I pretty much separate myself from what his father does with Matt. I know he loves him and wouldn't do anything to harm him. It's chaotic at his dad's house, but I've come to realize that it's not going to hurt him."

What did hurt Matt was Andrea saying things like "What's wrong with your father? Doesn't he have a bathtub at his house? It looks like you haven't had a bath in a month." She would see Matt's eyes well up with tears and eventually she recognized the harm she was doing and decided to drop it. "Matt's relationship with his father is more important than whether he takes a bath or not or if he gets to bed on time," she said. "I have to put things into perspective."

Even though their father may not be the best housekeeper or their mother may not be as strong a disciplinarian as you'd like, the parental involvement and caring far outweighs any inadequacies on either parent's part. Children who have two caring, involved parents gain a tremendous psychological advantage, says Hugh McIsaac, director of the Los Angeles Conciliation Court. "What is important is how divorced parents can cooperate in a way that makes sense for the children," he says. "I see kids who are now eighteen or older and they have both parents continuing to be involved and supporting them and they are very well-adjusted, solid kids. In some ways these kids are much better socialized than children from intact families. They know how to negotiate, how to handle conflict, how to handle transitions. What's most critical is that both parents work together, cooperate and plan things based on what their children's needs are and not their own." A rule of thumb is: Don't sweat the small stuff. Most of it *is* small stuff. Keep this in mind when you feel irritated by the way your ex-spouse raises your children.

We Can Work It Out

In more and more parenting partnerships, divorced parents are discovering ways to cooperate where their children are concerned. "I felt that my daughter, Sophie, was going to bed too late when she was at her mother's house and was frequently too tired at school," said the father of a five-year-old. "I thought she needed to get to bed earlier and get more sleep. I shared my concern with Claire that she seemed tired and we joked about the bedtime battles. We commiserated about the struggle and I told her the routine I had set up at my house. Claire agreed with me and said she would try to implement an earlier bedtime. I tend to be stricter, but I respect what Claire does and we regularly discuss things that concern Sophie. Sometimes we compromise and sometimes not.

"There was a period when Sophie was having bad dreams and I didn't know how to deal with it," he went on. "I called Claire and asked her what I could do. She was very helpful. We generally put Sophie's interest first. I'm sure that we've messed up from time to time, but we really work at it."

Everyone makes mistakes. It's unrealistic to expect perfection from the other parent, especially when he or she is redefining roles, assuming new responsibilities, and doing things for the first time. "His house is a pit!" complained one newly divorced woman. "It's a total mess but I just work on ignoring it and let him live life the way he wants to. It's his house. I keep reminding myself that it's none of my business. I steer clear of the issues that don't directly affect my daughter's well-being. In issues that do affect our daughter we pretty much agree. He's a good father and I am willing to let him parent our daughter his way when she's with him. He really loves her and that's the most important thing."

To maintain a parenting partnership you must respect the other parent's right to establish a separate relationship with the children. The basic rule, put bluntly, is to keep your nose out of the other parent's business. The more you allow your ex to develop a personal parenting style, the more involved and responsible he or she will be. Your children have the right to know and love both of their parents.

5. ACKNOWLEDGE WHAT THE OTHER PARENT HAS TO OFFER YOUR CHILDREN

It's easy to take your children's other parent for granted. You may feel that your life would be even easier if he or she weren't in the picture at all. But stop and think for a minute about what your ex-spouse contributes to your children's lives. "My ex does things with our daughter that I would never do," said Cynthia, a busy office manager who is very much an indoor person. "They go to tide pools together, he takes her on hikes and nature walks, she's learning about whales and dolphins. He's exposing her to all his interests and she is quite a well-rounded little girl as a result. Sometimes I think he babies her and is overly compulsive, but I feel lucky that she has a dad who loves and adores her and whom she adores. I think it's important that she has both of us."

Remember the qualities you were attracted to when you first met your ex-spouse. Those qualities still exist and are available to your children. Recognizing and appreciating what your ex-spouse has to offer your kids motivates you to work toward a more cooperative parenting arrangement.

One woman still carries anger about her former husband's sudden departure from her life, but she has learned to appreciate his steadfast reliability regarding their son, Scott. "When I start to feel resentful I remind myself of all the things Will has done, like paying the child support on time, spending time with Scott, helping him with his math homework, accepting collect calls from him when he misses the bus after school. All the little things that he does that enrich Scott's life and also makes mine a lot easier," she said. "For instance, Scott is applying to college and Will is helping me to figure out the financial aid forms. He's also been tutoring Scott in algebra for the SATs. I stop to imagine what Scott's and my life would be like if Will wasn't in the picture and I had to do everything myself. That brings things back into perspective very quickly."

Your ex may have been far from desirable as a marriage partner, but it's important to recognize what he or she offers your children. If nothing else, your kids will benefit from exposure to your ex's differing view of the world.

Let Me Count His or Her Virtues Exercise

When I ask participants in my seminars to write down their ex-spouses' attributes and positive qualities, a groan roars through the room and I hear people mutter, "She must be kidding!" That's when I jokingly say, "Okay, what would your response be if I asked you to make a list of his or her failures and shortcomings? There'd probably be a stampede to find your papers and pencils and you'd do it in a flash." Then, of course, there's a lot of laughter and nodding of heads. But when you focus on your ex's weaknesses you continue to make that person the bad guy, which adds fuel to a fire you need to put out.

In truth, your ex-spouse has both positive and negative qualities, as do you. When you were first attracted, you were smitten with the attributes and strengths. Remember? He may have been playful and spontaneous. She may have had a great sense of humor. These characteristics may have become obscured in the course of your marriage, but they still exist and can benefit your children. Even the negative traits have a positive side. For example, an irresponsible person may be carefree and fun; someone who is critical also may be discerning. Cultivate a generosity of spirit. You'll feel better and your kids will appreciate your acknowledgment of their other parent's good traits.

List at least five positive characteristics of your former spouse.

1. ______________________________

2. ______________________________

3. ______________________________

4. ______________________________

5. ______________________________

You did it! That wasn't so impossible, was it? You can keep your list to yourself or you may choose to share it with your ex-spouse. In either case, your recognition of the other's positive qualities will help you build a new relationship.

6. EXPECT TO FEEL AWKWARD AND UNCOMFORTABLE ABOUT THIS NEW WAY OF RELATING

You may feel uncomfortable when you first start to relate with your ex-spouse in a more formal manner. "I feel like a phony when we talk in such a polite, take-care-of-business way," one man complained. "I'm used to being much more open. It's really weird." I coach parents to stick with this awkward new way of relating even if they feel as if they are faking it. If you act as if you're business partners for a long enough time you will grow into the part.

A father in one of my seminars reported, "I decided to try out this idea of relating to my ex-wife as I would an associate. It felt strange at first. Here I was saying polite things like 'I can see that you're upset, but that's no longer my problem. Let's get back to the kids.' I kept up the façade while inside I just wanted to blast her. The good news was that I didn't get into a fight with her and we did get things clear about the kids."

There may be a gap between how you feel and how you act, but give yourself credit for controlling your emotions and forging this new relationship. Doing business when you'd rather be doing battle takes getting used to. Learning any new skill feels unnatural at first, but with practice, relating as parenting partners will become more familiar.

Remember when you first rode a two-wheeler? You probably felt unsure of yourself, but with time, bike riding became second nature. The same is true when learning a foreign language. Your mouth has to contort to make the strange new sounds, but eventually you become fluent. Learning to relate as business partners with someone with whom you were once intimate is a similar shift but a necessary one if both parents are to remain actively involved with their children.

MISSION POSSIBLE

Dana and Gene have two children and were married for twelve years. "We had been fighting for the last two of those years and I finally decided that I wanted out of the marriage," said Dana, a pediatric nurse, during her first counseling session. "I mustered up the courage to tell Gene, but it took another four months of fighting before he finally moved out." This sounded like the beginning of a story I'd heard a hundred times: Spouses fight, get a divorce, then continue to fight, using their kids as weapons. But as Dana unfolded the rest of her story, it took an unexpected turn.

"Gene is a great dad," she continued. "He's always been very close to the children and I decided that I would do everything possible to make it easy for him to stay involved. I have to give Gene credit. As angry as he was, he agreed that we would never use our kids as a negotiating point."

Their divorce was actually very tough. They had some major battles over money, but they also spent a lot of time designing a parenting plan they both could adhere to. Gene and Dana worked with a mediator to spell things out clearly and specifically, so now they don't have many conflicts about money, time, or responsibility. Within that framework, they can be fairly flexible. "We discussed how we would treat one another in the children's presence," Dana said. "We wanted to make things as smooth and consistent as possible.

"I've had to learn to compromise, but the kids seem to be doing really well, so the trade-offs are worth it," she went on. "Gene has the kids three days a week and they are with me for four days. The next week we switch and we split the holidays. The children have rooms and clothes in each house so they don't have to schlepp things back and forth. Gene and I talk regularly. We both work very hard at putting our children's needs and interests first.

"In the last years of our marriage we didn't communicate much at all," she said, obviously surprised at how the divorce has worked out. "We have a much better relationship now. Before there was always intense struggle for control, but now we have boundaries and we each know what our job is. It's just a lot clearer."

You may think that Dana and Gene are the exception to the rule and that a parenting partnership is only possible for "other people." But Dana and Gene are not that unusual. According to research, 50 percent of divorcing couples successfully establish a cooperative parenting relationship.[2] These people succeed for the same reason Dana and Gene did. They made their children their priority.

SENTENCED TO SOLE CUSTODY

When the subject of custody comes up in my seminars, parents sometimes raise their hands and say they'd rather not have the ex-spouse involved in the kids' lives at all. "My life would be a lot easier," they say. This may be true in the short run. But when it comes to the well-being of your children you have to look at the longer haul.

During a question-and-answer period at a recent conference on divorce, a woman told this story. "I fought furiously to have sole custody of my children. Sixteen years later I feel like the judge *sentenced* me to sole custody. I've served my sentence and I'm completely worn out." At the time of her divorce she was so angry that she never wanted to see her ex-husband again. She thought it would be much easier to have control, and to make the decisions about her kids' care. She got the complete control she wanted, pushed her husband out of the picture, and assumed responsibility. With no support or relief, her whole life centered on her kids. "I was a mother and a wife," she admitted at the conference. "So when I was forced to give up my role of wife, I clung desperately to my identity as the all-nurturing caretaker. Because of my fears and anger we all suffered. My kids missed knowing their father and having him in their lives and I was trapped raising two kids alone.

"If I had to do it over," she said, "I'd find a way to keep their dad in the picture. Sole custody is a heavy sentence."

Research indicates that children whose fathers are shut out experience greater stress and suffer more psychological and emotional distress.[3] Let's look at how some couples have made the transition.

ROME WASN'T BUILT IN A DAY

When some parents cannot establish a parenting partnership during the first stages of divorce, I help them plant seeds for the future. For example, take the case of Ben and Linda, married for nine years and the parents of an eight-year-old son, Gil. They came to me for counseling in the middle of the divorce process. They had separated twice before but had reconciled their differences. Now Ben had met another woman and wanted out. Linda was devastated. It became obvious to me that both Ben and Linda were too immersed in anger to begin to establish a co-parenting relationship.

I helped them to recognize that they were too caught up in mistrust and conflict to establish a parenting partnership. This is true for a lot of couples initially. Many people find that after the anger dissipates and trust is reestablished in terms of their parenting roles, they become more able to work with each other. I asked Ben and Linda if they wanted to develop a civilized relationship so they could continue to parent their child. Ben immediately responded, "I certainly don't want to forfeit my relationship with my son. *Of course* we have to find a way to make this work!" Apparently it hadn't occurred to him until I asked that question that they were endangering Gil's well-being.

THE RICOCHET EFFECT

Only rarely do parents agree to build a parenting partnership at the same time. Usually one person begins and the other freaks out and tries to bring things back to the status quo. Even though they may agree on what's best for the kids, the pull of the familiar is strong. Certain well-worn patterns of relating, no matter how dysfunctional and destructive, spell familiarity and security. This is especially true for families in which there was tension, fighting, and a high level of drama. As painful as it was, they become addicted to drama. They may know that a more positive emotional climate will be better for everyone concerned, but they feel compelled to maintain the familiar way of relating.

Remember, it takes two to tango. As long as you don't bite when your ex puts out the bait, you are less likely to fall back into an unhealthy pattern of relating. Keep affirming your commitment to this new business relationship and your ex-spouse will eventually give up and begin to play by the new rules.

Chapter 5

It's Not What You Say, but How You Say It

Communication for Cooperation

The truth remains hidden from him who is in the bondage of hate and desire.

Buddha

"After my divorce I never wanted to hear from my ex again," one woman told me. "The sound of his voice sent me into a rage. But when you have kids you *have* to talk to each other." She's not the only divorced parent who wishes her ex came complete with a mute button so she could push it and shut him up. Perhaps you would just as soon never speak to yours again; however, when your children's welfare is concerned, communication is necessary.

Unfortunately, some parents use verbal contact with one another to extract the symbolic pound of flesh. "Listen, you jerk. Don't accuse *me* of not being strict enough. The kids don't even have a bedtime at your house." "You're so selfish. I can't believe you didn't even send Adam a birthday card." This dumping of hostility on your ex comes from anger, hurt, and residual feelings of betrayal and loss. These emotions are a natural part of the separation process, but they can obscure your goal of cooperation for the sake of your children. Verbal attacks are counterproductive and they leave scars on your kids.

What you say to your former spouse today will shape your children's future. It's in your own best interest to learn the skills for cooperative communication.

I know it seems unfair to be asked to build a cooperative partnership with someone you mistrust. It may seem impossible to build *any* kind of partnership with someone who did you wrong, but divorce isn't about fairness or who's right. It's about letting go of old roles and destructive patterns of relating.

You are no longer your ex's intimate partner, but you are still parenting partners. This shift away from intimacy requires hard work and practice because you will be learning to communicate on a whole new level.

"After months of bickering with Natalie, I decided to stop waiting for her to become rational and see my point of view," reported my client Jonathan. "I was tired of hanging up the phone feeling smug and self-righteous. I was also tired of replaying our conversation ad nauseam. I decided that it was more important to be free of the emotional burden than to be right."

I am not suggesting that you become friends with the other parent. What I am advocating is that you establish a sound working, business relationship in which your children are your shared asset. Whether on a daily, weekly, or monthly basis you're being asked to resolve issues with your ex-spouse. Learning skills for effective communication will help you arrive at a satisfactory resolution.

This chapter offers guidelines for positive communication. You will learn to give information and ask questions in a neutral, nonprovocative manner, in other words, without pushing your ex's buttons. I know you're an expert at driving him crazy. I know you can say that magic word or groan at just the right moment and send her into a frenzy of rage. But it's time to stop seeking revenge.

WATCH YOUR LANGUAGE

To communicate successfully with the other parent you must learn a new language. If you still refer to the children's other parent as your wife or husband, you're still thinking of your relationship as intimate. Words are powerful; they shape reality. Used correctly they can help refocus how you relate to one another. Train yourself to refer to your children's other parent as Laddie's mother or Helen's father. This phrase more clearly defines his of her role both in your life as well as in the life of your kids. Here are eight keys to effective communication.

Communication for Cooperation

1. Be clear about what you want.
2. Keep it simple: Stay focused on one issue.
3. Use nonjudgmental language.
4. Ask questions in a neutral way, then pause for a response.
5. Don't make assumptions.
6. Stay in the present.
7. Listen actively.
8. Remember that timing is everything.

Let me elaborate.

1. BE CLEAR ABOUT WHAT YOU WANT

Be sure that the other parent understands what you are asking for. Be specific in your requests. People who are angry often use global generalizations, sarcasm, or accusations laced with blame and resentment.

"Why can't you be more responsible?" "You're never on time. I have to work too, you know." "Just because you are a party animal doesn't mean I have to accommodate your schedule. I'm not a baby-sitter." Each of these statements contains a hidden request, but because of the implicit put-down they provoke a defensive reaction. Once you know clearly what it is you want, you can make your request in a neutral, courteous tone. For example, Loretta, a slightly scattered young mother with flyaway hair and energy to match, has arranged for three-year-old Eddie to spend every weekend at his father's house. John picks him up from his mother on Friday afternoons at 4:00 and Loretta is supposed to pick him up at 3:00 on Sundays.

John, an always reliable if somewhat rigid mechanical engineer, often gets a frantic call from Loretta late Sunday morning. She announces that something has come up and she'll be along soon. One Sunday, when Loretta showed up two hours late, John exploded. "You're so selfish," he yelled. "Why can't you keep a bargain? We've been waiting for two hours." Loretta looked startled. "You're always complaining that you don't get enough time with Eddie," she yelled back. "And when you do get to keep him a little longer you complain about that too. There's just no pleasing you."

This interaction escalates into a full-scale battle and nothing gets accomplished. John doesn't resolve his frustration and Loretta never understands what John is asking. When John attacks, Loretta's instinct is to strike back. They're each left with more resentment and greater confusion.

It's important to remember that being clear with one another is easier if you don't let resentments build up. Most of us live with the misconception that if you ignore a problem, it will resolve itself. This rarely happens. The longer we let something irritate, the more likely we are to explode.

John might have discussed his displeasure with Loretta after the first or second time she arrived late. He could have expressed his frustration by saying, "I have a hard time when we agree that you'll pick Eddie up at three and you don't show up until five. It's difficult enough for me to make the transition from being with him to his leaving, but the uncertainty of when you'll be here adds to my tension and he feels it too. I'd like you to honor our agreement. Can I count on you to be on time?" This type of statement is far more specific. John lets Loretta know what the problem is, how it affects him, and what changes he'd like her to make. He is more likely to get a cooperative reaction when he doesn't blame her.

What Do You Do When They Just Won't Budge?

Sometimes one parent acts reasonably and the other parent won't cooperate. Liz, 5, and Betty, 8, will be on school vacation in a week, and both parents work. Deirdre, a tentative, shy woman who has just gotten her first job in a retail clothing store, calls her ex-husband, Tony.

"The kids are out of school next week," she tells him. "I'd like us to arrange a schedule." "I have to work," replies Tony, a temperamental house painter who hadn't been particularly cooperative during their marriage. "I can't take time off." "I'll be responsible for Monday through Thursday," volunteers Deirdre. "I'd like you to make arrangements for Friday and Saturday."

"We wouldn't be dealing with this mess in the first place if it wasn't for you," attacks Tony. "*You* wanted the divorce. Now *you* take care of the kids." Deirdre takes several deep breaths and realizes that this discussion is futile. No matter how reasonable and rational she is, Tony just isn't going to help make arrangements for his children.

Deirdre has several choices. She can jump into the ring, pick up her gloves, and start fighting. Chances are this will result in more bad blood, more frustration, and no resolution of the problem. Or she can recognize that her expectations of what Tony should do—reasonable as they are—will not often be met. And she can then decide to put her children first and do what's best for them in the long run.

If Deirdre encounters this kind of situation repeatedly, she may decide to investigate child care options independent of Tony. She may find a backup person who can care for the children during vacations or she can explore various after-school programs. Sometimes you're not going to get the cooperation you want and it's better to adopt a "What can I do to make this situation work" attitude and move on.

John, the exasperated mechanical engineer, faced a similar problem in his conflict over his ex-wife's chronic lateness. At one point John did indeed discuss Eddie's pickup time in a clear and rational fashion and Loretta agreed to be on time. The next Sunday rolled around and Loretta was forty-five minutes late. John has several options. First, he can ask Loretta what's not working for her. "You agree to pick Eddie up at three on Sunday, but something always comes up," he might say. "What should we do to make this arrangement work? Maybe five-fifteen is better for you?"

Or John can alleviate the problem by keeping Eddie at his house until preschool starts on Monday. Or he can wait until three, then leave her a pleasant note saying, "I waited until 3:15 and we went to the park." After not finding them home a few times she'll get the message. Or he can recognize that she can't or won't keep her word, accept that she'll pick Eddie up sometime between three and five, and be willing to wait. Each strategy allows John to take back control so that he doesn't feel like a helpless victim of Loretta's actions.

2. KEEP IT SIMPLE: STAY FOCUSED ON ONE ISSUE

When you have identified the problem that needs to be discussed, stay focused until it is resolved. During a difficult conversation people often introduce other controversial subjects which distract from reaching a resolution. For example, one former couple began to discuss where their daughter, Jenny, would go to school the next fall, but before long Jenny's mother had sidetracked the conversation. She asked who was going to take Jenny to her swimming lessons this week. Twenty minutes into the discussion, they realized that they hadn't moved any closer to resolving the issue of Jenny's new school.

It's tempting to bring up all of your various concerns in the course of a single conversation, but this usually overwhelms the other parent. It's important to set the conversation's agenda, decide on the subjects you are planning to address, and stay on track. Don't go on to a second subject until you have completed the first.

Think of your conversation as a business meeting to be conducted in an orderly manner. Review beforehand how you feel about the issue and what outcome you want. Prepare yourself. Know your agenda. Remember, your goals are to get your needs and the needs of your children met, maintain a sense of dignity, and enlist the other parent's cooperation.

Like any newly acquired skill, this businesslike approach to relating will feel awkward at first. Remember when you first learned to type, ride a bike, or speak a foreign language? You had to expend extra energy to master the new skill, but with practice it became second nature. The same is true here.

A word to the wise: Separate discussions about money from other issues. Money is always a highly charged subject that can change an otherwise benign conversation into a heated battle.

3. USE NONJUDGMENTAL LANGUAGE

Learn to use "I" statements in place of "you" statements. "I" statements communicate how you feel and what you want without attacking the other person. "You" statements, on the other hand, are judgmental. They point out what the other person is doing wrong. Imagine how you would feel if someone said, "You're always late picking the kids up." "You never give them a bath when they stay at your house." "You're always late with child support." "You can't even get the kids to school on time." "You don't call when you're supposed to." "You never come to school meetings or events." Your reaction would likely be defensive or furious or both. Combine those feelings with the fact that it is your ex-spouse who is making these accusatory statements and you have a recipe for disaster.

No one likes to be blamed or to feel that he or she is bad. Statements that begin with "You" are focused on the other person's character and usually have a blaming, judgmental tone attached to them. They don't give the other parent any information about the problem, how you feel about it, or what changes you want made. Making "you" statements is like dropping a smoldering coal into a pile of dried leaves. It's sure to produce a fire.

To communicate effectively you must take responsibility for your feelings. Then you have to give the other parent information about what it is you want. "I" statements force you to do just that. Take, for example, Gloria, a dark-eyed beauty who was raised in a large family under the firm hand of an Old Country father.

"Juan never has his homework done when he comes back from your house," she accuses Ernesto. "You always let him watch TV. He just runs wild." Hidden in these accusations is a desire or a demand, but most likely all he will hear is the implied message: "You're a bad father." Gloria would have been much more effective if she had said "When you let Juan come home without his homework done, I get upset. I think schoolwork should come first. I'd appreciate you making sure he gets it done."

Let's dissect what Gloria is doing in her second response. The formula for owning your feelings is to first state how you feel. Second, let the other person know what you think. Finally, state clearly and specifically what you want. When you ____, I feel ____. Because ____. What I want is ____.This formula lets Ernesto know what Gloria wants and why she feels so strongly. Here is another example of taking responsibility for feelings: "When the kids count on seeing you and you don't show up, I am furious. Not only am I inconvenienced, but they feel disappointed. I'd like you to keep the dates you make with the children." This statement is more likely to generate a cooperative response.

Attack the Problem Not the Person

Describing the problem and focusing on solutions is more effective than blaming the other parent. Separate the person from the problem. "There was a time when my ex wasn't spending enough time with Rachel," explained Marian, an aggressive, perfectly coiffed real estate agent who is always rushing from one appointment to another, but manages to set aside time for her daughter. "He's a financial consultant and is under a lot of pressure, but my heart would break when Rachel asked, 'Doesn't my daddy love me anymore? When is he going to come see me?' I wanted to call him up and just scream, 'We're all busy. I'm just as busy as you are! You're missing out on your little girl's life.' "

Instead she caught herself as she was about to dial his number and calmed herself down. She gave herself a pep talk: "Marian, you know how Mick reacts when you rant and rave. It never gets you anywhere. Now just take a deep breath and try to be more tactful."

When Rachel's father answered the phone, Marian told him calmly about her concerns. "I know your business trips are important, but Rachel hasn't seen you very much lately," she said.

"She's really feeling neglected. These trips come up periodically and we should make plans about how to handle them. Maybe you could schedule some special time with her before you go away."

In this more rational frame of mind Marian decided to attack the problem instead of her ex-husband. She correctly predicted that by sharing her concerns and invoking their common interest—their daughter—she would be far more successful in gaining his cooperation.

4. ASK QUESTIONS IN A NEUTRAL WAY, THEN PAUSE FOR A RESPONSE

One effective way of engaging the other parent in a discussion is to ask questions. Imagine that you are an investigative reporter who is interviewing your co-parent. Interviewers often act as if they don't know the answer to a question so they can get the facts from the other person's point of view.

Making statements generates resistance when asking questions may evoke answers. Answering allows the other parent to get his or her point across and helps you to understand that person's perspective. "What do you think about____ ?" or "Do you think it would be better to have Pat spend the weekend with you while I'm out of town or with his grandparents?" Questions educate and inform rather than criticize or attack. Unlike statements, they don't offer the other parent a target for reaction.

Once you ask the question, stop talking. Wait for the response. In negotiation, silence is your most effective tool. People who are uncomfortable with silence may ask a question and then jump in to offer a solution or quickly ask another question. Slow down, take a deep breath, and wait! This puts the burden on the other parent to come up with a suggestion or solution.

Melinda and Oliver came to see me about their four-year-old daughter, Norma. Oliver and Melinda were divorcing and the custody arrangement had not yet been formalized. Under the current arrangement Norma spent weekdays with her mother and some weekends with her father, although there was no clearly defined schedule. As I questioned them about how they felt about this arrangement it became obvious that Melinda, a tiny woman given to quick nervous movements, was dissatisfied; she wanted a structured routine. "How can we make the schedule more consistent?" Melinda asked Oliver, a strong, silent type who took firm stands, but had trouble expressing himself. "It would be great if you would agree to a regular weekly schedule. Then Norma would know exactly what to expect," she added before Oliver could get a word out. By answering her own question, Melinda never gave Oliver a chance to think about what *he* thought; she also avoided hearing his opinion.

Sometimes people rush in with a solution because they're afraid of what the other parent will say. Or they genuinely don't want to hear the other person's opinion because the response may not be the one they want.

I interrupted their conversation and shared my insight about Melinda's inability to let Oliver wrestle with her question. I coached Melinda not to let Oliver off the hook by asking another question, providing a solution, or making a comment. I suggested that she let him sit with the issue so she could find out what he thought.

Melinda asked Oliver the question again and this time waited for his answer. "I'm not sure that it's really necessary to have a regular schedule," he said slowly. "Things seem to work fine the way they are. I like the flexibility. Besides, Norma doesn't seem to mind." Melinda didn't like what she heard, but at least she knew what she was facing. Now we could explore their differences and find a compromise that would work for the three of them.

Some of the most successful negotiation occurs when one participant remains silent. Resist temptation, keep your mouth shut, and let your ex break the silence!

5. DON'T MAKE ASSUMPTIONS

When in doubt, check it out. Many parents think that they are mind readers, that they know what the other parent thinks, feels, or wants. Janice, a frazzled, discombobulated saleswoman who is settling into a new job after seven years as a stay-at-home mom, was furious at her ex. He had let Mandy miss the cutoff date to sign up for the soccer team. "Janice always took Mandy to soccer practice when we were married," retorted Ken, a mechanic who still seems dismayed by the dismantling of his family. "I thought that she'd continue."

These kinds of assumptions lead to misunderstandings and potential arguments. It's important to discuss your understanding of how things are going to be handled before either of you act on them or abdicate your responsibility. Ken should have confirmed that Janice planned to handle the soccer arrangements. Instead he assumed that because she had done so while they were married she would do so afterward, in spite of her dramatically changed schedule. Janice should have told Ken that she expected him to take care of the soccer sign-up. Instead, both parents made assumptions and their daughter was the loser. Don't leave things vague and ambiguous. Make everything explicit and verify your agreements. Otherwise, misunderstandings are inevitable.

Petra and Jack, for example, had discussed plans for the children's Easter vacation. Jack was to take the kids back east to visit his family. He assumed that Petra, a notoriously late sleeper on weekends, would bring the kids to his house at 10:30 A.M. on Saturday morning so they could make a 12:00 flight. When 10:30 rolled around and the kids were nowhere in sight Jack frantically called Petra. "Where are the kids?" Jack barked. "I thought you were going to bring them over to my house by ten-thirty." "Hold on, Jack," Petra answered sleepily. "I never said that! You know this is my only time to sleep in. I thought you were going to come here. The kids are waiting on the front steps."

It's important to clarify what you think the other person said and what your understanding of it is. You can use statements such as "Do you mean," "What I hear you saying is," "In other words," "Let me understand what you are saying," "It seems like . . ." Clarify by restating in your own words what you think the other person just said. Petra's saying "Let me see if I heard you correctly; you're going to pick the kids up tomorrow morning at ten-thirty" would have prevented the fiasco. Summarizing what was said would have cleared up any misunderstanding.

Offer the Benefit of the Doubt

Let's say you and the children's mother have agreed that she'll pick them up at your house and take them to school. You have a business meeting and she's fifteen minutes late. Don't assume that she is trying to make your life miserable, ruin your plans, or get back at you. Give her the benefit of the doubt. Something may have happened that held her up. Perhaps she got stuck in traffic, had a flat tire or an emergency. Suspend judgment until she can explain.

"I try to cut Bruce some slack whenever I can," reported Nancy, a hyperorganized mother. "I remind myself that no matter what he does, he really wants to do the right thing. I say it to him and I tell myself. There are times when he messes up, but if I treat him as a person who wants to do right by his kid it prevents a horrible fight and encourages him to improve. This doesn't mean I'm naïve. I know he's unreliable and that I can't count on him. Yet I find that holding both thoughts simultaneously—that he is basically unreliable, but he does want to do right by his son—helps me to have a compassionate point of view."

6. STAY IN THE PRESENT

Don't bring up past history. When you get frustrated with the other parent, you know that one of the easiest ways to send him or her off the deep end is to bring up past failures. We all have a museum of war relics from our marriage and while it's tempting to hurl memories of wrongdoing at the other parent to validate our point, *this never works.*

"Remember the time you were supposed to bring the kids to my mother's house for a family dinner and you arrived three hours late?" "Remember the year we had to pay a five-hundred-dollar penalty because you didn't get the taxes done on time?" The recipient of these taunts has been convicted of the crimes of lateness, irresponsibility, or selfishness, but how much closer are you to resolving the issue? A more likely result is the construction of another barrier.

Stay in the present. Stick to the issue and deal with it in the here and now. If the problem is lack of consistency between father and child, speak to that. If she's late picking the kids up, discuss her lateness. If he forgets to make lunch for his son, confront the issue without bringing up past transgressions. Tell him how you feel when he doesn't give you notice of his vacation plans with your daughter. Let her know your concerns when she's late picking up your son after football practice. Talk with him about how you feel when your son calls you at work and says he doesn't have any lunch. Let the other parent know the impact the problem has on you and the children. Face the problem, but do it without including past history. A statement about how you feel right now conveys the necessary information without triggering a defensive reaction.

You can't change the past, but you can shape the future by dealing with issues in the present. The goal is not to build an airtight case so you can sentence the other parent for past crimes. The goal is to build a working relationship so that your children's needs are met. You can choose to look behind you or to look ahead. It will be far more satisfying if you turn your attention to where you would like to be instead of where you have come from.

7. LISTEN ACTIVELY

Imagine for a moment that you are a scientist and that the other parent is an alien from another planet. (That shouldn't be too hard.) These aliens have different customs, traditions, religions, values, and ways of thinking. Your job is to learn as much as you can about them and their point of view. To do this you have to pay careful attention so you can see their perceptions, feel their emotions, and hear what they express. You have to try on their reality. In other words, you have to put yourself in their shoes. Most likely, they believe as fervently in their point of view as you do in yours.

Listening actively gives the other parent the satisfaction of being heard. To do it, you acknowledge what is being said by restating what you understood. "This is the first Christmas we're not going to be together as a family. I'm not sure how to handle the time with the kids." A reflective response would be "You sound worried about not having enough time with the children at Christmas. How do you suppose we might work things out?" Or "I just don't know what to do with Timmy. This is the second time he's been benched for hitting another kid on the playground. His teacher sent home a note saying one more incident and he'll be sent home." A careful listener might respond, "It seems you're anticipating the worst. I can understand why you're upset, but let's see if we can figure out what's bothering Tim and how to help him."

Reflecting back to your co-parent what you think he or she has said accomplishes two things. First, the other feels heard and understood. Second, this approach promotes further discussion and fosters a sense of cooperation.

Acknowledgment Doesn't Mean Agreement

Don't misunderstand: Just because you acknowledge what the other parent says doesn't mean you agree. It simply means you heard. You can understand perfectly what the other parent says and completely disagree. Take the case of Sebastian, an impeccably groomed corporate psychologist who won't go out without dressing in a suit and tie. He has just received his six-year-old daughter's first report card. She got one B, three C's, and a D in arithmetic. Horrified, he calls his ex-wife, Glenda, at her art gallery. "I can't believe what a bad report card Sylvie got," Sebastian fusses. "What's going on? Maybe she needs a tutor! There's no excuse for such poor grades."

Glenda's reaction is reflexive. "I can't believe it," she shrieks silently to herself. "The kid is in first grade and he's acting as if she just blew her SATs. He's laying the same trip on Sylvie that his parents laid on him, and look at what a compulsive nut case *he* is. His whole day is wrecked if the toothpaste cap isn't screwed on tight and now he's putting his craziness on her!"

Fortunately, Glenda catches herself before sharing her analysis of Sebastian's traumatic childhood. Asserting her best self-control, she responds, "You sound upset, Sebastian. You seem concerned about Sylvie's grades and you're wondering if she needs extra help."

"Yes," he responds. "I want her to bring her grades up. Maybe she just isn't getting enough attention in class."

"I don't think it has to do with the teacher, Sebastian," replies Glenda. "Remember, Sylvie is just starting first grade. It's been a big adjustment for her. I'm concerned too, but I don't think things are as bad as you're making them out to be. She still has a good shot at college! Let's each spend time helping her with her math homework and see if she improves."

Glenda refrained from saying what she was thinking, comments she knew would provoke a fight. She reflected back Sebastian's worries while clarifying her own point of view on the problem. This let him feel his concerns were being addressed while encouraging a cooperative effort.

Share Your Own Feelings Too!

Feelings play an essential role in effective communication. It is as important to acknowledge the other parent's emotions as it is your own.

Barbara's son, Henry, 5, had been stealing toys and candy from the supermarket when they went shopping. When she called Doug, a hearty, back-slapping building contractor, to talk about the problem, she mentioned that Henry had been waking up at night. "Maybe I should take him to a therapist to find out what's bothering him," she said. "Over my dead body," snapped Doug. "All kids steal stuff. You're making a mountain out of a molehill." "Doug, I can hear that you are upset and you don't see Henry's stealing as a problem, but I'm really worried about him and I need some advice," countered Barbara, an elementary school teacher who tended toward caution in all things. "I'm not just going to march him off to a shrink. I can understand why you're upset if that's what you thought. I'm sorry if that was the impression I gave, but I'm really worried."

"Why don't you talk to your shrink and ask what she thinks before we go any further?" Doug replied grudgingly. "That way we don't drag Henry through a lot of unnecessary scrutiny."

Barbara had been faced with anger and resistance. She could have reacted by saying, "Why don't you face the fact that Henry has a problem. You're always so blasé." In fact, Doug's carefree attitude toward what she perceived as serious problems had been a factor in their divorce. But that comment would have put a roadblock in the path of any further discussion. Her reflective response let Doug know that she heard and appreciated his concerns. This allowed each to air differing points of view until they came to a satisfactory resolution.

Allow the Other Parent to Let Off Steam

In the course of conversation you'll often encounter the other parent's anger and frustration. There are several ways to deal with these negative emotions. One is to permit him or her to let off steam by sitting through the complaints and objections.

"If I don't include Charles in the decision-making process there is a ten-minute lecture," said Aliza, who is originally from Colombia. "How do you feel when Charles flies off the handle?" I asked.

"It's very painful. I feel like I'm being worn down, like a child who is being castigated for not doing something right," she answered. Aliza's solution is to escape through visualization. "You know the lead apron you wear at the dentist's office when you're getting X rays? Well, I put on my imaginary lead apron to protect myself from his barrage of negativity. I used to be devastated. I felt like a bad person. Now I just let that stuff bounce off my lead apron." Aliza listens for a while and lets him vent, then she brings the conversation to a close without escalating her own rage.

It would be easy for Aliza, who was raised in an emotional Latino home, to react to Charles's angry attacks with a bitter quarrel. Instead she has found a way to cope with Charles's hotheaded anger while protecting herself. She has discovered that until Charles lets off steam nothing is accomplished. Rather than interrupt him, she decided to sit quietly without responding to his attacks. Aliza's strategy makes it easier for them to talk more rationally next time.

8. REMEMBER THAT TIMING IS EVERYTHING

As a rule, it's best to talk with the other parent during normal office hours. This helps structure the relationship as one in which you conduct business. You will need to express your preference so that the other person knows the boundaries of your availability. Of course there will be exceptions, but in general it's best to keep to a nine-to-five schedule.

Think back to when you were married. What was the best time of day for you to talk to your ex-spouse? What time was the worst? "I learned not to talk to my husband before dinner," said one divorced woman. "He was always so grumpy when he came home from work. If I had anything important to discuss, I waited until he had a chance to unwind." This information continues to be useful even though you are divorced. Plan your discussions for a time of day during which the other person is receptive.

You're in This Together

Imagine for a minute that you and the other parent have been shipwrecked at sea and you're stranded in a lifeboat. You have limited supplies, space, and resources. You have a choice. You can see the other person as a hindrance to survival and you can waste precious energy fighting over the limited resources. Or you can remind yourself that you have a common goal: You both want to survive. In order to accomplish this goal you'll need to shift your thinking and separate the problem from the person. The problem now is to raise healthy, happy kids. To be effective, you'll want to consider each child's needs, just as on the raft you would have to consider the need for water, food, first aid, and shade. Fulfillment of these needs is a shared problem. Your focus changes from "How do I feel about this person?" to "How can we solve our mutual problem?"

When you face your children's needs jointly, when you adopt the attitude "We're both in this together; what can we do to make it work" the situation seems more manageable, and you discover options you never knew existed.

Despite appearances to the contrary, you both want what's best for your children. The more you can focus on this common goal, separate the person from the problem, and accept the task as a shared one, the more successful you will be.

> The Golden Rule is do unto others as you would have them do unto you. Treat your parenting partner as you would like him or her to act toward you.

Communication Inventory Exercise

Awareness is the first step in changing behavior. Once you become aware of how you're communicating and how effective you are, you can evaluate what changes are needed. In my seminars, I assign this communication inventory as one of the first home assignments.

First, recall the last three or four conversations you've had with your children's other parent. Then take a few minutes to answer the following questions:

1. What was the tone of the conversations? On a scale of 1 to 10 (1 being calm, cordial, and cooperative, and 10 being a raging argument), how would you rate the tone of your contact? 1 2 3 4 5 6 7 8 9 10

   If you rated yourself in the 1 to 5 range, congratulate yourself. If you fell into the 6 through 10 range, you have work to do.

2. What are some of the most irritating things he or she does in a conversation? Consider tone of voice, mannerisms, evasive tactics, etc. Make a list of the things that irritate you.____________

   ____

3. What issues spark your anger?____________________

   ____

4. What can you do to defuse your reactions?________________

   ____

5. What do you do to upset or provoke him or her?____________

____

6. What are some of the blocks to effective communication between you and the other parent? Check the ones that apply.

   _____ Conversation detours

   _____ Blaming tone

   _____ Unrealistic expectations

   _____ Jumping to conclusions

   _____ Ambiguous questions

   _____ Bringing up past history or mistakes

   _____ Discussing personal issues

   _____ Not listening to the other person

7. How can you apply some of the eight keys to effective communication presented in this chapter to enhance your discussions? Think of at least one specific technique that you can use in your next conversation. Make a commitment to give it a try.

Remember, the goal of conversation with your ex is not revenge but rather courteous communication about your children. The first step in making changes is to recognize what you're currently doing—both what's working and what needs improvement. This awareness alone will begin the process.

Don't expect your communication style to change quickly. Changing old patterns takes time, so it helps to see this process as an experiment. Implement some of the suggestions offered here for the next month. Notice how they affect your discussions with the other parent. Remember, learning any new skills takes time and a lot of practice. Be patient with yourself and celebrate even the smallest improvements.

Chapter 6

Dealing with Difficult Exes

An eye for an eye and we all will be blind.

Mahatma Gandhi

How do you deal with someone who threatens to take you to court every time you refuse a demand? Who harasses you by walking into your house in the middle of the night? Who shouts obscenities at you? How do you negotiate with someone who restricts your access to your children? Or who threatens to hurt you? Or who repeatedly calls to check on the kids despite your requests for privacy? How do you deal with someone who wants to see your children only when it's convenient for him? Or who agrees to one thing and then does exactly as she pleases? In other words, what can you do when your best efforts at cooperation fail?

It would be nice if everyone had an ex-spouse who is rational, reasonable, and mature enough to handle postdivorce issues. Some people are simply too angry, unreliable, immature, or unstable. In his book *Coping with Difficult People,* Robert Bramson, Ph.D., developed several profiles of difficult people that I have adapted and applied to divorcing spouses.

Difficult former spouses tend to be self-absorbed and insensitive to the needs and concerns of their ex-spouse and children. They are often unreliable and irresponsible, particularly when it comes to child care and maintaining visitation schedules. These people justify their actions and blame the other parent for the difficulties that inevitably arise. As you read this, you may be thinking that this profile describes your ex perfectly, that you are the good guy and he or she is evil incarnate. But even if you feel relief at recognizing that your ex does, in fact, fall into the category of "difficult person," the two of you still have to interact on a regular basis. While you may be the rational, responsible partner, you, too, probably do things that perpetuate your ex's behavior.

While you may wish for a miraculous change in your ex, you likely won't get it. You can't wave a magic wand and, like Cinderella's fairy godmother, transform the other person. But you can change your own attitude. First, you don't have to bite every time your ex puts out the bait. You have the power to defuse the difficult behavior by setting limits, adjusting your expectations to realistically match your ex's limitations, or simply not reacting. When you alter your response you change the dynamics of the interaction and your ex will be forced to relate to you differently. In fact, this is the only action that will bring about change.

Many difficult people come across as strong, powerful, and decisive when, in reality, they are driven by fear, distrust, and weakness. Think about it for a moment: If your ex didn't feel threatened, there would be no need to attack or undermine you. The strategy is to overpower you, but the need arises from feelings of inadequacy and insecurity. Regardless of your ex's underlying motivation, your own best interest demands that you learn to minimize his or her difficult behavior.

Difficult ex-spouses fall into five categories. These people require "Special Handling." Like a package filled with fragile material that requires extra attention, these individuals need especially careful treatment to minimize their negative effect on you or your children. The first step is to identify and understand your ex's behavior. Once you understand the motivation you can begin to develop a coping strategy. But first let me identify the five types of difficult spouses:

1. The Angry Attacker
2. The Control Freak

3. The Intimidator
4. The Placater
5. The Uninvolved/Unreliable Parent

Now let's look at each type in greater detail.

1. THE ANGRY ATTACKER

Rodney, a short, pudgy, and mild-mannered certified public accountant, recalled a particularly disturbing incident with his ex-wife, Fay. Rodney works in a family-owned sportswear company with approximately fifty employees. He's worked for the same company for fifteen years and has a reputation for being even-tempered and fair-minded. Only Fay could test the limits of Rodney's patience.

They divorced because Rodney had found living with Fay intolerable; she would fly into a rage at the slightest provocation. Their marriage seemed more like an episode of *American Gladiators* than a loving relationship. After years of bickering, Rodney finally moved out of the house.

Several months after Rodney had asked Fay for a divorce she called his office no fewer than a dozen times during a single day. "I tried to reason with her," Rodney explained. "But she just kept screaming obscenities until I finally hung up on her. By the seventh call I had had it. I shouted at her until I realized that arguing wasn't getting me anywhere. I just wanted to kill her. I took a deep breath and told her that if she called me again I would call my attorney to get a restraining order preventing her from calling me at work. I figured that that would put an end to her calls. But no, she just kept calling. I was so embarrassed. The people in the front office had to tell her I wasn't there."

Rodney didn't get to the end of his rope overnight. He had tried using reason and logic, thinking he could convince Fay to change. When this proved ineffective, he would defend himself and enter into the argument. The simplest conversation would escalate into full-scale conflict. "Fay's like a little whirlwind that builds into a tornado," Rodney observed. "When we were married, she was mad at the world. Now that I'm no longer in her cherished circle I've become her target. She wants to destroy me."

The turning point finally came when Rodney figured out that it was pointless to reason with Fay. Fighting was simply her modus operandi. He stopped defending himself. When she screamed at him, he simply repeated the same phrase over and over: "I'll only discuss issues related to our son and I won't continue this conversation until you calm down." There were times when Fay continued to hurl obscenities and he would hang up and wait for the dust to settle.

Rodney's new strategy of setting limits, both in terms of the topics he would discuss as well as how he would be treated, took Fay by surprise and gradually led to a decrease in attacks. However, it was never easy for Rodney to deal with his ex-wife. He dreaded his conversations with her and over time decided to minimize the amount of contact he had with her by handling the majority of their business through letters and notes.

Fay is a classic example of an angry attacker. These types of difficult spouses are verbally abusive; they try to intimidate with accusations, criticism, harassment: "You're a cheap bastard." "You're an unfit mother." They frequently throw temper tantrums to intimidate you into backing down. They are like angry, out-of-control children who desperately need clearly defined limits and time to unwind.

Angry attackers have a strong need to prove that they're right and you're wrong. They are impatient. When you don't see their point of view, they use aggression to gain a sense of importance and superiority. Their motto is "victory at any price." For the most part, they feel utterly justified in their anger. These individuals are more bark than bite. When you refuse to engage in their attacks, set limits about what you will tolerate, and minimize the amount of contact you have with them, their behavior gradually will begin to improve.

2. THE CONTROL FREAK

Controllers don't trust that you will do things as well as they can. They wholeheartedly believe that their way is the "right" way and they want to make sure that you conform. If you were married to a controller, he or she most likely handled the family finances, made logistical arrangements, and preferred to be in charge.

Control freaks need to maintain control, especially over those things they hold near and dear, including their children. Divorce is especially unsettling to them because the order and structure they so desperately need have been disrupted. Control freaks fall into two categories: the nitpicker and the manipulator.

Lillian was an overorganized, overwrought nitpicker. Even her short brown hair was tightly curled. Harvey was a laid-back, ex-hippie type. Their divorce was marked by intense fighting and accusations of infidelity and irresponsible behavior. These charges continued during the period initially following their divorce and caused bitter fights over property as well as custody of their seven-year-old son, Cliff. When the court awarded Harvey joint custody, Lillian suddenly showed anxiety about being separated from her son.

Each time Harvey, a thirty-eighty-year-old electrician, came to pick up Cliff for the week, Lillian would come to the door with the boy's suitcase and a packet of information containing his appointments, his homework schedule, his permission slips for school trips, and reminders about his wearing his glasses and taking his vitamins.

"I can't believe it," Harvey complained. "You'd think that I was a complete moron if you saw the notes she had given me. It's not like I've never taken care of Cliff. She seems to be getting more and more freaked out as time goes by."

Lillian had always been a take-charge woman. During the marriage she had managed their money, made their social plans, and generally run their lives. She had been protective of Cliff and over-involved in his life. But it wasn't until she had to let her son go to his father's every other week that her anxiety began to escalate. She worried about what happened while Cliff was with his father, whether he got to bed on time, whether he wore his helmet when he went Rollerblading. Lillian was filled with fear and Harvey felt as if his ex-wife was invading his privacy. He resented her lack of confidence in him. The more Lillian pressured Harvey, the more resentful he became.

Lillian never let up. She accused Harvey of being an inadequate parent. "You don't make him wear his glasses, he doesn't get his homework done, and perish the thought that he should take a shower every day," she would say. These attacks widened the rift between them until Harvey became uncommunicative and cold. As a result, Lillian's mistrust increased. She threatened to take Harvey to court to change the custody arrangement.

Harvey was at his wit's end when he came to see me for counseling. He didn't understand why Lillian was acting so irrationally. "After ten years of marriage, you'd think she'd trust me. I've always been there for Cliff. I show up every week like clockwork. It's not like I'm an ax murderer," Harvey complained. "I had to listen to her while we were married, but I don't have to put up with her crap now!"

Harvey's anger was justified, but his strategy was making matters worse. After several sessions in which he vented his frustration I recommended that he ask Lillian about her concerns. I explained that when someone is feeling as anxious as she was, offering more information rather than less relieves the anxiety and generally makes the person easier to deal with.

We discussed the fine line between maintaining his autonomy and sharing relevant information. He could easily let Lillian know about his taking Todd to a computer class or give her an update on visits to the dentist. Harvey's willingness to include Lillian in this limited way eventually alleviated her desperate need for control.

The Manipulative Ex

The other type of controller uses a more calculated approach. Francine, a tall, thin woman with salt-and-pepper hair, had been married to a manipulator. Despite her height, she seemed small and beaten when she came to me for help. Her shoulders were hunched over and she hid behind a veil of bangs and a pair of horn-rimmed glasses. As she sank into the couch tears rolled down her cheeks. "Things started out pretty well between Russell and me," Francine explained. "During our separation we agreed that we would each have our son half time. There were times when

Russell hated me for leaving him, but we both put Jerry first and we respected each other as good parents."

But when the divorce trial didn't go Russell's way, Russell flipped out. Up to that point he had had control of their assets and he manipulated Francine through money. After the judge ruled in her favor, he could no longer intimidate her. "The only way he can control me now is through Jerry," she said.

Jerry, who was almost thirteen, had decided he wanted to live with his father and stepmother during the school year. While this was painful for Francine, she knew it would be good for her son and agreed to the change. She agreed that Jerry would spend holidays and summers with her, as well as every other weekend and one night every other week.

Francine continued to receive child support at a reduced rate, but she soon realized that Russell's ultimate goal was to restrict her access to her son and ultimately eliminate his obligation to pay child support.

"Every time we talk on the phone he's verbally abusive," Francine said. "He calls me a liar and a game player and says that Jerry doesn't like to come to my house. He says the only reason my son sees me at all is because of guilt and the pressure I put on him. I know that's not true. But Russell keeps hammering at me until I feel squished. And now he's dragging me back to court to take away my weekday visit with my son." Going to court cost Russell more than he pays for a year's worth of child support. His motivation was not Jerry's welfare. It was about power and control. He was manipulating Francine, Jerry, and the legal system too.

Francine had gone out of her way to be cooperative despite Russell's harshness, but her efforts had failed. Every time she spoke to her ex-husband she ended up feeling anxious and powerless.

After hearing about their emotionally charged phone conversations, I suggested that Francine minimize her contact with her ex-spouse. The conversations were unproductive and toxic. I recommended that she communicate by letter as much as possible. Francine was reluctant to accept my advice. She worried that Russell could use something she had written against her in court, so I suggested that she ask her attorney to review any correspondence before she sent it to her ex-husband.

I also recommended that she let the attorneys negotiate the custody and child support issues. I pointed out that despite her efforts at cooperation, her ex-husband was not going to respect anything short of a court order. I empathized with her frustration at having access to her son restricted. And I counseled patience, suggesting that she make the most of the time she does have with her son and that she reach out to her friends and family for support.

Dealing with either the nitpicker or the manipulator can be painful and trying. But regardless of what your former spouse may say or do, make your own commitment to easing the tension. In many cases, time works wonders to relieve a difficult situation.

3. THE INTIMIDATOR

Carla and Mark had fought bitterly before they separated. Carla, a legal secretary and the mother of two young children, had returned to work shortly after each of their births. Mark was an immature, impulsive man who couldn't hold a job. He blamed his bosses for problems at work and took out his anger and frustration on his ex-wife. "Mark's always been a bully," Carla explained. "When he finally left he took all the credit cards and cleaned out the bank accounts. I was left with my house, which my parents had bought for me before we were married, my sons, and a lot of bills."

Mark is six three and muscular, and he uses his stature to intimidate people. When they were married he lost his temper regularly. Once he shoved Carla so hard she shattered the glass in the sliding glass doors. He used to turn over chairs and throw things against the walls. Carla was scared about what he'd do now that they weren't living together.

Mark is a classic example of an intimidator. His sense of betrayal is so strong that he can't control his impulses. Whenever Mark loses his temper, he feels his actions are completely justified. His judgment is severely impaired and he has no concern for the consequences. His primary goal is to avoid feeling his pain, especially the pain of divorce.

"One night shortly after our separation Mark came to my house in the middle of the night and stood on the front lawn screaming at me, calling me names, and accusing me of trying to ruin him," Carla said. "He insisted that I come out and talk to him. When I refused, he threatened to drive his car through the front of the house. I was so terrified that I called my attorney and got a restraining order against him. Then I had a locksmith change all the locks."

One of the most difficult aspects of dealing with an intimidator is admitting how psychologically unstable the person is. The violent, irrational behavior represents serious, long-term emotional problems. People who must deal with this type of personality often try to defend themselves with reason. "I was the peacekeeper in our marriage. I walked around on eggshells all the time," Carla said. "When Mark would get upset I would try to make him calm down, but it rarely worked."

Mark still tries to intimidate her both physically and emotionally, and she's still frightened of him, but she has as little contact as possible. She does most of her communicating through her attorney. "It costs money," she says, "but it's worth it. When we have to exchange the children we do it either at the police station or in the fire station parking lot, where I feel safe. He's crazy and that's probably not going to change. I don't want to subject myself to his abuse anymore, so little by little I've figured out a way around it."

There are several keys to dealing with an intimidator: (1) Recognize that you are dealing with someone who is emotionally unstable, unpredictable, and irrational, (2) set and maintain clear, firm limits, (3) avoid engaging in fights, threats, or accusations, (4) minimize the amount of contact you have, and (5) remove yourself from an abusive situation immediately. Let your ex know that you will do whatever is necessary to protect yourself and ensure your safety and that of your children. Like Carla, you may need to get a restraining order, change the locks and your phone number, minimize the amount of contact, and exchange your children in a public place. These preventive measures will lessen the stress and minimize the opportunities your ex has to threaten you.

When intimidation extends to your children, stronger measures may be necessary. One of my clients, a nurse who had been married to a doctor, had been physically abused throughout her marriage. In fact, her ex had a long history of hitting his women, especially when they fought his unrelenting control. When his daughter from a prior marriage had started dating and begun to resist his rules, he beat her until he broke her arm. The incident ended in a criminal trial and he lost all rights to her custody.

My client had two children with him, a boy and a girl. Throughout their divorce and in the decade since, the doctor had repeatedly petitioned the court for custody of the girl. Never had he shown any interest in his son. The daughter, now entering puberty, suddenly decided she wanted to live with her dad and his third wife.

"I'd like her to move in with him," said Sara, a large and outspoken woman, "because that's what she really wants, but I'm terrified of what will happen when she starts going out with boys. When he gets mad he does real damage."

Still, Sara was tired of fighting. She had battled this man in court for thirteen years. He had much more money than she did and could afford a platoon of lawyers. Now he was threatening Sara with a court-ordered psychiatric evaluation. She was ready to give up and let her daughter go.

I suggested she give free rein to her lawyer, who had served her well over the years and who recommended she keep on fighting. I also recommended that she attend a support group for battered wives. She had been divorced from this abusive man long enough, and come so far in her own personal growth, that she had forgotten some of her fear and rage. Sara needed to get angry all over again, not for herself but to protect her daughter.

4. THE PLACATER

Placaters are the people who march under the banner "Peace at any price." They frequently agree to do something and then fail to come through. They say yes when they mean no and have little or no regard for the consequences when they change plans. These difficult exes create chaos by saying one thing and doing another. They can't be trusted to give a straight answer.

Nicky was seven when his parents separated. His mother, Rochelle, works for the phone company and his father, Andy, is a supervisor for a computer software company. Andy's affair with a woman at work went on for two years before he was able to tell Rochelle that he wanted to leave her and marry the other woman. Nicky lived with his mother and saw his father every other weekend.

The school year had just started and Rochelle wanted Nicky to take some after-school classes in wood construction and in clay sculpting. Rochelle called her ex-husband to ask him if he would pay for the classes. Andy was agreeable and promised to send a check to cover the cost. Rochelle signed Nicky up and paid a deposit. A week went by with no check. When the time came to pay the balance of the tuition she called Andy and discovered that once again he had said yes when he really didn't want to. Now he was backpedaling and refusing to pay. Rochelle had already made the commitment; her son was looking forward to the classes and she couldn't afford the expense.

"I should have known better," Rochelle said with a sigh. "Andy will say anything to avoid a confrontation. His standard operating procedure is to agree to something and then to do exactly as he pleases. It drives me crazy." Rochelle had lectured him about his spinelessness and how he hurt his son when he didn't keep his bargains, but she now realized that trying to change him was like trying to change the spots on a leopard. Instead she developed a strategy to deal with his placating behavior.

Now when she asks Andy to take care of their son or to pay for something extra, she gives him plenty of room to object. She has learned to ask if he has any reservations or foresees any difficulties with their agreement. This way, she forces him to cope with his ambivalence before she makes plans that involve him. When dealing with slippery people, you're better off putting agreements in writing. Reconfirm plans and give yourself enough time to make alternative arrangements.

5. THE UNINVOLVED/UNRELIABLE PARENT

Unreliable spouses are immature; in many respects they are more like children than adults. They assume responsibility for their kids only when it is easy and convenient.

Lisa teaches political science at a local community college and

Grant is a branch manager at a discount appliance store. Their joint custody of ten-year-old Ava provided that she spend one week at Lisa's and the next week at her father's. One day Lisa was on her way to work when Grant called. She could hear in his voice how upset he was. Ava had the flu and he was bringing her over so Lisa could take care of her. In the past Lisa would have let him off the hook and canceled her classes. But this had happened one time too often. "Whenever something came up that was inconvenient or hard to deal with he would come running to me," Lisa said. "Well, I was tired of rescuing him." Instead she told him that if he wanted joint custody he would have to take more responsibility. This approach blew up fast; Grant had an airtight rationale and he accused Lisa of being unreasonable. Lisa realized that Grant wouldn't give up unless he was forced to.

In utter frustration Lisa decided to respond differently. First, she acknowledged how difficult it was to deal with a sick child and then she told Grant that she knew he could figure out how to take care of Ava. She said she was needed at work and not available to cover for him. Then she made a couple of suggestions about what he could do to get help, hung up the phone, and went to work. Granted, Lisa was nervous about what Grant would do, but she knew she had to break the pattern of coming to his rescue every time he sent up the red flag.

That night she called to see how Ava was doing and discovered that when he was forced to handle a situation on his own, Grant coped very well. He stayed home from work in the morning, then arranged for a neighbor to take care of Ava in the afternoon.

The next week Lisa arranged for Ava to stay with her father while she went on a business trip. Grant was supposed to pick Ava up after work so Lisa could catch a 7:30 plane. At 6:15 Lisa started to worry; if she didn't leave in the next fifteen minutes she would miss her plane. There was no sign of Grant. She called his office, but no one answered. She hoped he was on his way, but by 6:30 she was at her wit's end. Frantically, she called her parents and asked if she might drop Ava off with them on her way to the airport. Luckily, her parents were home and willing to help. Lisa and Ava dashed out of the house and left Grant a note that said "If you want your daughter, pick her up at my parents' house."

"I finally realized that I just can't count on Grant," Lisa said. "He's too unreliable." The next time Lisa has to be somewhere important she'll make alternate plans so if he doesn't show up, she won't be stuck. "Some of us still believe in Santa Claus," Lisa admitted. "I wanted to believe that Grant would grow up and do the right thing, but he rarely does." Lisa realized that it was time to stop wishing that her ex-husband would be different. She developed a strategy to avoid continual disappointment, and in this way also avoided futile confrontations.

WHEN STEPPARENTS ARE DIFFICULT

Fifty percent of divorced parents remarry. The addition of a stepparent dramatically alters the dynamics of your reorganized family. The quality of the relationship between the new stepparent and the biological parent can either help or hinder family relationships. A stepparent can be a positive influence by bringing a more balanced perspective into a tense situation or by taking over the exchange of children between two hostile parents. On the other hand, some stepparents can increase hostility between ex-spouses.

A year after her divorce was final, Veronica's ex remarried. Now whenever she calls to speak to him, the new wife interferes. "Any time I call my children's father at home it's like trying to get past a security guard," Veronica complained. "She wants me to clear my conversation with her before I can talk to him." When Veronica does finally get her ex on the phone, his wife stands in the background coaching him about what to say. "He wants to be cooperative, but it seems like he's afraid of her reaction if he doesn't put up a fight," Veronica complained to me. "Archie was so much easier to deal with before she came into the picture."

Some stepparents create friction and conflicts where they didn't exist before. Many resent their new spouse's involvement with the former family. Some react more strongly to the ex-spouse than the biological parent does; others actively promote an escalation of hostility. Some stepparents come on too strong, trying to take on the role of second parent. Their overzealousness may be a genuine attempt at establishing their new family, but it often threatens the biological parent. A biological parent has a hard enough time accepting that another person is filling a role that biological parent considers his or hers alone. When a new spouse moves in before the postdivorce family has had time to solidify, feelings of intense competition may be ignited. The relationships that occur as a result of remarriage are complex and challenging. Your children need time to adjust to the new stepfamily. This adjustment can be delayed by negative dynamics between one biological parent and the other's new spouse. I have touched on just a few of the issues that arise as a result of remarriage. Consult both the Suggested Reading List as well as the Resources at the back of the book for further information.

When dealing with a difficult ex or stepparent, it helps to have a strategy for coping. In his book *Getting Past No,* William Ury suggests several steps for dealing with difficult people in the workplace. I have adapted some of his strategies to coping with your ex-spouse.

Five Strategies for Dealing with Difficult Exes

1. Hold realistic expectations.
2. Prepare for the interaction.
3. Don't simply react; do the unexpected.
4. Create distance between you and the difficult behavior.
5. Set limits.

Now let's look at each strategy more closely.

STRATEGY 1. HOLD REALISTIC EXPECTATIONS

Think back on how your ex-spouse acted while you were married. Was he critical, angry, and antagonistic? Did she nag you unmercifully? Was he irresponsible and unreliable? Did she regularly say one thing and then do exactly what she wanted? Did he or she have a strong need to run the show?

Your ex's personality during the marriage probably indicates how he or she will continue to act. Don't expect the other person to make a radical change in character simply because of a divorce. Most people remain true to form in both their strengths and weaknesses. If they were responsible, committed parents before divorce, that behavior will probably continue. But if they were controlling or irresponsible during marriage, that probably won't change either. Your challenge is to accept who your ex is and stop trying to change him or her. Once you have come to terms with the fact that your ex is not who you would wish him or her to be, you can let go of your disappointment and anger and develop a strategy for dealing with his or her difficult behavior.

A client of mine provided a perfect case in point: Peggy, a copy editor at a business magazine, had agreed to have her six-year-old son, Jeremy, at her house at 7:00 so his father could pick him up. This time was inconvenient for her since she had an invitation to a dinner party that evening. But Gary, an extraordinarily handsome, struggling musician, had a late appointment and she wanted to accommodate him.

As Peggy was driving up the hill to her house at 7:02 she saw Gary driving down the hill toward town. "That looks like Daddy," cried Jeremy. Peggy couldn't believe that Gary had refused to wait two minutes. She and Jeremy pulled into the driveway and went inside. No dad. No note. They waited and waited and Jeremy asked sadly, "Doesn't Daddy want me to come to his house today?" Peggy reassured Jeremy. "There must have been some mistake. I bet he'll be here soon. Why don't we leave a note on the door saying that we went over to Carol's for dinner and that he can pick you up there."

Just then, Gary drove into the driveway. He was forty-five minutes late. "Where were you?" asked Peggy. "I was here at seven," responded Gary. "We were here at seven-oh-two," replied Peggy. "Wasn't that you driving down the road?" "I couldn't wait. I went into town to grab a bite to eat," Gary said matter-of-factly. "You fed Jeremy, didn't you?" "No," muttered Peggy. "You always like to go out to eat with him, so I had him wait for you." As Gary stood in the middle of the living room she took Jeremy into the kitchen and hurriedly fixed him a sandwich.

"I'm late for my dinner party," growled Peggy. "Would you clean up after Jeremy finishes eating? I have to go." She stormed out of the house.

Peggy was an hour late for her dinner party and missed the meal completely. When she returned home, she found ketchup flung from one end of the kitchen to the other and food all over the floor. Not only had she missed the dinner, but she had come home to a mess.

"I just wanted to kill him. It was so hostile," she cried. "Here I go out of my way to accommodate his schedule, making myself into a pretzel, and look how he treats us. And the sad part is that poor Jeremy pays the price. What a jackass! I wish that man would disappear. May his soul rot in hell!"

Although she had plenty of information, Peggy forgot who she was dealing with. Gary always had been self-centered and irresponsible. His music, his friends, his life had always come first. Time and time again his behavior had indicated that he just wasn't going to change. She thought she had adjusted her expectations to more closely match his reality; however, she still expected him to treat her the way she treated him. It hadn't worked. This leopard wasn't about to change his spots either.

After several sessions, Peggy came to terms with the reality of her situation. She needed to recognize who she was dealing with and act accordingly. Only then would there be less disappointment and frustration for her and Jeremy.

When you deal with a difficult ex, don't expect miracles. You'll only set yourself up for heartache. Anticipate the problems that occur regularly and take the necessary action to protect yourself and your children.

STRATEGY 2. PREPARE FOR THE INTERACTION

Human beings are like reaction machines. Experience and our own nature program us to respond automatically to certain stimuli. When dealing with a difficult ex-spouse you need to practice what you are going to say and how you're going to say it. An athlete prepares mentally before a big event with visualization or repetition of key movements. An actor recites her lines over and over. You can practice talking with your ex-spouse by rehearsing in front of a mirror or with a friend. Mental rehearsal is especially important when you are working to change a pattern of destructive interaction.

Start by imagining yourself talking with your former spouse the way you want to. Visualize yourself refusing to react, setting limits, clarifying the plans you have agreed to, offering information, or doing whatever is necessary to circumvent predictable behavior. After you have run through the interaction in your mind several times it's time to ask a friend to practice with you.

This technique is called role playing. Ask your friend to play the role of your ex. Coach your friend on the abusive, critical, threatening, or placating phrases your ex-spouse uses. Now the two of you act out a discussion with your former spouse. Practice using the coping strategies and communication skills you have learned in this and previous chapters.

If you find yourself reacting in that old familiar way, stop the role play and start again. Keep replaying the interaction until you can successfully stay out of the conflict. Changing your part of the interaction requires self-control and a lot of practice. Be patient with yourself. Changing old patterns is difficult; you may need time before you can master this skill.

STRATEGY 3. DON'T SIMPLY REACT; DO THE UNEXPECTED

You probably have one of three reactions when confronted with difficult behavior: You want to strike back, defend yourself, or give in to get your ex off your case. Unfortunately, these reactions reinforce, and in some cases *encourage,* the troublesome behavior. You're not only up against your ex's demeanor but your own reaction as well. Your response can intensify the very behavior you want to stop.

You can't change your ex, but you do have control over yourself and your reactions. The first step is to control your own behavior.

You need to maintain your balance. Regardless of what your ex says or does, stay focused on your goal of doing what's best for your children. Your challenge is *not* to react!

One effective way to change the tone of your interactions is to do the unexpected. This will disarm your former spouse. The fact is, most people do react predictably. When Fay harassed her mild-mannered accountant ex-husband, Rodney, his reaction to her was anger; when Lillian pressured Harvey for information about their son he automatically became noncommunicative and unavailable; and when Grant refused to take responsibility for his sick daughter, Lisa threatened his right to joint custody. These reactions were all habitual. To break the destructive cycle you have to reverse the dynamic. Rodney finally set limits on how much of Fay's harassment he would tolerate. Harvey gave Lillian more information about their son rather than shutting her out. And when Gary was late to pick up their son, Peggy made other arrangements and planned for the future.

The key is to do the opposite of what you normally do. To disarm your former spouse you must first establish a measure of respect by refusing to play the game. Take charge of the situation by changing the rules and controlling your reaction. By doing this you say "You may not like me, but you must take me seriously and treat me decently." Doing the unexpected catches your ex off guard and breaks the vicious cycle of action and reaction.

Recognize the Early Warning Signs

Be aware of early signs that your conversation is deteriorating. One of the best barometers is your body. Notice how you're feeling. Is your stomach tied in a knot? Do you have a lump in your throat? Is your heart pounding? Are your palms sweaty? These are signs that you are losing your composure, that you need to get some distance from the situation.

We all have certain emotional buttons. When they are pushed we react. Some people react bitterly to criticism, others see red when they are threatened; still others are infuriated by people telling them what to do. Ask yourself about your own emotional buttons. Recognizing them helps you to control your natural reaction. If your ex-spouse criticizes, remind yourself not to take it personally. Remember the adage we heard as children "Sticks and stones may break my bones, but words will never hurt me." Keep that in mind when you deal with your ex-spouse.

When you are under attack, you may find it helpful to remind yourself that your ex doesn't know a better way to communicate. As you detach yourself from the situation and stop reacting, you will notice that the bullying behavior subsides.

STRATEGY 4: CREATE DISTANCE BETWEEN YOU AND THE DIFFICULT BEHAVIOR

When you find yourself facing a difficult situation with your former spouse, step back, collect your thoughts, and look at your ex's behavior objectively. To help create a sense of detachment, imagine that you are looking down from the balcony of a theater, imagine that he or she is standing on the stage. From the balcony you can evaluate the situation calmly, almost as if you were a third person. By observing your ex-spouse from this perspective, you can distance yourself from your natural emotions and reactions.

Our ex-spouses are particularly difficult to view objectively because they touch off a series of reactions that quickly become part of the game. An excellent tool that breaks destructive patterns of reaction is labeling your former spouse's behavior. In ancient mythology, calling an evil spirit by name was one way to ward it off. The same holds true for you in relation to your ex. By naming the game you can break the spell he or she casts.

Some people resist categorizing someone else, especially with such simplistic labels as angry attacker, intimidator, or placater. I recognize that human beings are complex and can't be reduced to a single label. But by placing your ex into a particular category you can begin to depersonalize his or her behavior. Take a moment and decide which category suits your ex. Once you identify your ex as a type you will recognize that he or she gives others the same treatment. After she filed for divorce, one of my verbally abused clients was surprised to find that her husband was famous for yelling at everyone, his staff, his partners, even his clients! And she'd thought she was special! If your ex is a placater you may realize that this is her coping mechanism in every other area of her life too. By naming the difficult behavior you can remind yourself that your ex-spouse's actions are based on his or her own shortcomings and not take them as personally.

Understanding Can Help

Understanding why your ex acts as he or she does can be useful. An exercise that I use in seminars and support groups is to take an 8½″ x 11″ piece of paper and fold it down the middle. On one side, list your ex's difficult, annoying behaviors. Then put yourself in your ex's shoes and on the other side of the paper write what you think is the motivation for each behavior. I realize this won't be easy, but if you can get even a glimmer of why a person acts in a particular way, you may be released from the negative patterns of interaction. For example, an ex-spouse who is overly controlling and repeatedly calls to check on the children is most likely motivated by insecurity and a lack of trust. Understanding this may mitigate your impatience.

Once you have done the first part of this exercise, take a clean sheet of paper, again fold it in half, and on one side list your responses that helped minimize the difficult behavior and on the other side list responses that caused your ex's behavior to escalate. Make a list of at least five responses from the past that have worked to defuse a situation with your ex-spouse. Then think about how you can use those strategies in future interactions.

STRATEGY 5. SET LIMITS

Establishing new boundaries after divorce is always necessary, but it is even more important when dealing with a difficult ex.

Some people are diehard rule breakers. You set a limit and they immediately take on the challenge. They feel compelled to exceed it. "I was sick and tired of Dave calling me first thing in the morning," exclaimed Lynn, a hardworking escrow officer. "I told him that I was willing to talk with him about the children, but that I would prefer to do that during the day. Maybe I didn't make myself clear, but Dave kept calling every morning before eight when I was getting the kids ready for school. No matter what I said he wouldn't stop. Finally I decided to leave my answering machine on and not take his calls."

Dave, an early-to-bed, early-to-rise building contractor, was still angry that Lynn and he had divorced, so he continued to intrude on her personal life. No matter how clearly Lynn stated her preference, Dave was bound and determined to ignore her. Rather than get into a fight, she took the situation into her own hands and disengaged from his intrusive behavior. After a couple of frustrating weeks Dave gave up and called her at her office. For her this was a big step in redefining their relationship.

In some cases it is even more urgent that clear limits be set. When you are dealing with an angry attacker or an intimidator you must make clear what you are willing to tolerate and what you will do if your boundaries are not respected. Unfortunately there is often a testing period when your ex will try to bypass your newly defined limits. Stick to your guns. The longer you maintain your boundaries, the clearer it will be that you mean business. Your ex will gradually begin to respect these changes.

Irreconcilable Differences

One of life's heartbreaks, whether we are married or divorced, is that certain differences are simply irreconcilable. Some issues are never decided satisfactorily, some patterns never change, despite your best effort, and some problems remain complex, painful, and troublesome. No matter how hard you work some issues never end up neatly and tidily resolved. They may always be a struggle. They may always be an irritation. They may always be unclear. These areas of ambiguity are the ones that cause the knots in your stomach until you learn to surrender.

There is, don't forget, a fine line between surrender and submission. I am not advocating that you become a doormat or allow the other parent to abuse or mistreat you. What I am suggesting is that you find the wisdom to accept the things that aren't going to change and cultivate the inner strength to move on. Give up the unwinnable battle. Put down your sword, not in defeat, but in victory—victory over yourself and your need to be right, victory over trying to change the other person, and victory over the urge to get even. Put your children first. Make them the cause you champion.

There was a period in my life, shortly after my divorce, when I had numerous revelations about Ama's father and what he needed to do in order to be a better parent and live a more fulfilling, productive life. I spent months talking at him about my insights, to no avail. Finally, in absolute frustration, I realized that no amount of talking, explaining, or cajoling was going to change him. He had made his choices and wasn't about to alter them to suit my "superior" methods. With hindsight I realize that the energy I expended trying to change him wasn't completely altruistic.

I felt smug in my ability to see his shortcomings. I liked my brilliant plan for how he could improve himself. I had a mission; I was on a crusade. Only finally after months of arguments, frustration, and knots in my gut did it dawn on me: If he hadn't listened to my character-building advice while we were married, he certainly wasn't going to listen now.

Once I gave up my crusade and accepted him for who he was and still is, flaws and all, our relationship improved dramatically. I found far greater inner peace and discovered new ways of communicating that were less stressful and ultimately more satisfying. (I have to confess, I still have moments when I want to redesign his personality, but with every year that passes they are less frequent and easier to control.)

You are beyond the point of changing your ex-spouse. It's time to accept him or her for who he or she is, with both deficiencies and strengths. The only change you can make now is in how *you* communicate.

Chapter 7

Where's Poppa?

Keeping Both Parents Involved

We should take him to court and have the judge tell him that he has to come and see us. The judge could make him visit us.

Leroy, ten years old

Abbie, now 22, was only seven when her parents divorced. Afterward, her dad was never an important part of her life. "I see him as weak, not someone you can count on," she said. As a little child, Abbie tried to keep hold of her daddy. She'd call and ask him to take her to play at the park, but half the time he stood her up. "It's almost like if he starts to communicate with me he'll have to get too involved. That idea is too overwhelming so he keeps me at a distance. I've been excommunicated by him so many times. Now I just can't try anymore unless he wants a relationship with me, nothing I do is going to work. I'm resigned to the idea that when my dad needs a daughter in his life, then he'll come to me, but I can't keep pursuing him."

Abbie, unfortunately, is stereotypical. Fifteen million American children—one quarter of all children under eighteen—are now growing up with little or no contact with their fathers. In 1970, 12 percent of children lived with their mothers alone; by 1988 this figure reached 24 percent.[1] Absent fathers are twice as common as they were a generation ago, and there is no relief in sight.

Research conducted at the University of Pennsylvania by sociologists Frank Furstenberg and Kathleen Mullan Harris shows that after divorce noncustodial fathers have minimal contact with their children. Between 1976 and 1987, 42 percent of the children in the study had not seen their fathers at all during the previous year. Only 20 had slept at their fathers' houses in the previous month, and only one in six saw their fathers once a week or more.[2] Research links a father's absence to psychological stress, poor academic performance, higher incidence of drug abuse, and teenage suicide.[3] Clearly, a father's time and attention are crucial to the well-being of his children.

This chapter is for both moms and dads. Some sections are geared more toward one parent than the other, but I suggest that you each read the whole chapter. A mother (or a father who has primary custody) will learn how to encourage the noncustodial parent to maintain the connection with the children, and how to make transitions between parents easier. A father (or noncustodial mother) will learn how to stay involved with the children and how to make them feel secure. (If the two of you share joint custody, you will still find this chapter helpful.) You will also find a section on how to make transitions easier on *you* when the children leave for the other parent's house. The goal of this chapter is to help you find constructive ways for both parents to stay involved.

Any way you cut it, divorce is hard. The trauma can be minimized, however, when children have continuous, open, easy access to both parents.[4] Rather than prescribe a particular form of custody, I am going to suggest a formula for maximizing parental involvement. Studies show that after divorce, about 90 percent of children live with their mothers. Given this reality, I direct this section of the chapter to mothers.

Sociologist Frank Furstenberg has said, "Men regard marriage as a package deal . . . they cannot separate their relations with their children from their relations to their former spouse. When the relationship ends, the parental bond usually withers."[5] Research also says that men who stay connected to their children during the first year after divorce will continue to stay involved.

That's why you need to start off on the right foot. Society tends to downplay a father's role in his children's lives. If you can counteract this prevailing attitude, your children will have a better chance of keeping their father in their lives. There will always be some fathers who do not want to be responsible for their kids, but they are the exception.

Loss of easy access to their children is what drives most fathers to become absentee parents. As the primary care giver, you control access to your kids. You can make seeing the kids a piece of cake or a walk through a minefield. If you use this particular contact with your ex-spouse as a time to pick a fight or make him jump through hoops, he may give up contact with your children simply to avoid a confrontation with you.

A man whose wife initiated the divorce may stop seeing his kids. This withdrawal can last as little as the few months it takes to pull himself together or it can go on for years. "It was so painful seeing my son and realizing that we would never have a close father-son relationship," one male client explained in a therapy session. "I can't tolerate the idea of being a Sunday dad. For me, it's easier to let go completely and not see him at all." In the course of his therapy I helped him face his feelings of loss and sadness. He ultimately recognized that avoiding the pain of the changed relationship with his son would be easier for him, but it would be a great deal harder and far more damaging to his son.

That case was easy because the man was exceptionally aware of his feelings. Many men, however, blame their lack of involvement on anger toward their ex-wives, legal hassles, or feeling uncomfortable alone with their children. They rationalize that their wives rejected them, so their kids must have done the same. Angry and hurt, they stay away. Other men retreat into their work or new social life; they attribute their lack of involvement to busy schedules or a new relationship. The truth is, they avoid contact with their children out of feelings of pain and guilt.

KEEPING DADS INVOLVED

Surprisingly, a recent survey of 142 divorced fathers conducted by Charles Hoffman of California State University at San Bernadino found that 69 percent of them viewed involvement with their children as very important. Many credited former wives with their continued involvement. And yet Hoffman also found that most of those same men see their children two weekends a month or less. You can't force a man to see his children, but you can encourage him to stay connected. Here are six tips for keeping dads involved.

1. Encourage frequent contact and open communication.
2. Let your ex know you want him to be involved with your children.
3. Ask the children's school to send report cards and notices to their father and encourage him to attend school functions.
4. Call your ex occasionally to share good news about your kids.
5. Help your children acknowledge his birthday and significant holidays.
6. Make visitation as pleasant as possible for all of you.

Let's look at each point in more detail.

1. ENCOURAGE FREQUENT CONTACT AND OPEN COMMUNICATION

Your children need to talk with their father regularly. Maybe you can help set up a regular phone time or a call before bedtime so he can hear how their day went and verbally tuck them into bed. Don't interfere with these calls to have your own conversation with him or to argue about money or scheduling. This should be their private time to connect, free from any interference so they can talk openly. Your differences with him have no place in their relationship.

"I call my kids every few days just to see how they're doing," Cary said during a counseling session. "The other day, my daughter, Babs, and I were joking around when she suddenly turned cold and acted bored. She almost stopped talking except for a couple of 'I don't knows' and 'uh-huhs.'

"Then I heard her mother's voice in the background asking who Babs was talking to. She must have walked in in midconversation.

I guess Babs didn't want her mom to think we were having too good a time together," Cary said. Apparently Babs's mother often listens to her one-sided conversations with her dad and interjects snide remarks. Or she asks to get on the line and hassles him about something. "I want to be able to talk with my kids without my ex-wife eavesdropping on our conversations," he said sadly.

Your children will benefit from a separate relationship with their father, and ultimately so will you. If, on the other hand, you make their communication an obstacle course, you risk his becoming an absent-father statistic.

Adopt a Hands-off Attitude

You will be tempted to become involved in the relationship between your children and their father. Many mothers admit to interrogating their kids about their conversations with their fathers, "What did he want? How is he doing? What did the two of you talk about?" But even these innocent questions feel intrusive and can be disruptive to their relationship.

Frankly, this hands-off approach is one that parents in intact families would do well to emulate. Every child has some rights to privacy. "My son has a whole separate relationship with his dad," said Gilda, a tall, dark cosmetics saleswoman who is proud of the restraint she is showing. "In the beginning I would question him about their conversations, how they spent their time, and what he did at his dad's house. But I saw it made him uncomfortable. He really didn't want to report to me about his dad. I don't ask. I wish I could. It's hard to let him have a separate life that I don't have any control over, that I don't even know about. But I just wait for him to tell me, and I keep a tight rein on my curiosity."

2. LET YOUR EX KNOW YOU WANT HIM TO BE INVOLVED WITH YOUR CHILDREN

For many fathers, caring for their children is a foreign experience. In addition to our culture's dismissal of the father's importance in the lives of his children, there is the reality he may well have had an absentee father of his own when he was growing up. Although the culture is changing, there are still many men who have spent little or no time alone with their kids. For them, the prospect of giving day-to-day care can be frightening.

The man in the following story was typical in this regard. Fortunately, his ex-wife stepped back and let him try his wings. "I was terrified when I first thought about taking care of my son alone," confessed Jared, a recently divorced father of a three-year-old. "When I was married I went to my job and my wife stayed home and cared for our son. My career was my main focus and I didn't pay much attention to him. I saw my role as provider and as a support to my wife, not as a full participant." Jared had never changed a diaper, never cooked a meal, never given his baby a bottle. "The only thing I did was play with him and hold him when my wife asked me to. My father wasn't involved with me, so I didn't even know what I was supposed to do." In some ways his relationship with his son has been enhanced since the divorce. He has been forced to reassess his role as a father. He's become a much more involved parent. "I can't take for granted that he'll be part of my life," he said. "Now that Tyler is with me a few days a week I've had to learn how to cook and take care of him."

Acknowledgment Can Go a Long Way

After divorce, many men feel isolated and cut off from their families. You can help your ex, and indirectly your children, by acknowledging how difficult the adjustment is. Many problems can be averted by letting your ex-husband know that you recognize the importance of his role in your children's lives.

One of my clients had fought hard for custody of her kids. Michele, a fluffy-haired blonde who had hardened herself during a bitter divorce, was now ready to take a softer stance. "I decided to swallow my pride and let Hank know how much the kids need him," she said. "I knew he was struggling to fix up his new place and make it nice for the kids. I told him, 'I know how hard getting settled in your new apartment has been.' I let him know how important he is to the kids. 'They really look forward to seeing you,' I said. It worked like magic; this guy who was such a jerk all through our divorce looked me in the eye and said, 'Thanks, I really needed to hear that.' "

3. ASK THE CHILDREN'S SCHOOL TO SEND REPORT CARDS AND NOTICES TO THEIR FATHER AND ENCOURAGE HIM TO ATTEND SCHOOL FUNCTIONS

Many schools function as if the intact nuclear family were still standard-issue. They send information notices and report cards only to one home. They leave room on their forms for only one address and telephone number.

Let the school officials know that you want all information about your children and their school events sent to both homes. I recommend you do this regardless of the other parent's involvement or proximity. My daughter's father lives out of state and I request that her school send copies of report cards and notices about events, meetings, and conferences, regardless of the fact that he is too far away to attend. My reasoning is that the more information he has about his daughter and her education, the more likely he is to take an active interest.

"I helped educate my daughter's school about families with two divorced, involved parents," a father in one of my seminars recently reported. "I used my computer to redesign their application and emergency forms. I made enough room so families with parents at two separate addresses could be included on the form. At the bottom of my completed forms, I wrote in bold letters: **Father is actively involved in the lives of his children. Please send all information regarding the children to both parents!**"

School: A Common Meeting Ground

Encourage your ex-spouse to attend school conferences, back-to-school night, and other school events. You can tolerate any discomfort you may feel being in the same room together when you see the pleasure your kids get when both of you are present. My client Woody hesitated to attend his child's back-to-school night.

He had been divorced for only a few months and he was still nervous about being in a public place with his ex. That afternoon his son called and asked if Woody was coming to see the volcano he had made as a science project. With reluctance Woody agreed to go. "I'm so glad I did," Woody said later. "When I saw my kid's face when I walked in, my anxiety disappeared. He wanted me to meet his teacher and see his work."

At times when you can't both attend a parent-teacher conference, set up an alternate meeting. School conferences and events can be positive experiences in which both you and your ex-spouse take pride in your children and remember that no matter how difficult your marriage may have been, together you produce these wonderful people. If problems arise, a parent-teacher conference can be an opportunity to coordinate your efforts and come up with a common plan. In any case, your children get the message that they have two caring, involved parents who are concerned about their education and development.

4. CALL YOUR EX OCCASIONALLY TO SHARE GOOD NEWS ABOUT YOUR KIDS

Much of the talk between divorced parents is about logistics, scheduling, and problems. This "maintenance talk" is necessary, but an occasional phone call to let the other parent know about a child's success in learning a new skill, winning an award, getting a part in a school play or a good report card can help forge a cooperative relationship. Sharing the highlights of your kids' lives is easily neglected when you are busy and have limited contact with your ex. Remember to include your children's other parent in happy events. Make copies of awards received or reports on which your children worked especially hard. Send photographs, badges from swim meets, the latest art project. By including him in the everyday joys of your children's lives, you build a positive rapport with your ex-husband while you also strengthen the parent-child bond.

5. HELP YOUR CHILDREN ACKNOWLEDGE HIS BIRTHDAY AND SIGNIFICANT HOLIDAYS

This is especially important for young children who depend on you to remember important dates. Make a point of reminding your children of their father's birthday, and their paternal grandparents' birthdays, and other important occasions. Until your children are old enough to assume responsibility for buying cards or gifts, you need to help. (Gifts are optional if money is a problem. You may want to encourage your children to save their money so they can buy their father a gift.)

An alternative to buying presents is providing supplies so your children can make their own. A gift doesn't have to be elaborate; in fact, the most meaningful presents are usually the ones your children create themselves. This is a way for them to express their love for their parent or grandparents. Three of the most cherished presents my daughter has given her father were a frame made of noodles painted gold with her annual school portrait glued in the middle, a bird feeder that she made by stuffing peanut butter and birdseed into a pine cone, and a painting she entitled *The Fuchsia Fairy* which to this day has a prominent place on the wall next to his desk. Help your kids remember the important events in their father's life and make an effort to celebrate them. It will mean a lot to them and even more to him.

You help set the tone for the father-child relationship by acknowledging the importance of keeping two parents involved in your children's lives. Do it for your kids. They need and deserve both of you.

6. MAKE VISITATION AS PLEASANT AS POSSIBLE FOR ALL OF YOU

Visitation between the children and the noncustodial parent can be awkward, uncomfortable, even painful. The visitation relationship is a complex one. Comings and goings, especially, can be emotionally draining and tense for everyone involved. The noncustodial parent lives by a time clock with the meter running. The custodial parent has to shift gears from being a single parent to simply being single. On top of that, she is faced with abrupt separation from her children. Despite these stresses, the relationship between a noncustodial father and his children is extremely important. Your children long to see him.

As the custodial parent, you can influence the atmosphere surrounding the visits. Your attitude affects how your children handle their time with their other parent. Take a moment and imagine that the court awarded your former spouse sold custody of your children and you have been granted "reasonable visitation." How would you like the transitions handled? How much time would you like to spend with your children? How would you like to negotiate holidays and vacations? Put yourself in the other parent's shoes and you will get a clearer idea of how to make the visiting process go smoothly.

Mothers sometimes don't understand the difference to the kids between having a father at home where they see him regularly and when he lives someplace else. When a father is no longer under the same roof, everyday interaction becomes difficult, and in many cases impossible. Help with homework, discussion about chores, dinner and bedtime conversations are gone. Now the time spent together is artificial, usually centering on planned activities such as dinner at McDonald's, trips to the mall, a movie. The nature of the relationship is altered dramatically by its new structure.

Nevertheless, visits with Dad, no matter how infrequent or unnatural, are important. The hardest part of visitation is often the transition. The kids feel like batons in a relay race; they're being handed off and they just hope they won't be dropped. Their parents are nervous wrecks; they know the handoff is the part of the race that needs the most finesse. In this section you will learn how to make transitions easier on everyone involved. And these following five steps can make the transition easier on your children.

Comings and Goings: Helping Your Kids Make the Transition

1. Prepare for departure.
2. Establish routines for comings and goings.
3. Don't "do business" with your ex.

4. Acknowledge your children's feelings.
5. Expect off-the-wall behavior.

Let me elaborate.

1. PREPARE FOR DEPARTURE

Let your children know ahead of time what the schedule is and when they will go to their other parent's house. Young children also benefit from a fifteen-minute warning and another reminder five minutes before the scheduled departure. This helps them disengage from their current activity and shift gears before leaving.

Hali is five and an expert at traveling between houses. Her mother, Kathy, is a teacher who is skilled at keeping little children focused on the coming task. "We make the transitions positive," Kathy explained. "I remind Hali that her dad is going to pick her up. About half an hour before he comes over I announce that her daddy will be here soon. This really seems to help her to shift gears and get ready to go. I tell her I'll miss her, but that she is going to come back in a few days and that her daddy is really looking forward to seeing her."

2. ESTABLISH ROUTINES FOR COMINGS AND GOINGS

"Kitty used to get clingy and cry when her father would pick her up," said Betsey, the mother of a seven-year-old. "She would carry on that she didn't want to go or throw a temper tantrum." Betsey and her ex talked about the transition and decided to ritualize it as much as possible. Now her dad picks her up from school at 4:30 on Thursday afternoons. They do the same thing every time: Drive to the market for grocery shopping, go back to his house, unload the groceries, and then cook dinner together. Since they've started the routine, Kitty hasn't had one tantrum. "She does get upset when we change the schedule," Betsey says. "She has a calendar in which she marks her visits so she knows when she is going to see her dad again." This visual reminder helps Kitty to feel in control and to facilitate the transitions.

The more consistent you keep the pickups and drop-offs, the easier they will be on your kids and you. Children thrive on routine. Transitions can be as programmed as bedtimes or mealtimes. Buy your children a calendar so they can plot their visiting schedule. The more they can depend on a predictable pattern for the transfer from one house to another, the better they will feel.

3. DON'T "DO BUSINESS" WITH YOUR EX

Asking your children to relay information to the other parent during visitation is an obvious no-no, but there are other kinds of exchanges that also must be avoided. Avoid the temptation to use visitation for any other purpose than the exchange of children. The ex-husband of one of my clients asked her to bring their daughter to a specific street corner so he could pick her up and take her to a special church service. My client agreed. Then he asked if she could bring along a painting that was part of the court-ordered divorce settlement. That's where my client balked. "He knows that painting means a lot to me," said Debra, a fiery redhead with flashing Irish eyes. "He also knows how emotional I am. I'm going to be really angry the day I hand him that painting. I don't want my daughter there when it happens." Debra knew herself well enough to protect her daughter. She also wanted to protect the sanctity of her daughter's time with her dad. The transition between homes is hard enough to manage without taking along your parents' emotional baggage.

4. ACKNOWLEDGE YOUR CHILDREN'S FEELINGS

When your children are leaving to go to the other parent's house or coming back to yours they may say something like "I don't like you and I want to stay at Daddy's house" or "I don't want to go, I'll miss you." This can be hard to take. Try to remember that your children are feeling the stress of the transition between one house and the other, as well as the separation from a parent. Instead of reacting to their words, try to acknowledge their feelings. "I know it's hard for you to leave your father" or "You sound mad about not being able to stay with him" or "You seem sad about leaving me." These reflective responses will help your children feel they have been heard and understood. By acting as a sounding board for your children's feelings, you also help to relieve their stress.

Chad, a five-year-old, lives with his mother, Judy. His father picks him up every other Saturday and they spend the weekend together. One Saturday, just before his dad arrived, Chad said, "I can't go to my dad's today. I have to stay and play with my friends." Judy replied, "Don't be silly. Of course you're going. Your dad's coming to pick you up. Now come in here and get ready."

C: But we're playing Ninja Turtles and I'm Leonardo.
J: You love going to your dad's. You know you have fun when you're there.
C: I don't want to go. I want to play with my friends.
J: (Getting really annoyed) Chad, you can play turtles when you get back. Now get ready.
C: (Bursting into tears) I want to stay home and play.

Chad was trying to explain his feelings and Judy was responding to him with logic and reason. They could have been speaking two different languages. Judy couldn't acknowledge Chad's feelings because of her own pain and guilt. When she described the incident in a support group, she admitted feeling guilty about Chad shuttling between two houses and not having a "normal" family. It also reminded her of the loss she felt at not having her family together and all of the changes she had been forced to make since her divorce.

Judy might have empathized with her son's apprehension and ambivalence. She might have said "It's hard to have two homes. Sounds like you wished you didn't have to go back and forth between our house and Dad's." She didn't have to solve the problem; all she needed to do was to listen to her son's pain and confusion, then acknowledge and accept it. This is difficult when your children's pain pushes your own tender emotional buttons. But to help them cope with their feelings, you have to differentiate their feelings from your own. This also will go a long way toward easing transitions.

Allow Your Kids Their Enthusiasm

Another aspect of acknowledging feelings is to allow your kids to express their excitement about their time with their other parent. Maxine, the mother of eight-year-old Brian, was wrestling with this issue in her therapy. "Brian's father has him for weekend fun time," she complained. "When Brian is with me, I keep to a scheduled regimen. We eat dinner, read stories, take a bath, and it's off to bed. I do all the disciplining because his father is very unstructured."

When Brian comes home bubbling with stories of all the neat things he and his dad did, Maxine feels like snarling. "I feel like I'm the meany and he's the party guy," she says. "Sometimes I feel like I'm competing with him." Nevertheless, she's learning how to hear Brian's excitement about his father without feeling it is taking something away from her and her relationship with her son. "I do all the hard work and they have such a great time," she went on, "but the one time I did criticize his father when he was telling me about their great time at the baseball game, Brian got upset and defended his dad. I realized that I had to make it safe for him to share his enthusiasm with me."

If you are the custodial parent who takes on the major responsibility for day-to-day care, it can be hard to hear that your children had a wonderful, fun-filled experience with their other parent. However, it is essential that you separate your feelings for your ex-spouse from those for your children. Your kids need reassurance that they can love and enjoy both parents. One way to communicate this to them is by being supportive when they share their excitement.

5. EXPECT OFF-THE-WALL BEHAVIOR

Take a moment to put yourself in your children's shoes. Recall how you feel when you return home from a vacation or even a business trip. Don't you usually feel slightly disoriented and grumpy the first few hours after you return home? Time is needed to decompress. After being away, I like to open my mail or wash some dishes as a way of reorienting to the everyday routine. Your children have the same need when they make the transition from one house to the other. Expecting them to be off-the-wall will ease your stress about their reentry and help their readjustment.

I can still remember a time when Ama was six and returned from a weekend with her father. He brought her back to my house on Sunday night, gave her a kiss good-bye, and said he would see her soon. No sooner had the door closed behind him than Ama began to cry inconsolably. When I asked what was wrong, she screamed, "I want my daddy." She carried on for half an hour and I was terribly upset. Finally, I called a friend who had been divorced for a couple of years. She reassured me that her kids also had a difficult time when they returned from seeing their father and suggested I take a warm bath with Ama to calm her down. With a bit of a struggle Ama and I got into the tub. I drew pictures on her back with soap until she settled down and finally stopped crying. I was so relieved. After the bath, I got her into her pj's and tucked her into bed. I said to her, "I can see it's hard for you to leave your daddy and we will figure out a way to make it easier on you." I realized that I had to do something to prepare for her reentry so that we wouldn't have to go through this trauma whenever she spent time with her father. From that point on, however, I expected a certain level of acting out when she came back from his house.

Reentry should be as predictable as departure. Plan to do a calming activity together when they return. This can be as simple as playing a board game, watching a video, cooking together, or having a snack. The point is to help your kids get back into the routine of your house. These activities can have a calming effect on your kids as well as help them reconnect with you.

YOUR ADJUSTMENT

"Visitation is a weekly abandonment," Alexis mourned during a therapy session. "I feel schizophrenic. One minute I'm a mom, the next minute I'm alone. I have built my life around my kids and when they leave, I feel lost." Alexis finds life difficult when her kids walk out the door and she's left alone in an empty house. She looks forward to their coming home. She realizes that she's become too dependent on them and that her dependence isn't good for any of them. When her children leave she becomes obsessed with her schoolwork and all the things she has to get done. She doesn't know how to nurture herself. She finds a million excuses why she can't. "I'm much better when my kids are around and I have a purpose and a routine," she said. "They are my buddies. I feel a big void when they are with their father."

The transition from being a parent to being alone can be difficult and painful. However, there are several things you can do for yourself to ease this transition.

Create a Ritual for Yourself

A consistent routine eases your children's transition. The same may help you to make the shift from parenting time to alone time. This is what two participants in my support groups have done.

One man has a standing racquetball date for Sunday afternoon. He takes his children back to his ex-wife's house and then goes directly to the racquetball court for a game with his friend. "I used to feel lost when I would drop the kids off," he said. "Now that I know I have something to do and people to be with, the transition is a lot easier on me. I still hate going back to an empty house, but the time in between with friends has made a difference."

The other, a woman, has gotten into the habit of taking a hot bath when her daughter leaves on Thursday evenings. "It's become such a nice ritual to help me to shift gears from being a full-time mom to being a woman," she said. "I light some candles, put on a tape of some soothing music, and lie in a relaxing bubble bath. I've really gotten into it and now I make it a habit of starting my time off with a soothing bath." Be creative. Think about what would help you to make the transition easier on yourself and then commit to doing it. You must take care of yourself when your children are away.

Make Plans with Friends

It is too easy to feel isolated and alone when you spend so much of your time and energy focused on your children. I recommend to the participants in my seminars and support groups that they make plans with a friend before their children leave. This provides at least one adult social activity to anticipate. I frequently hear single parents complain about missing adult social companionship. The majority of their time is spent working or with their children. If this is the case for you, now is your chance. Being with another adult helps you to shift into a healthy self-centeredness. This event can be as simple as a movie, dinner out, or a trip to an athletic event or art opening. Many single parents are so pressed for time that they spend the majority of their time away from their kids catching up on chores and errands. I recommend that you spend some time socializing while your kids are away.

Make A Wish List of the Things You Would Do If You Had More Time

Your list can include anything from hang gliding to getting a massage. Don't censor yourself; think about what would be fun. Then, while your kids are away, do at least one thing from your list.

Liana, for example, felt limited by her job as a bank clerk. She had been an art student, but what was once a burning interest had all but disappeared during marriage. At my suggestion, she made a wish list and at the top of her list was taking an art class. "I got the community college catalogue and found several classes I wanted to take," Liana reported during a support group meeting. "It was easy to decide on the one to take because it coincided with my kids' time with their dad. I chose a stone-carving class. I've never done anything like it, but it just seemed so different from standing behind a teller's window all day. I liked the idea of pounding on a rock.

"The people are really nice. I picked out my stone, and I've started to pound away," she said with excitement. "It's very therapeutic. I love to see the chips flying off the rock. I can't believe I've waited so long to do this."

I realize that these suggestions may sound artificial and you may feel awkward at first, but do them anyway. Once you start to use some of these techniques to ease the transition they will begin to feel normal and natural. The better care you take of yourself, the more recharged you will feel when your children return home. When my daughter first went to her father's I would feel lost and alone for the first few hours, but before long I began to cherish time to myself. Before I knew it, it would be time to put on my mother's hat again.

STAYING INVOLVED

If you are a noncustodial father (or mother) this section is for you. When you were married, you may have left the lion's share of the child care to your ex-wife, but don't let your lack of familiarity stop you from staying actively involved. As the noncustodial parent you well may feel like an outsider. You may assume that your kids don't really need or miss you, but this is far from true. Your children want and need your continued involvement. But how do you do this now that you have limited access to your kids?

Three factors are key to your children's sense of security: your *reliability, consistency,* and *commitment.* Your kids need to know that even though you no longer live in the same house, they can still count on you. When you make plans and then postpone or cancel them, are late with child support payments, or fail to have regular consistent contact, your kids interpret this as a lack of caring. They start to believe that they are no longer important to you. This can damage their self-esteem.

Don't let your ex-spouse's attitude prevent you from staying connected. "The first year after our divorce Leah was very angry," one man told the support group. "She would put me down in front of our daughter. I felt like she was trying to scare me off from seeing her. She would change the time of my visits or schedule activities for my daughter on the days I was supposed to spend time with her." He finally realized that he had to address his ex-wife's resistance. He made it clear that he wasn't going to allow her to interfere. He told her that he needed her cooperation. Eventually she began to act more civilly. "I guess she realized that it wasn't in anyone's best interest to keep my daughter," he said. "But I had to stay committed to being with my kid or I could have been chased off."

Establishing a new parenting relationship takes time and can be fraught with complex feelings, but your children count on you to work out some way to continue as their parent. These are six keys to staying involved.

1. Make a place for your kids in your new home.
2. Spend time alone with each child.
3. Encourage your kids to have friends over.
4. Make your time together as normal and natural as possible.
5. Establish rules, routines, and responsibilities for your children.
6. Make a commitment to be actively involved in your children's lives.

Let me elaborate.

1. MAKE A PLACE FOR YOUR KIDS IN YOUR NEW HOME

Reuben, the father of Max, 13, and Sam, 15, has had the boys every other weekend for ten years. His ex-wife, Brenda, called me and asked if she and the boys could come for a counseling session.

"I don't know what to do," she said. "The boys don't want to go to their father's house and I don't know how to handle it." She sounded distraught. I had seen the family on and off over a five-year period, so the boys felt comfortable talking with me. Sam started the session with a complaint. "Last weekend was the pits," he said. "No matter how many times I talk to my dad about having a separate bed, he never listens. Max and I have to sleep in the den on a pull-out sofa bed and he was tossing and turning all night and I couldn't sleep." Sam adamantly refused to share a bed with Max anymore. "I'm not going to go over there until he gets a place for me to sleep. Plus, we don't have anyplace to put our clothes. We have to keep them in our bag and everything is wrinkled. I feel like a guest. Why can't he make the den our room so we feel like it's our home too?"

Max chimed in. "Yeah, I don't want to sleep with Sam either. It's weird and besides he snores. My dad is a real wimp. When we ask him about separate beds he has some lame excuse like 'I can't afford it' or 'There isn't enough space.' My mom offered to give him one of the beds from our house, but he won't do it. I don't want to go to his house anymore either."

Max and Sam felt hurt that in those ten years their father had not made a place for them in his home. While they were young, they were willing to adapt to his living arrangement, but now they are more vocal.

At the very least, your children need a bed and a place to keep their belongings. If you have limited space, this storage space can be a shelf in a closet or a couple of dresser drawers, but they need to feel that your home is their home. Put their artwork and photographs up in an obvious place; help them to feel a part of your new environment.

2. SPEND TIME ALONE WITH EACH CHILD

You don't necessarily have to go anyplace special, just set aside time for you and your child to be together and talk without interruption. This could be as simple as a fifteen-minute period before bedtime. Take this time to find out what your child is interested in and how he or she is feeling. Share your feelings as well. In my seminars I suggest that parents establish a bedtime routine in which their children tell the best thing and the worst thing that happened to them that day. This structure lets them share what is on their minds. They will know that they can count on this time to talk about anything that may be bothering them.

You may also want to arrange for a special visit from each of your kids separately. This gives each a chance for the undivided attention he or she craves now that you are no longer living together. Stan and Virginia have been divorced for eleven months; they have two children, Jason, 6, and Jan, 11. Stan moved into an apartment two blocks away. The children spend one night a week and every other weekend at his new house. Before the divorce, Jason and his father were especially close. They went to dirt bike races on weekends, Stan helped with his son's Cub Scout den and he refereed at soccer games.

One evening Virginia called Stan and said, "I just tucked Jason into bed and he looked so sad. When I asked him what was bothering him he burst into tears and said, 'I miss my daddy.' " When Virginia had questioned him further, he complained it just wasn't the same when his daddy didn't live with him. She told his father, "Stan, I know you are consistent in seeing the kids, but what do you think about spending some extra time with Jason, just the two of you?" Stan was happy to make time for his son. The next day he came over after school to tell Jason and Jan about his new plan. Jason would spend Saturday alone with his dad. On Wednesday night, Stan and Jan would have a special time together. Jason's face lit up. It was clear that this extra one-on-one time was something he needed badly. Stan was also conscious of taking time with each of them when they came to his house together. Sometimes he and Jason would go out in the yard and kick a soccer ball around while Jan worked on her homework. At other times, he and Jan played a board game while Jason was playing with his action figures. This gave them the attention and special time they were missing.

Make Your Kids Feel Special

If you have a new love interest or are recently remarried, you need to take care that your children do not feel replaced by your new relationship. The majority of visitation time should be spent with your children. Be sensitive to your children's feelings when you introduce them to a new person in your life. Jim had been seeing me in counseling for about a year after his divorce. He had been dating Anne for about six months and wanted his elementary school age kids to meet her. "I'm really nervous about introducing my kids to Anne," Jim said during a session. "Since my divorce she's the first woman that I really feel serious about. I want my kids to meet her, but I don't know how to do it so my kids don't feel bad." I told Jim his concern was valid. After a divorce, children are afraid of losing the noncustodial parent. They can easily feel threatened and jealous of a parent's new love interest. Jim had been wise to wait until this point to introduce Anne to his children. I suggested that he encourage them each to invite a friend to a weekend activity and that he tell them that he would be bringing a friend as well. I also reminded him that the activity should be time-limited and that the major portion of the weekend should be devoted to him and his children.

Jim called his children a few days before their weekend together. "I'm going to bring a friend with us when we go ice-skating and I wondered if each of you would like to invite a friend to come along as well?" he said. His children were delighted to bring their friends and this smoothed the introduction to Anne.

Remember, your time with your kids should be spent primarily with them. Introducing a new person to them gradually will make them feel cared for and secure. This will go a long way in preventing problems down the road.

3. ENCOURAGE YOUR KIDS TO HAVE FRIENDS OVER

As your children get older, social events begin to play a bigger role in their lives. Their friendships take center stage. Although your time with your children is precious, it is helpful if you occasionally invite their friends over to your house. One twelve-year-old complained to her mother, "I don't want to go to my dad's house. It gets in the way of seeing my friends." Her mother suggested that she ask her father if he would be willing to let her have a friend spend the night from time to time. When Paula presented the idea to her father he was more than willing. He encouraged her to call her friends from his house and made it known that she and her interests were important to him.

Fourteen-year-old Manny had become hesitant about spending time at his father's house. His father insisted that Manny spend the entire weekend with him and his new wife. With some coaching, Manny was able to confront his dad about his frustration. After several conversations Manny's father agreed that one day of the weekend Manny would spend with his friends and the other day they would be together as a family.

As your children get older, their friends and their social life become more important. It is important to respect your children's changing needs. Stay open to their ideas and feelings and include their friends in your life.

4. MAKE YOUR TIME TOGETHER AS NORMAL AND NATURAL AS POSSIBLE

To avoid being a Disneyland Dad, encourage your children to bring homework, school projects, activities, or art supplies to your house. You want them to feel at home when they are with you and for your relationship to be as normal and as natural as possible. Bringing the things they do on an everyday basis to your house will help them to feel comfortable in your new surroundings. Another benefit: When your kids bring their work and activities to your house, you aren't under pressure to entertain them.

The Disneyland Dad

The following story will be recognizable to nearly every noncustodial father. "For the longest time I felt like I had to entertain my kids when they came over to my house," Patrick confessed during a support group meeting. "I can't believe the contortions I went through to win them over. I would take them to arcades and fill their pockets with quarters so they could play endless games of Pac-Man and Super Mario Brothers. At home I would either play hours of Monopoly or Pictionary or let them watch TV all afternoon. I never felt good about how we were spending our time, but I didn't know what else to do. I felt obliged to entertain them so they would want to be with me."

With the group's support, Patrick realized that his role as social director wasn't working. He retired his lanyard and whistle and asked his children to bring their homework and projects along when they visited. For the most part, things are now much more normal. "Sure, sometimes they can be demanding," he says, "but our time together feels much more natural. I hate to admit it, but I was starting to resent my kids. Having to be 'on' all the time was stressful. I wish I had done this sooner."

Your time together should be as "regular" as possible. Your kids don't want to be entertained, they want to have a normal relationship with their dad. You set the tone. If you continually take them out and entertain them, that is what they will grow to expect. As much as is practical, create a routine in which some of the time you do fun things together and part of the time they are responsible for their homework and entertaining themselves.

Noncustodial parents often want their time with their children to be fun, but overindulging them or giving them carte blance isn't good for anyone involved. It's natural to want your limited time together to be special, but make it special by doing something that strengthens your relationship.

Having your children with you for short intense periods can be difficult, especially if you have children of different ages. Accept that this is an artificial situation. If your family were still together, your children wouldn't be your weekend sidekicks. One thing that doesn't help is overcompensating for the loss of your intact family. This is like feeding your children marshmallows because they are hungry; ultimately a marshmallow is neither satisfying nor nurturing. Your children need a father, not a social director.

5. ESTABLISH RULES, ROUTINES, AND RESPONSIBILITIES FOR YOUR CHILDREN

When your children are at your house, they should have clearly defined rules and routines. This adds to their sense of normalcy and security. Establish house rules that include a bedtime, expectations about appropriate and inappropriate behavior, and chores you expect them to do. The latter don't have to be overwhelming; they can be as simple as having one child empty the garbage and another help fold the laundry.

If you have errands to run or projects to do around your house, include them. Let them feel a part of your new life. Have them help water the plants, mow the lawn, make minor repairs. Even if your children complain, your rules and chores will add a dimension of reality to your time together.

6. MAKE A COMMITMENT TO BE ACTIVELY INVOLVED IN YOUR CHILDREN'S LIVES

Going through a divorce and establishing a new household can be draining, but your children count on your continued involvement. Talk with them by phone daily. One father told me that he missed reading his kids a bedtime story, so a couple of times a week he would call and read a story to his two children by speakerphone. Make a date for a regular phone check-in. Ask your children about their day, their friends, their after-school activities. By taking an active interest in their lives and staying in close contact you give your kids the message that they are important and that you love and care about them. You may have divorced your ex-spouse, but you didn't divorce your kids. Be an involved, committed dad. The rewards are tremendous. And your kids are counting on you.

THE REJECTING PARENT

Some ex-spouses refuse to be involved with their children. Take the case of Camilla's ex. She had been married to Victor for ten years and they had three children. She walked into a support group meeting looking pale and depressed. "It doesn't really matter how close you live," she said through her tears. "My ex-husband lives five miles from our house and works even closer, but he doesn't see his kids unless they beg him." The previous Sunday her daughter had spent fifteen minutes on the phone begging him to come see her. All he would say was "It's better this way." He justified his absence by saying that he has a new family now and he doesn't have enough time for both, Camilla said.

Her son asked Victor to take him to baseball practice. Victor said he didn't think he could, but that he'd call him by Thursday to let him know either way. Thursday came and went and Victor never called. "He never calls," said Camilla. "He's trying to drop out of the picture, but my kids won't let him. They keep calling him. He only comes for major events like birthdays. It hurts to know that he doesn't want to see our kids. I don't know what to say to them."

Some of these rejecting parents never were very involved. Some just don't care. Others feel uncomfortable in their new parenting role with their children. Seeing the kids can stimulate guilt in fathers who initiated the divorce. For fathers who were left by their wives, seeing the kids may stimulate an unbearable sadness and sense of longing for their family. Some men may not know how to deal with their children's needs. Or they may simply feel awkward in this new arrangement. Whatever the reason, some parents simply bow out and there is little you can do to change their behavior. However, before you throw in the towel and cut off contact completely, consider the impact this will have on your children. Remember, whatever little time they spend with their other parent is for them, not you.

Other parents mean well but can't get it together. They were not reliable during their marriage and they won't be reliable now they are divorced. They may show up late to pick up or drop off their children, or they may agree to see their kids at a particular time and not come at all.

Gretchen was a solidly built chiropractor who received little support of any kind from her ex-husband for her two children, Sonia, 7, and Cal, 9. She came into her therapy session clearly upset. Her face was red and her eyes were brimming with tears. Before she sat down, she said, "I'm so mad I could scream," then she burst into tears. Her ex had made arrangements to take the kids for the weekend. They were excited because they hadn't spent much time with him lately. Both were packed and ready and killing time until he came to pick them up. The appointed hour came and went. She called his house but there was no answer. "Cal was getting especially restless," she said. "He wanted to know where his dad was and why he was late. I kept reassuring him that his father would be there soon, but after an hour and a half I was fuming. Not only were my kids upset, but I had made a date for that evening with my boyfriend. I had to change my plans. Two hours later, their father waltzed in. He was puzzled by my anger. I wanted to kill him, but the kids seemed so happy to see him."

I empathized with Gretchen's feelings of frustration. Then we thought about what she could do to prevent this from happening again. I suggested that once she had calmed down she could let him know that in the future she would wait a half hour past the arranged pickup time, then she would leave with the kids. I also suggested that she let him know how his unreliability affected his children.

Despite the chronic disappointment, most children, especially young ones, would rather have any kind of contact with their parent than none at all. The only thing you can do to help is to listen, empathize with their hurt and frustration, and handle the matter as calmly as possible. If your ex-spouse gives you an explanation for his or her unreliability you can offer that to your children. But the truth is that the unreliability is probably more upsetting to you than it is to your kids.

THE HIGH PRICE OF UNINVOLVED FATHERS

There are several common repercussions when fathers are absent from their children's lives. Boys whose fathers don't stay involved may lack self-confidence and pride in their own masculinity. Boys rely on their fathers for the development of their sexual identity. They model themselves on their fathers by sharing interests, adopting their values, and having playfully competitive interactions with them. They measure themselves against their fathers in their budding abilities and skills.

Girls also pay a price when fathers disappear. Girls who grow up without a male figure in their lives feel rejection; they long for their fathers. Later they tend to be unsure of their femininity and insecure in their relationships with men.[6] They do not look to their fathers for their sexual identity, but they look to them for validation of their femininity.

Fathers help children of both sexes gain a sense of independence from their mothers. Dad's involvement makes the necessary separation from Mom easier.

When your children's father is not available, it's essential to provide trustworthy male role models. These men can be teachers, camp counselors, athletic coaches, scout leaders, male relatives, etc. Irene, the single mother of a ten-year-old son, has been divorced for eight and a half years. Her ex-husband moved out of state and has no contact with his boy. "For the past eight years I have had a male best friend, Joe, who is married," Irene explained. "He comes over to my house regularly and spends time with Clyde. He buys him gifts and they do things together. He takes Clyde to Dodgers games, they go to Boy Scouts events together, and they putter around the garage repairing old tools. Joe is a stable factor in Clyde's life."

Mothers whose ex-husbands are out of the picture inevitably report that their children crave male attention and contact. Emily, the mother of two girls, told the support group that her daughters would frequently ask why she didn't have a boyfriend. I helped Emily to understand that hidden in their question was a longing for a male figure in their lives. Emily was not interested in dating, but she was eager to offer her girls a relationship with a substitute father figure. We brainstormed, looking for men who might be available to her kids. Eventually she spoke with her brother about his spending more time with his nieces. He was unmarried and had always been fond of the girls but had never made much effort to spend time with them. When Emily talked to him about her need, he was receptive. She also asked the dads of some of her children's friends if they would include her girls in occasional activities. Be creative. Reach out to your family, friends, and church group for help. Everyone will benefit from the relationship.

A PAINFUL REMINDER

When sons exhibit traits and behaviors of the former husband, some mothers become overly critical and others unintentionally distance themselves. A mother's identification of her son with his father can drive a wedge between them. This can also occur between girls and their mothers, but it is more common with mothers and sons.

"I had to let go of the anger and resentment toward his father," Sheila said in counseling. Her son looks just like his father and has a lot of his traits. "He often reminds me of Fred and I say to myself, 'Through Burt I'm doomed to deal with Fred for the rest of my life.' I look at Burt and I see his father. I see his mannerisms and his way. When we were married Fred used to get angry and not speak for three days and now Burt does the same thing. He withdraws and won't talk to me." Sheila had to keep herself from saying "You're just like your father." She had trained herself to recognize the similarities between her son and her ex-husband and she is learning to separate her feelings toward her ex from those toward her son. This process can be difficult, but it is essential that you do not project the negative feelings you may have for your ex-husband on to your children.

THE LONG-DISTANCE PARENT

Distance shouldn't prevent a parent from keeping up contact with his children. Truly long distance will certainly change the nature of your relationship with your kids, but it shouldn't prevent you from communicating your love and your interest in your children's lives. It simply means that you have to work harder to stay in touch.

If you are the custodial parent and bear the major portion of responsibility for raising the children, you have a lot to cope with. You also have the joy of watching them grow. If you are the long-distance parent you will be missing out on the day-to-day events of your children's lives. You don't have the burden of responsibility, but neither do you have the joy of frequent contact and interaction. There are costs and benefits to each position. More important is your goal of doing what is best for your children. If you have custody, this means making your kids accessible to the other parent. Courtesy and cooperation are the keys to making a long-distance arrangement work.

Take the case of Adele and Tim and their two children, Adrienne and Louis. During the first two years after their divorce Tim remained actively involved in his children's lives. He saw them every other weekend and periodically during the week. Then Tim's company transferred him out of state and this drastically altered the contact he could have with his children.

Adele came to me for counseling. "Since Tim has moved away, both kids seem to be having a hard time," Adele explained. "Louis is angry all the time and Adrienne asks when she's going to see her dad. They really feel his absence. He calls occasionally, but the children need more contact." I agreed with Adele's perception and suggested that she call Tim and discuss a trip for the children to visit him as well as a regular date for phone calls. I also encouraged her to have Adrienne and Louis write to their father or to get permission to call him collect.

Adele was clearly relieved at her next session. "I called Tim last night and told him how the children were feeling," she said. "He was missing them too, but he wasn't sure how to stay in touch with them long distance. He thought a regular phone date with the kids was a good idea and agreed that it would be easier to have a schedule. We arranged for Adrienne and Louis to fly out over the Presidents' Day weekend and talked about the children spending part of their summer with him." This was just the beginning of a new plan, but they had made a good start. After they finished their discussion, Louis and Adrienne got on the phone. They made a date to talk with their dad every Wednesday night at 7:00. "I could see their relief when they hung up," she said. "Now they know specifically when they can count on hearing from him. It's not like having their dad here, but at least they still feel his caring." Long-distance parenting is a tremendous challenge to everyone involved. Logistics and distance make staying in touch much more complex, but your children want the contact.

Here are seven ways to make the long-distance relationship work.

1. Establish a specific day and time to talk to your children by phone. Be sure it is compatible with their schedule and does not conflict with their other parent's plans. Call at least once a week, preferably more often. If your kids are old enough, encourage them to call collect if they want to talk. This keeps the lines of communication open in both directions. If money is a concern, make your calls after the rates go down, either in the evening or over the weekend.

   To give a more natural feeling to your conversations, encourage your kids to keep a list of things they want to talk about during your phone dates. If they do, you'll know more about their day-to-day lives and concerns. A good relationship is a two-way street, so you too can jot down reminders of things you want to share with your children.

2. Kids love to get mail. Send letters, postcards, or notes as tangible reminders that you are thinking of them. Unfortunately, many long-distance parents feel awkward about writing; they are at a loss for what to say. To make this easier Melanie Rahn developed a kit called The Written Connection. The kit includes suggested topics, information about how to write to children of different ages, ideas for inexpensive things to send, plus a guidebook. To order a kit contact The Written Connection, 2633 E. Indian School Road, #400, Phoenix, AZ 85016, or call 800-334-3143.

   When writing to your children, keep the communication light and positive. Many absent parents have a tendency to preach at their kids to demonstrate their effectiveness as a parent; this only acts as a turnoff to your kids. Younger children like cartoons, jokes, or cute photos. Older children appreciate articles of interest, anagrams, or secret codes that only the two of you understand.

   When replying to your children's letters, be sure to respond to their questions or comments specifically. This fosters a genuine dialogue between you. Send a stack of self-addressed, stamped envelopes to make it easier for your kids to write. You may also want to include several envelopes addressed to the children's grandparents to encourage correspondence between them as well.

3. If you haven't yet done so, ask your children's school for copies of their report cards and notices of activities. Knowing what occurs in their school life makes you better able to ask your kids intelligent questions.

   Encourage your kids to send photocopies of reports, art projects, and schoolwork. Let them know that you are interested in what they are doing. Tell them you want to be as much a part of their lives as possible.

4. Make audio- or videotapes to send to your kids. If your children are used to your reading to them at bedtime, make an audiotape of their favorite stories. Add a personal good-night message at the end of the tape.

Your children will also enjoy a videotape of your new house, both inside and out, and of your neighborhood, your pets, the nearby parks, or other points of interest. This can be especially reassuring if they haven't yet visited you in your new house.

5. Make a photo album for your children. Be sure to include pictures of you, your relatives and friends, and, most important, pictures of you and your children together. You may want to make a scrapbook of their last trip to see you, including, for example, photos of all of you together, ticket stubs from trips to the zoo, concert programs, pretty leaves you collected, even place mats from restaurants you frequented.
6. Make a date when both you and your children will watch a special program or sporting event on television and then talk about it with them afterward. This helps create a sense of immediacy and it's a way to share common interests.
7. Express appreciation to your children's other parent for keeping the lines of communication open and for helping foster your relationship with your kids. Think of this conversation as a wise business investment in your future relationship with your children.

LONG-DISTANCE PARENTING WITH CHILDREN UNDER THE AGE OF THREE

Young children require more frequent contact in order to maintain a relationship. At this age they have limited cognitive ability. If contact is sporadic and infrequent, they have a hard time sustaining a mental image of you. If you must be away from your children while they are young, it is even more essential that you stay actively involved in their lives to establish and maintain a solid relationship. These are four ideas to help do this.

1. Send a young child a handmade book of photos about the two of you with a simple text under each photo. For example: "Here are Daddy and Laurie at the zoo feeding the monkeys."

"Mommy and Alex are riding bicycles in the park. Remember the sticky peanut butter and honey sandwiches we had for lunch?"

2. When you spend time with your kids, give each one a special object to remember you by. This could be a stuffed animal, a favorite cup, a special seashell. Instill the message in your child, "Every time you use or look at this you will remember our special time together and how much I love you. You're very special to me."
3. If your child is under two it may be best if you go to see your child at his or her home rather than expect the child to come to see you. Children under the age of two can easily become anxious when they are away from their custodial parent for an extended time. It may be better both for your child as well as for your time together if you go to visit and spend time together each day, but allow your child to sleep at home. This may not always be necessary, but it is important to gauge your children's ability to be away from home based on their ages, temperaments, and your relationship with them. Some two-year-olds who are confident, secure, and adaptable may be able to handle a five-to-seven-day visit, assuming that you have maintained a close relationship.
4. To prepare for the visit, talk with your children's other parent and become familiar with their daily routines. Reacquaint yourself with their food preferences, sleeping habits, and favorite activities. The more you can make your children feel comfortable, familiar, and at home while they are with you, the better your time together will be. Ask their other parent to send their favorite clothes, their cherished stuffed animal, and some familiar toys and books.

   As much as you may resist this idea, I recommend that you encourage your child to bring a photo of his other parent as a way of staying connected. This photo can be very comforting for a young child.

   While your child is at your house, encourage frequent phone calls with her other parent. You may also want to have a calendar in her room. If she asks how long it is until she sees her mommy again, you can offer tangible reminders of how long she will be with you and when she will return to her other home.[7]

REENTRY

To help your children with reentry, be sure they get a good night's sleep the night before they return to their other home. Nervous energy and excitement combined with travel and the change in time zones can be stressful.

Remember that your children are going through an intense transition. They have been in a very different environment and are coping with a good-bye from their other parent. That's not easy for anyone. They may feel sad or angry, as well as excited about seeing you. For many children, the change from one home to the other can be very disorienting and upsetting. Remember to be patient. Help ease them through the transition by providing them with their familiar routines.

If you are the parent who is distant, make a date to talk with your kids shortly after they have returned to their other home. Despite your fear of being a superficial influence on your children's lives, your involvement can be significant. This, however, will take commitment and more effort than ever.

If you are the custodial parent, you are also more crucial than ever in helping children maintain a relationship with the distant parent. You control the access. Other than holidays and vacations, the phone and mail are the main lines of communication between parent and child. Make them available. The amount of time children spend with a distant parent is less important than the degree to which they maintain a relationship and feel valued.

Chapter 8

Making It Legal

Choosing an Attorney and Other Issues

To win one hundred victories in one hundred battles is not the acme of skill. To subdue the enemy without fighting is the acme of skill.

Sun-tzu, The Art of War

When my husband and I decided to divorce in 1978, the average young parents' lifestyle and the cultural climate were dramatically different from those of today. We were renting a small adobe house in Santa Fe, New Mexico. We owned no property and we had few possessions. When we decided to end our marriage I contacted a mutual friend who happened to be a lawyer and asked if he would handle our divorce. We set up an appointment and my soon-to-be-ex and I went down to his office. Within an hour we had agreed on child support, divided our joint property, and signed a divorce agreement. We traded our friend, Steve, a pair of cross-country skis for his services. Our story may be hard to believe in this era of litigation, custody battles, and huge attorney's fees, and I do understand that when property and financial assets are involved, divorce can be far more complex.

However, wouldn't it be wonderful if everyone could have a clear-cut, amicable divorce? Although our marriage was a shambles, my ex-husband and I were lucky in that we were young, naïve, and had lived simply. If we had waited until today to divorce, things would have been far less congenial.

As I watch many of my friends go through treacherous divorce proceedings, I am struck by the impact their lawyers' styles have on the tone of the legal process. Several of these people started out committed to a cooperative, working relationship. But when they entered the legal system they found that tension increased, tempers flared, and their relationships with their almost-ex-spouses deteriorated exponentially as their divorces took on lives of their own.

What was once a personal relationship is now discussed in terms of awards and stipulations and is relegated to the domain of attorneys, judges, and court reporters. Before you filed for a divorce you probably never dreamed of the complex legal ramifications of ending your marriage. Now you are entering the Twilight Zone of the legal system.

There are numerous books written by lawyers on divorce law and procedures, but I thought it important to discuss the impact of the legal system on the parenting partnership. In this chapter, written with the expert advice of several family law attorneys and mediators,[1] you will learn (1) how to choose an attorney who will minimize the adversarial nature of divorce, (2) how to keep the lines of communication open with your ex-spouse, and (3) how to choose among the various forms of child custody.

CHOOSING AN ATTORNEY

Your selection of an attorney is one of the most important decisions you will make. Divorce is like a chess game with someone else playing the game for you. What makes the greatest difference in how the divorce is handled is the philosophy and style of the attorneys. Most people don't recognize the degree to which an attorney orchestrates the entire divorce procedure. You have no control over your spouse's selection, but you can choose your own advocate with care and consideration for how he or she will handle your case.

I recommend that you pick the lawyer who will represent you in the same way you would select a contractor to remodel your house. Before hiring someone, you would check his references and talk with people who have used his services. You would find out about his reliability, honesty, and workmanship, and inspect some of his prior jobs. In selecting an attorney you want someone who understands your goals and priorities and who will advocate your interests while working toward a fair and reasonable settlement.

As you begin to interview attorneys you will realize that attorneys vary in the way they deal with their clients, in how they handle cases, and in their philosophical approach. In a study of attorneys, social psychologist Kenneth Kressel found that attorneys run along a continuum from "advocates" to "counselors."[2] Aggressive advocates take pleasure in the legal challenge of divorce and emphasize "winning." These attorneys prefer to take charge and they frequently escalate conflicts between divorcing parents. Their goal is to get the best deal for their client without regard for the long-term consequences of their actions.

Advocates often advise a client to cut off direct communication with the ex-spouse, an action that may incite rage and retaliation from the other party. "My attorney is like a small shark," said Rhoda, a perfectly coiffed pharmaceutical saleswoman with tired eyes. "He's the kind of guy who brushes up against your leg and you think that didn't hurt, and then you look down and your leg is gone." Rhoda's lawyer was bright and knew the ropes, but he advised her to stop talking to her ex and that's when things turned sour. "We started out on pretty good terms, but once my lawyer took over everything changed," she said. "In the end I got a much bigger settlement than I ever expected or even really wanted. But now I have to deal with this angry, bitter ex-husband for the rest of my life. I don't think it was worth it." Don't assume that the tougher your attorney, the better you will be represented. If you get a gladiator who pushes the other side too hard and achieves an enormous emotional and financial conquest, your victory may reveal itself as hollow in the years to come.

Attorneys who see themselves as counselors tend to be more psychologically aware and family-oriented. They are concerned with the emotional climate of the divorce as well as with the legal aspects. These attorneys provide their clients with practical advice and support and are concerned with their clients' and their children's welfare. They are interested in finding solutions that will be fair and equitable for both sides. "But I think there are a lot of lawyers who are very aggressive and go for the jugular," says family law attorney Glen Hardie. "The attorneys who are most successful, as far as getting good results for their clients, are the ones who can hold back from fighting. Inevitably, when I have another fair-minded attorney on the other side, we are each much more effective." The most successful divorce attorney is the one who achieves fair, cooperative settlements out of court, not the one who is continually in litigation.

INTERVIEWING AN ATTORNEY

"I knew when it came to the actual divorce, my ex-husband would make things tough," said Fran, a timid woman whose ex had been verbally abusive. "If we had to go to court, I wanted a lawyer who could go the distance." She interviewed several people, but when she met Joan something clicked. "I needed someone who could stand up to any firebombs he might throw. Joan was interested in my getting a fair deal, but she was even more concerned about my mental state. It was almost as if she were psychologically trained." Fran chose a highly skilled professional who was both compassionate and able to protect her interest.

Before deciding on an attorney, do some research. Get referrals from friends and business associates and, if possible, other lawyers. Seek an attorney who is a family law specialist rather than someone who handles divorce cases only occasionally. Choose someone who can be an advocate when one is needed but who will not get you into expensive and unnecessary legal battles.

Interview several attorneys before making a decision. Ask questions. Find out how long they have been in practice, their views on joint custody and mediation. Ask what percentage of their cases are settled out of court. And, above all, trust your intuition. As you listen to the attorney talk, ask yourself, "Does this person solve problems or create them?" The answer should be your litmus test.

A key factor in choosing an attorney is deciding how involved you want to be in the process. Do you want a take-charge type of lawyer who is going to handle all aspects of your case and simply report the outcomes? Or do you want to be consulted at each step and offered options on which to base decisions?

"I was such a basket case when we started the proceedings that the divorce seemed to have nothing to do with me," confessed Wendy, a perky young mother of two who had married at eighteen. Her much older husband had always taken care of the major decisions. "I felt intimidated by my lawyer," she said. "He had a big office and all these people working for him. I didn't know anything about legal matters, so I let him take over. He was costing me a fortune, but everything seemed to be going fine. Then he sent several inflammatory documents to my ex without my permission." Wendy spoke with a family friend who was also an attorney and was advised to read all communication with her ex-husband before it left her attorney's office. She also requested that her attorney tell her all the options so that she could make more informed decisions.

You may be tempted to wash your hands of the entire process and let your attorney handle your divorce. Avoid this temptation. You must maintain control of decisions that will affect you and your children for the rest of your lives. In order to do this you have to be a real participant in the legal process. Think of this as your part-time job. Plan to spend time reading your legal papers. Keep your own divorce file. See that your attorney keeps conflict to a minimum. It is crucial that he or she understand your goals and objectives. The two of you need to agree on how your case will be handled.

The Interview

Most attorneys will not charge for the initial half-hour interview. I recommend that you speak to at least three lawyers before making a choice. Make it clear each time that the meeting is an interview. Following are some questions that will help you choose legal counsel that is right for you. You may want to ask some of these questions on the phone before you set up a meeting.

1. How long have you practiced law? What percentage of your practice is divorce cases? Are you a family law specialist?
2. Will you be handling my case personally or do you work with associates?
3. Do you have trial experience and are you prepared to go to court if necessary? What percentage of cases do you settle out of court?
4. How familiar are you with the court system, personnel, and procedures?
5. What is your philosophy regarding divorce? Have you ever been divorced?
6. How do you feel about joint or shared custody? What are your thoughts on mediation or face-to-face negotiations with the other side?
7. What, if any, is your experience with reducing the adversarial nature of the legal process?

You should feel comfortable and confident when speaking with your attorney. After each interview, ask yourself: "Did I feel that he or she understood my needs and wishes? Were we in agreement on how I wanted my divorce to be handled?" Sometimes the choice will depend on a personal intuitive factor. One of my male clients chose a female lawyer because he wanted to set his feminist wife at ease. One of my female clients chose a large male attorney because she was physically afraid of her husband. Remember, you are doing the hiring. Your attorney will be working for you. Choose someone who will represent you in a way that is consistent with your attitude.

LEGAL FEES

Divorce is like a sleeping volcano. When it erupts into hostility, the legal fees, like the fire and smoke, can rise into the stratosphere. Divorces frequently end up costing more than anyone expected. If you don't maintain control of yours you may find yourself dipping into savings, investments, or an inheritance to pay your legal fees.

Fees are frequently an area of contention between attorneys and their clients. Be sure to discuss this issue with the attorneys you interview. Many will have a prepared statement that describes their services, billing arrangements, and average retainer. Here are some additional questions.

1. How do you bill for your services? Do you have a flat fee, or do you charge by the hour?
2. How much is your initial retainer? Do you draw against the retainer or will I be charged an hourly fee in addition?
3. What is the average cost for handling a case like mine?
4. Do you bill for phone calls and correspondence?
5. How do you keep track of the hours spent on my case? Will I receive an itemized bill?
6. Do you have a standard agreement outlining your charges, billing procedures, and services? (If they do not have such an agreement will they draw one up for you?)
7. What can I do to keep my legal fees to a minimum?

Regardless of what you and your spouse have agreed on, expect to pay your own legal fees. There are always exceptions, but this is frequently the case. If you are unable to pay the entire bill, most attorneys will work out a monthly payment plan.

When considering the cost involved in dissolving your marriage, keep in mind that an attorney's most precious commodity is time. He or she deserves to be compensated for the time spent on your behalf. On the other hand, you are entitled to an accurate record of your attorney's hours. One way to maintain control of your divorce and the time spent on it is to ask for copies of all the documents generated on your behalf. This keeps you informed of any actions taken and makes you a more active partner in the process.

Money-Saving Ideas

You may feel as if your attorney is financing a trip to Tahiti on your legal fees. To reduce legal expenses, you must learn to monitor the time you spend with your attorney, both in person and on the phone. Talk is anything but cheap when you do it with your lawyer. Here are some tips that can help you to minimize your fees.

1. Limit your discussions with your attorney to legal matters. Don't use your lawyer as a counselor or therapist. Your attorney may be a good listener but the meter is running and your fees are mounting as you discuss the emotional issues of your divorce. Your lawyer doesn't need to know how awful you felt when your best friend and her husband invited your ex to her birthday party. If you need emotional support or a place to vent your feelings, a trained psychotherapist is far less expensive.
2. Whenever possible, talk with your attorney's secretary rather than speak with your attorney directly. The secretary can set up appointments, confirm correspondence, and handle nonlegal information.
3. Prepare for both your phone and in-person meetings. Make a list of the points to cover and refer to it.
4. Resist the urge to call when you can handle the matter in writing. It's easy to run up your legal bill on the telephone, especially if your attorney is supportive.
5. Seek help from your attorney only when help is feasible. Refrain from complaining about issues your attorney can't resolve. For example, an ex who is sarcastic on the phone may be maddening but is not worth the cost of your lawyer's attention.

Remember your goal is not to win or to punish your ex, but rather to come to a reasonable, fair resolution. If you and your attorney share this goal, and your ex is willing, you can reach resolution at a moderate cost.

MEDIATION

The premise of mediation is that the decisions about a divorcing couple's future and the care of their children should be made by the pair, not by attorneys or judges. When tempers flare and couples can't communicate constructively, a mediator is useful.

Mediators are unbiased professionals who assist couples to reach out-of-court settlements on issues such as custody, division of property, and spousal support. Mediators do not take sides or decide issues. Their job is to help the parties come to mutually acceptable agreements.

Mediation tends to be less expensive than retaining two attorneys and marching off to court, but the decisions reached in mediation are not legally binding. They still require the services of an attorney to finalize them. Mediation is frequently confused with arbitration in which there is also an impartial third party. In arbitration, however, the spouses agree to bow to the decision made by the arbiter. The mediator, on the other hand, never makes a decision but rather acts as a guide to help each person arrive at a decision that feels fair. If no agreement is possible, either party can return to the more adversarial process. Another benefit of mediation is that parties who reach a mediated settlement are more likely to follow through on the agreement.

Even if you are working with an attorney you may want to consider using a mediator to resolve specific issues, especially those pertaining to the children. Hugh McIsaac, director of the Los Angeles Conciliation Court, says that "children do best when parents reach a settlement using mediation." Some parents use a mediator only to resolve custody or visitation issues. In fact, many states require mandatory mediation for couples involved in custody disputes. It is not uncommon for couples to return to mediation after their divorce is final to settle new child-related issues. Regardless of which route you take in dissolving your marriage, you may want to consider putting a clause in your divorce decree stipulating that if either party wants to amend the existing agreement, mediation is employed before further legal action is taken.

Choosing a mediator is like choosing an attorney. Get referrals from attorneys who have seen their work and interview several before deciding. Find out their background and training in mediation. Most mediators are either attorneys or mental health professionals. Mediation is used to resolve all kinds of disputes, so find out if your mediator specializes in divorce and family mediation. Those who are attorneys are not allowed to give you legal advice while acting as a mediator, so don't expect that kind of help.

Before choosing a mediator, decide if he or she seems fair. Impartiality is the mediator's primary attribute. Is the mediator understanding and compassionate? Do you feel rapport and trust with this person?

Mediators are like air traffic controllers. They sit in the control tower and direct communication by helping each party to remain focused on the issues at hand, concentrating on the future rather than the past and attacking the problems rather than each other. Mediators assist each person in compiling the necessary information to make informed decisions, in giving priorities to each person's needs and goals, and working out solutions that are agreeable to both parties.

Mediation is better suited to fostering family cooperation than is the adversarial legal process. Consider mediation when dissolving your marriage or at any time when there are disputes that could be settled by an impartial third party. Mediation is an alternative worth considering at any point during your divorce.

CUSTODY

One of the primary concerns of divorcing parents is custody of the children and visitation schedules. Custody is the assignment of legal and physical responsibilities for the care of your children. While custody laws vary from state to state, most require that the form of custody be specified before the divorce is finalized.

There is one common pitfall that parents easily fall into during the course of custody negotiation. Parents often see children as possessions to fight over rather than young people whose needs and rights must be protected. Custody is about children's access to their parents and vice versa. The focus of your custody settlement should be (1) when the children will be with each parent, and (2) how each of you can continue to parent them effectively. These considerations are essential to your children's health and well-being. I strongly recommend that you do everything possible to reach a constructive custody agreement rather than resort to a destructive, costly court battle.

The two most common forms are sole and joint custody. Most people think of custody in terms of where the children will live, but the courts make the distinction between legal and physical custody.

Sole Custody

In a sole custody arrangement one parent has the primary responsibility for the children and the autonomy to make all the decisions regarding their care. The custodial parent makes all medical, educational, religious, and legal decisions without having to consult the other parent. The noncustodial parent is given visitation rights. Sole custody used to be the norm, but this is changing for several reasons. In the past when sole custody was granted, mothers were the custodians of the children with fathers being granted visitation on alternate weeks. This was a tremendous burden on one parent, and the children had insufficient contact with the noncustodial parent, usually the father. When sole custody is granted these days, more frequent contact with the noncustodial parent is usually included.

Joint Custody

Joint legal custody is gaining in popularity. In this arrangement, both parents share in the important decisions and responsibilities for their children, regardless of physical residence. Their commitment is to continue parental involvement in their children's daily lives. Joint custody does not necessarily mean that the children divide their time equally between the two homes.

Some states make the distinction between joint legal custody and joint physical custody. In joint legal custody, both parents participate in important decisions and responsibilities regarding their children even though the children may spend most of their time in one parent's home. In a joint physical custody arrangement, the children will divide their time more equally between two homes. The amount of time spent in each home varies depending on the family. Some families divide the time into days, weeks, months, school years, or even whole years. In this form of custody, children genuinely have two homes and live in both places. The hallmark of successful joint custody is a commitment to the ongoing connection and regular participation of both parents.

Split Custody

In a split custody arrangement, each parent has sole custody of one or more of the children. This form of custody is rare because it separates siblings. Courts generally think that children should grow up together, yet in some cases this form works best. Say, a teenage daughter wants to live with her mother while her younger brother wants to remain with his father. When this is the case, a visitation schedule is arranged between the children and their non-custodial parent.

IS ONE FORM OF CUSTODY BETTER THAN ANOTHER?

The jury is still out as to which kind of custody is best for children. The consensus is that children need regular contact with both parents and their fathers' continued involvement in their lives, but there is no simple answer about which form of custody is best. The research that compares joint custody to sole custody has been too limited to make definitive conclusions.[3] Joint custody does give children a better chance to continue relationships with both parents, but custody alone cannot predict how well a child will adjust to divorce. Most custody experts agree that good adjustment depends less on the form of custody than the absence of parental conflict and a nurturing relationship with both parents.

Studies report that children living in joint custody families tend to have higher self-esteem, but joint custody is not for everyone. Some families are not prepared to maintain two homes. Others can't sustain the high degree of cooperation required. In families where there is a great deal of conflict, children do better when visitation is highly structured and contact between parents is less frequent. If you are entrenched in an ongoing conflict with your ex-spouse, joint custody is not recommended.

Because so much depends on the circumstances of each individual family at any given time, no simple prescription is possible. The most effective custody depends on what will work best for you and your children. You want the situation that will provide the greatest stability, consistency, and parental involvement. Regardless of what you decide, as the children grow, parents remarry, and relationships change, the custody arrangements will need to be altered. Be creative when considering which form of custody will work best. There is a lot of room for variations and options within each.

DIVORCE NIGHTMARES

The two nightmares that haunt family law professionals are physical and sexual abuse of children and parental kidnapping. According to Hugh McIsaac, actual abuse occurs in about 2 percent of divorce cases, though accusations are far more frequent. Cases in which accusations of spousal or sexual abuse are used to keep noncustodial parents away from their children are extremely painful for everyone concerned. When emotions run high it is easy to imagine the worst of your former spouse and jump to conclusions that are not based on factual evidence. If you have reason to believe that your ex-spouse is abusing your children, contact your local office of Child Protective Services so that the charges can be investigated.

If you are the parent who has been falsely accused of abuse, there is a support group you can contact: Victims of Child Abuse Laws (VOCAL), P.O. Box 11335, Minneapolis, MN 55411 (612-521-9741).

The second nightmare is parental kidnapping. Kidnapping is a federal offense, but every year thousands of children are kidnapped by their noncustodial parents. In the majority of cases the abductor's primary motivation is to inflict pain on the former spouse, not out of love for the children. According to a study done by the U.S. Department of Justice, Office of Juvenile Justice and Delinquency Prevention, 60 percent of the incidents involved the violation of written custody orders. The remainder violated verbal understandings. Kidnappings from schools or day care centers were rare, a mere 2 percent. Nearly half of the kidnapping episodes were brief, lasting between two days and a week. And according to the study, 48 percent of the custodial parents or guardians knew where the children were. According to the National Center for Missing and Exploited Children, parental kidnappers often have a history of spousal abuse or violence, death threats against the custodial parent, or child abuse.

Unfortunately, there is very little protection against parental abduction. In most cases, visitation rights will not be revoked or limited unless the custodial parent has concrete evidence of a physical threat or the probability of an abduction.

Federal laws protect you and your children should they be abducted to another state. Children taken to another country present a far more difficult situation. The Hague Convention on the Civil Aspects of International Child Abduction is useful in dealing with countries that are signatories, which include Australia, Great Britain, France, Portugal, and Canada. But third world countries that have not signed the convention can present major problems for custodial parents. If your child has been abducted to a foreign country, contact the consulate of that country. However, there are several precautions you can take if you suspect that your ex-spouse is going to abduct your children.

TIPS TO PREVENT PARENTAL KIDNAPPING

First and foremost, trust your intuition. If you suspect your children are in danger, take action. Most kidnappers will make a threat before the actual abduction takes place. If you have received threats, take them seriously. Here are some suggestions to prevent parental kidnapping:

1. Keep a file on your ex-spouse in case tracing is needed. Be sure to include social security number, driver's license, credit card and bank account numbers.
2. Alert your local police so they will be prepared to intervene immediately if the need arises.
3. Alert your child's school. Ask school personnel to notify you if someone suspicious shows an interest in your child. Ask officials not to release your child to anyone other than yourself or someone you have delegated. The school should have written instructions as to who can pick up your child.
4. Without frightening him or her, discuss your concern with your child. If you are the primary caretaker, let your child

know that he or she is not to go anywhere without your permission. (That includes the other parent.)

5. Send a written request to the U.S. Passport Bureau asking that your child not be granted a passport when application is made by the noncustodial parent. Your request will require a court-ordered certified copy of your custody agreement.

The best protection against parental abduction is to do everything possible to maintain a good working relationship with your ex. The exception will be the psychologically unstable parent, but that kind of person will also be presenting other custody problems.

Chapter 9

Money

How Important Is It?

Prosperity is living easily and happily in the real world, whether you have money or not.

Jerry Gillies, Money Love

People fight over two things in divorce: kids and money. This is partially because our society sees money as much more than a means to survival; money is also the culture's major symbol of power. People who are ending marriages often use the financial settlement to measure their victory or failure in the divorce itself. But divorce needn't be a contest over who ends up with the bigger piece of the pie. Divorce can be a means of getting out of an unsatisfying relationship, establishing financial independence, and building a new life. Money, of course, is an important part of the equation, but there is a vast difference between negotiating an equitable settlement and taking your ex to the cleaners.

In the film *The War of the Roses,* Michael Douglas and Kathleen Turner portray a couple who fight to the death for emotional and financial supremacy. Even after the divorce they remain trapped in a grotesque bond as they fight over the material debris of their marriage. This movie should be required viewing for all who are about to file for divorce in the hope they won't make the same mistakes. The couple in the title role lose sight of the purpose of their divorce and get caught in the basest form of greed and competition.

During divorce many of us feel vulnerable, helpless, and scared, as if our very survival were threatened. We're concerned about our basic needs for food, clothing, and shelter, so we cling desperately to our material possessions and financial security. Not only do we depend on money for the necessities of life, but we unconsciously connect it with emotional security. We confuse our basic survival needs with our needs for love.

Of course, having enough to pay your monthly bills, hire a baby-sitter, send your kids to camp, or go out to dinner and a movie certainly makes life less stressful. And having a cushion to fall back on during emergencies can alleviate the worst of your everyday worries. But money-in-the-bank money doesn't necessarily give you total peace of mind. The only way you are going to attain that is by taking charge of your life and gaining control of your finances.

In this chapter you will learn how to separate your financial fears and fantasies from the practical reality of providing for yourself and your children. A greater understanding of your attitudes toward money will bring you one step closer to taking charge of your finances, which itself will give you greater personal satisfaction. First let's look at the emotional side of your financial life.

MONEY INVENTORY

This is an exercise I use in my support groups to help participants understand money's significance to them. For many of us money has a psychological meaning that goes far beyond the practical purpose of paying the monthly bills. We frequently associate money with love, security, and power, see it as a yardstick to measure self-worth.

Most people who are faced with financial stress feel inadequate, insecure, powerless, and hopeless. The goal of this inventory is to help you to discover the role money plays in your emotional life.

Take a few minutes to answer the following questions. Be honest with yourself. Simply understanding the meaning you give to money will enable you to untangle the emotional from the practical aspects of your finances.

1. How do you feel about being on your own financially? ________

____

2. Is your attitude about your ability to survive financially and earn a decent living generally optimistic or pessimistic? __________

____

3. When finances get tight, do you panic and imagine yourself as a bag person or do you see it as a temporary situation? ________

____

4. When you're feeling frustrated, lonely, or depressed, do you head for the nearest mall for some temporary relief through shopping?

____

5. Does your self-esteem rise and fall with your bank balance? ___

____

6. Does your blood boil when it's time to write the monthly child support check? Are you ever tempted to withhold the check because you don't like the visitation arrangement or the way your ex spends the money? ________________

____

7. Do you ever judge the success of your divorce by the size of your settlement? ________________
8. Do you ever buy your kids "guilt gifts" or feel compelled to match what their friends have or do? ________________
9. Does money equal security? If yes, how much money do you need in order to feel secure? ________________

____

10. When you're angry with your ex about a late or delinquent child support payment, do you ever threaten to withhold access to the children as a way of getting even or applying pressure? ______

____

11. Do you ever send the child support payment late or refuse to contribute to your children's extra expenses as a way to punish your ex-spouse? ________
12. Do you ever resent your ex's financial wealth and fantasize about how to make him or her pay you more? ________
13. Do you ever take pride in causing your ex-spouse financial hardship? ________
14. Do you ever ask your ex to account for his or her spending habits? ________
15. How confident are you about your ability to earn a decent living? Answer using a scale of 1 to 10 (1 being absolutely terrified and 10 being absolutely confident). (Please be honest with yourself. Remember this is just for you. If you are unsure of yourself, this questionnaire will help you recognize your need for more emotional and practical support.) ________

    ____

A greater understanding of your attitude toward money and its role in your life will make you better able to meet the financial challenges you face. The first step in doing this is to sort your emotional from your financial needs. Money will buy you food, shelter, and services, but not companionship or peace of mind.

MONEY TRAPS AND HOW TO AVOID THEM

People entangled in a hostile divorce use money to manipulate or control as a means to get revenge. These are some of the most common money traps. See if you recognize yourself in any of these situations.

- Polly and Luke had been married for seven years. In their settlement Luke agreed to pay $250 per month in child support for their five-year-old daughter. Polly works as an elementary school teacher and counts on the monthly checks to make ends meet. Luke and Polly recently argued about changing the visitation schedule. The following month Luke didn't send the child support. When Polly questioned him, he said that he wasn't going to send it until she was more cooperative. Luke withheld the check as a means of punishing Polly. But ultimately it was their daughter who suffered.

- Christopher and Hilary were married for eleven years. Two years after their divorce, Christopher remarried. Gradually, Hilary demanded more and more money. "He may have a new young wife, but I'm going to get the satisfaction of making him pay," she said. Hilary was successful in her revenge, but no amount of money was going to alleviate her sense of loss and betrayal.
- When Ginny married Anthony she gave up her career as a computer programmer and stayed home to have two children. Seven years later, Anthony filed for a divorce. In the settlement Ginny was awarded the house and generous monthly child support. Anthony moved into a modest bachelor apartment in order to make his monthly payments, but Ginny refused to look for a job. She continued to live in their large suburban house while Anthony made the heavy mortgage payments. Ginny was using financial dependence to remain connected to Anthony.
- Gordon had been divorced for two years and began to suspect that his ex-wife wasn't using the child support exclusively for the children. Gordon remains actively involved with his two teenage children. Lately he's sent the checks directly to his older son. That way, he thought, the money was more likely to go to the kids. He wanted his children to know who was paying for their expenses. He was also perpetuating the conflict with his ex-wife.

Each of these people felt they were winning a victory by causing their ex-spouse a financial hardship. If you recognize yourself in any of these examples, reread the chapter on getting an emotional divorce. When you are late with your monthly support payments, demand excessive amounts of money, or deprive your ex of material possessions, you are the one who loses in the end. You may feel a momentary sense of satisfaction, but the truth is sad: Using money to gain revenge is less a sign of power than an indication of your inability to let go of the past.

Even when you feel justified, using money as a weapon is never appropriate. I understand that you may be furious with your ex and want payment for the pain and hardship you have suffered. You may feel that money is your only leverage. But before you act in a way that may be counterproductive, stop to imagine your children standing between you and your ex-spouse. Visualize them experiencing the effects of what you are about to do. Then ask yourself, "Are my actions going to serve me and my children or will they cause more harm than good?" This will buy you time to reconsider.

Making your ex suffer will add to the stockpile of animosity that already exists between you. Your goal should be to disentangle yourself from the past. Revenge only prolongs your suffering and prevents you from standing on your own two feet. Looking out for your own best interest doesn't mean making your ex walk over hot coals; what it *does* mean is that you do the best you can to work out an equitable agreement.

Your marriage certificate was not a guarantee to a lifelong pension fund. As you become self-supporting you realize that *you* have the power to take charge of your life and meet your own needs. This realization will be a tremendous boost to your self-esteem. Financial self-sufficiency also frees you from the fears and uncertainty of being dependent on your former spouse. The more independent and self-reliant you become, the more freedom you will have to redefine your relationship with your ex-spouse.

LET'S GET FISCAL: MAKING ENDS MEET

Now let's look at the more practical aspects of becoming financially independent. Getting an emotional divorce is necessary; equally essential is a financial divorce. Financial divorce means separating your assets, establishing your own credit, setting up your own checking account, and making financial decisions on your own. This may be the first time in your life that you are on your own financially. The thought may seem frightening, but it is another opportunity for you to take charge of your life.

For women, the usual fallout from divorce is a lowered standard of living: A custodial mother generally exists in an economic situation that is far more precarious than that of a custodial father. Following divorce, women's standard of living drops an average of 30 percent in five years, while men's rises 8 percent.[1] The drop is sharpest for women and children who were relatively well off before divorce. The financial demands of raising a family alone have helped in the coinage of a new economic term, the "feminization of poverty." The most obvious new class of poor is composed of mothers and children. Discrepancies in male and female pay scales add to women's burden. According to a 1982 federal advisory council report, if the wage gap between the sexes were wiped out, one half of female-headed households would be lifted out of poverty.

Most divorced parents expect a change in lifestyle. With the exception of the very wealthy, those of you who stretch your income to cover two households will have less cash available than when you were married. This requires adjusting your lifestyle to match your new situation. A diminished lifestyle may be far from ideal, but you can learn to adjust to it. The next section gives you some tools for getting back on your feet. Since divorced mothers suffer the greatest economic change, this section is directed toward women and their needs.

6 Steps to Financial Independence

1. Recognize that you *can* change your financial situation.
2. Examine your priorities and learn to economize.
3. Set realistic financial goals.
4. Make a budget.
5. Increase your earning power.
6. Cultivate an attitude of gratitude.

Let's look at each point in great detail.

1. RECOGNIZE THAT YOU *CAN* CHANGE YOUR FINANCIAL SITUATION

You *do* have the power to change your financial situation. Chances are slim that a white knight will ride up and rescue you. Now is the time to take back your power and trust in your own ability to make things happen.

There is a story about a woman who huddled in her basement as a hurricane swirled around her house. The neighbor on her right offered to take her to safety. She turned him down. The neighbor on the left did the same. Again she said no. A police officer came by and pleaded with her to leave. The woman refused. "I'm a good person," she said. "I have faith, God will save me."

Unfortunately, she died in the storm, which annoyed her no end. When she arrived in heaven she complained, "God, I've always been a good person. Why didn't you save me from that storm?" God looked at her and threw up his hands, saying, "Heaven knows, I tried. I sent two neighbors to get you. I even sent the police!" The moral of the story is: Pay attention to the resources available to you. You are your greatest asset. You have talents, skills, and abilities. Now is the time to call on them.

Daphne, a slender, graceful, one-time waitress, had divorced Ian, a successful businessman. Their two daughters, eight and ten, lived with their mother. Daphne hadn't worked during her twelve-year marriage and was terrified of being on her own. Even after two years she continued to be completely dependent on her ex-husband. Ian held her financial dependence over her head. Unless she catered to his every whim, he would threaten to cut her off. Ian demanded open access to the children, he frequently dropped by the house unannounced, and he occasionally coerced her into sex.

As time went on, Daphne felt more and more humiliated. One day she decided she couldn't tolerate the situation one minute longer. She had to find a way to establish her autonomy. She wrote him a note saying, "The party's over. Stay out of my house and out of my bedroom. You can see the children under the circumstances outlined in our divorce agreement. Our personal relationship is over."

Then Daphne called her good friend Rose, told her what she had done, and asked for help. The two women spent the afternoon discussing Daphne's talents. Although Daphne hadn't worked during her marriage, she had volunteered at her temple laying out their newsletter and designing their fliers and ads. She was also a terrific cook and party planner and a talented jeweler. The two women discussed Daphne's talents and salable assets and decided that the most immediately salable talent was her jewelry making. People raved about the jewelry she wore; she was often asked where she got her unusual earrings and pins. She had made pieces as gifts for friends and they were always worn with great enjoyment.

Daphne borrowed two thousand dollars from her parents and started her own jewelry-making business. She had business cards and fliers printed up and announced a home jewelry show for a Saturday afternoon a month before Christmas. She was amazed at the turnout. She sold everything she had and took orders for six more pieces. Over the next couple of months she began to take her jewelry to local stores and started getting regular orders. Within six months she had a sales representative showing her work and within a year she had three employees.

Don't underestimate yourself. You probably have talents you take for granted and skills you don't consider salable. Take stock of what you have to offer. Spend some time discovering what you do every day that may be a hidden asset. You don't have to start your own business, but begin to think about how you can use your talents to increase your earning power.

Resources Inventory Exercise

Don't take yourself and your talents for granted. A woman in one of my support groups was asked by her son's Boy Scout troop, her church, and his school to organize fund-raising benefits, which she did successfully. Before she did this inventory she didn't recognize her organizational talents as a valuable skill. Really look at all the things you do on a daily basis that you may take for granted but that can be used in developing your career. Take a few minutes to answer the following questions.

1. What skills and abilities have you developed while running a household and raising your children? List at least five. ________

   ____

2. What are your hobbies and interests? ____________________

   ____

3. Which of your skills, talents, or interests can be used to increase your earning power? ______________________________

____

4. What are three things you can do to start to change your financial situation? Pick one and begin to act on it. ______________

____

2. EXAMINE YOUR PRIORITIES AND LEARN TO ECONOMIZE

Take some time to decide what matters most to you. Most divorced parents have to adjust their lifestyles to a more limited budget. You have to economize, reassess your priorities, and cut expenses in order to live within your means. "I hadn't worked full-time while I was married and I wasn't sure that my part-time work would carry me once I no longer had my husband's support," Margaret told the members of a support group. "I only knew that I couldn't maintain the same lifestyle. At first I went into a panic; I was afraid I wouldn't have enough to pay bills. Then I developed health insurance phobia. At that point I felt completely overwhelmed." Margaret had to make some compromises, so she took a full-time job and moved in with her mother. "I didn't like giving up my privacy, but I realized the kids and I could live a better life by sharing a home," she said.

"I always had a housekeeper, now I can't afford one," she added. "But the kids come home after school and my mother is home for them. When I travel for my job, they are with Grandma. She helps them with homework and is a great support. It's a real relief not to have to do everything alone."

Margaret had a beautiful house and never worried about money. Now she has to watch every penny. "Instead of going out to dinner and the movies, we make a pizza and rent a video or we have a potluck with friends," she said. "My kids are learning that there's a budget now." Margaret has learned that life is full of trade-offs. Her loss of privacy is worth the benefits of lower rent and her mother's help with her children. Ask yourself what trade-offs you can make that will help ease your financial stress. Here are some comments about the trade-offs participants in my support groups have made.

- "Friends who have a lot more money I don't meet for dinner because it costs between fifteen and twenty dollars to eat out. Instead, I meet them after dinner for a movie or I just go out for a drink."
- "I never thought about paying for a baby-sitter before. Now when I go out I have to figure the evening will cost about twenty-five dollars by the time I pay for entertainment and a sitter. That's not within my budget. I didn't want to give up going out, so I decided to start a baby-sitting co-op with some of the other parents in my area. No one pays for a sitter; we just trade time. Now I can go out without blowing my budget."
- "No one believes me when I say I do my own home repairs. I can hardly believe it myself. I never considered myself to be very handy, but I bought a book on home maintenance and it's saving me a good chunk of change. So far I've replaced a leaky faucet, fixed a broken light switch, and repapered my bathroom walls. Not only am I saving money, but I feel so mechanical!"
- "I didn't want to move out of my house, but it was too big and too expensive to manage on my own. A friend suggested I get a housemate. I realized that would be a great way to reduce my monthly expenses. After all, I did have an extra bedroom with its own bath and a private entrance. I put an ad in the local paper and within a week I had a new housemate. She pays a quarter of my mortgage and utilities. She has a great dog that my son loves and I'm surprised at how much I enjoy her company."

Get creative and find ways to live within your budget.

3. SET REALISTIC FINANCIAL GOALS

Start plotting your own financial course and charting your financial future. By setting goals you'll have a road map of where you are going. Once you have clearly defined goals, you can begin to move toward them. Close your eyes and imagine your ideal life five years from now. Allow yourself to see as much detail as possible. Where are you living? What kind of career do you have? How much do you earn? What investments are you making? Consider your financial future and allow yourself to fantasize about how you would like it to be.

Now take a pencil and paper and divide your goals into three categories: short-term, intermediate, and long-range. This will help you to see what steps you need to take immediately. I ask participants in my support groups to establish goals. Following are some examples of what people said.

Short-term goals: I want to
pay off my credit cards.
ask my boss for a raise.
take a course in accounting at the community college.
open an IRA account.
set aside enough money for my daughter's birthday party.

Intermediate goals: I want to
send my kids to summer camp.
pay off my car loan.
start a money market fund.
enroll in a hotel management program.
be able to move to a different neighborhood.

Long-range goals: I want to
make a down payment on a house.
invest in the stock market.
start a college fund for my children.
buy a brand-new car.
buy a computer.

Mapping out your financial goals helps you plan for your future. Having a sense of where you want to be a year from now makes the daily compromises more tolerable.

4. MAKE A BUDGET

Some people consider a budget as an admission of failure, but a budget is merely a tool to help you to gain control of your finances. I have made several budgets over the years, none of them very elaborate. The purposes were twofold: First, I needed an idea of my monthly expenses and how much I had to earn each month to pay my bills. Second, I needed to reassure myself that I wasn't going to end up on the street pushing a shopping cart. When I would start to panic about my financial situation, I could use my budget as a pacifier.

I would read over the figures, take a few deep breaths, and talk to myself as a sensible friend would: "See, you can pay your bills based on the amount of money you are earning." Or sometimes I would say, "You need to cut back on your spending so that you can meet your monthly bills. You can do that." Then I would go over my budget and find where I could cut my spending or increase my income. I used my budget as a compass to keep myself on course.

When you make a budget, work out something that is realistic and livable. Your budget is not supposed to be a punishment; its purpose is to give you greater freedom. It is also a blueprint for financial independence. Start by making a list of your monthly income, including child support payments. Then list your monthly expenses, including house, car, insurance, food, clothing, debts, loans, etc. By looking at how much comes in right now compared to your monthly expenses you can get a handle on how much money you need to cover your basic expenses.

As you work with your budget, gradually include items from your list of financial goals. For example, if paying off credit cards is one of your goals, set up a section of your budget that includes that category. At first you may only be able to put twenty-five or thirty dollars a month into that account, but don't be discouraged. When you have a plan you will be surprised at how much more conscious you will be of your spending.

A certain amount of security comes from knowing what's expected of you each month. Once you know where your money is going, you can start to economize. Don't think of your budget as a fence between you and fun and the things you enjoy but rather as a way of gaining financial freedom.

5. INCREASE YOUR EARNING POWER

One way to improve your financial situation is to increase your earning power. This may require improving your education, asking for a promotion, getting further training, or turning a hobby into a salable skill or commodity.

"When I got divorced I took a job that I said I would never do; I worked as a housekeeper," said Marie, a pert Midwesterner who had followed her husband to the West Coast only to see her marriage dissolve. "I had to swallow my pride to clean other people's houses, but I wanted to go back to school and get a bachelor's degree in psychology." Cleaning houses let her set her own hours while supporting herself and her son. She mopped and scrubbed for three years until she finished her B.A. and was hired as a consultant. There she developed a series of classes to help children talk about their feelings. "I decided that I was on a roll and I applied for a master's degree program in counseling psychology," she said. "It took a few years, but little by little I was able to increase my income and do work that I really love."

Getting more education or starting your own business won't change your financial situation overnight, but it's the first step in earning a better living and attaining a sense of personal fulfillment.

"I was earning eighteen thousand dollars a year plus getting four hundred dollars per month child support. That's what we had to live on," remembered Meg, the still young mother of two grown children. "I had agreed with Joel to buy him out of the house, so I borrowed twenty thousand dollars from my father and he helped me out for a while by paying my mortgage payments." Even with his help, she was just barely scraping by. She couldn't afford to work as an office manager, so she decided to go back to school and become a court reporter, taking classes three evenings a week while working full-time.

"It was very stressful holding down a full-time job and putting in long hours taking night classes, but that was the only way I could have dug myself out of that hole," said Meg. She stuck with it. "It took me two years, but after that I was making almost twice as much as I did before. And I really loved my work!"

Getting more education or training can increase your earning power. Let yourself dream. Consider where your passion is, what excites you, and then take steps to find work in that area. You may have to continue at your present job while you take the additional training, but there is nothing more satisfying than reaping the financial rewards of your efforts.

As you take these steps toward your career your self-confidence will increase. Self-esteem isn't measured in dollars and cents but by how you feel about yourself. Financial independence is part of the foundation for healthy self-esteem. Knowing you are capable of providing for your family will give you a great deal of peace of mind.

6. CULTIVATE AN ATTITUDE OF GRATITUDE

Most of us spend so much time thinking about what's missing from our lives that we forget to appreciate what we do have. We look at what we've lost or we compare ourselves and our situation to someone else and inevitably come away feeling deprived. But focusing on the lack in your life won't help you to cope successfully with your present situation. In fact, it will only contribute to your feeling more helpless, hopeless, and dissatisfied. Appreciate what you do have rather than what you think you should have.

A certain level of financial security is necessary, but we spend so much of our time and energy focused on the pursuit of money that we lose sight of what's really important. We can live very well without many things we once considered essential. Living simply and learning to appreciate the value of nonmaterial things can add tremendous richness to your life.

Much of our frustration comes from the discrepancy between what we think should be happening and what's actually happening. We all have a fantasy of how "it's" supposed to be. When reality doesn't match the fantasy, we are disappointed. If we let go of what we think is missing from our lives and appreciate what's good about our reality we'll be a lot happier. What it boils down to is looking at what you want versus what you actually need. A need is something you require for your own and your children's well-being. A want is something you hope will satisfy you and make you happy. For example, I may want a new Mazda RX7 when what I need is a decent reliable car. In reality, most of us need very little, but we have a tremendous appetite and desire for things.

Sometimes we fall into the "if only syndrome." We think that if only we had more money or a new car or a new wardrobe, then we'd be happy. But that isn't where happiness lies. We can reduce a lot of our stress by staying focused on what we actually need rather than desperately trying to fill an emotional void with material desires. The writer Spencer Johnson once said, "We can never get enough of what we don't need!" Take a look at what really makes you happy. Learn to appreciate the nonmaterial assets in your life like good friends, a beautiful sunset, a precious moment with your kids, or a meaningful conversation with your parents. These nonmaterial blessings are the true riches of life.

The key is your attitude. You can use your situation to beat yourself up and feel deprived or you can use it to build strength. There are two basic emotions in life: love and fear. Ask yourself, "Am I operating out of love or am I driven by fear?" If fear is your motivator, don't be surprised if you've fallen into the trap of "scarcity thinking." You think you're not going to have what you need, you become frightened and insecure, and you question your ability to survive.

Instead of indulging in this kind of thinking, use the same amount of time to affirm that you *will* be taken care of and that you will have what you need. To paraphrase Keith Richards of the Rolling Stones—you can't always get what you want, but if you try, it just may happen you get what you need.

Consider what you actually need to take care of yourself, then make a commitment to cultivate an attitude based on love rather than fear. Focus on what's positive in your life, and surprisingly, you will feel a greater sense of security.

CHILD SUPPORT

Of crucial importance to most divorced parents is child support. In 90 percent of divorced families, the mothers have primary custody.

Noncustodial fathers are required by law to contribute to the costs of raising a child, but 41 percent of them walk away without a child support agreement. Even with an agreement in place, child support payments are frequently low and unreliable. Despite increasingly tough child support enforcement laws, a Bureau of the Census survey found that between 1978 and 1988, the average amount of child support that divorced men paid fell nearly 25 percent. Only one half of mothers who were entitled to child support received the full amount; one quarter received partial payment; another quarter received nothing at all.[2]

Divorced men are more likely to meet their car payments than their child support obligations, even though (as one study in the early 1980s found) for two thirds of them, the amount owed for their children was *less* than their monthly auto loan bills.[3] Nationwide, $4.6 billion is owed by fathers to children of divorce. Whatever strategy is used, child support collection has been disappointingly low. Studies have found that the only tactic that seems to awaken the moral conscience of negligent fathers is mandatory jail sentences.[4]

Forty-three percent of custodial mothers have an annual income of less than ten thousand dollars.[5] Child support scarcely makes up for the gap in income between men and women. If you are a noncustodial father, *make your child support payments regularly.* Not only is this required by law, but when you don't, your children interpret your lack of financial support as a lack of love and caring. Your child support payments are not only essential for your children's welfare, but they also send a message to your kids about your commitment to their well-being.

IF YOU'RE NOT RECEIVING CHILD SUPPORT

In 1987 court-ordered awards averaged about $2,710 per child a year, less than the estimated requirements for raising children at poverty level. Even if this amount were paid regularly, it covered less than a quarter of the average costs of raising one child.

If you are entitled to monthly child support but have not received payment, several avenues of recourse are open to you. Before you take any legal action, however, I recommend that you make every effort to work things out directly with your ex-spouse. If he doesn't take you seriously and start to make regular payments, let him know that you will take legal action. If that doesn't produce results, contact your lawyer or mediator, the local district attorney's office, or your local family support service.

Each state has established a Child Support Enforcement Agency (CSEA) expressly for the purpose of helping custodial parents collect child support payments. You do not have to be a recipient of Aid for Dependent Children to qualify for its help. Under Title IV D of the Social Security Act child support can be withheld from the wages of the negligent parent. According to Wayne Dass of the Los Angeles District Attorney's Office, half of all delinquent child support payments that are collected come from garnisheeing the negligent parents' wages.

Parents are required to pay child support before car loans, mortgages, credit card debts, or other claims made against their earnings. The CSEA can also place a lien on the parent's property, or intercept an income tax refund in order to collect child support. Let me reiterate, this assistance is available regardless of your income level. You do not have to be receiving welfare to take advantage of these services.

If you are not receiving child support payments on a regular basis, organize your documents and contact your local child support agency. Take your court documents mandating child support, the nonpaying parent's social security number, address, telephone number, place of employment, and other relevant personal data to your local child support agency. A caseworker will be assigned to you, who will assist you in filing your claim. It is essential that you keep accurate records of child support payments that were made and those that are delinquent. As you begin this process, keep in mind that your caseworker is handling numerous claims. In Los Angeles County a single caseworker handles an average of twelve hundred cases. Maintain frequent contact if you want to monitor the progress on your case.

Collecting child support is a complex and frustrating effort. There is no one recipe for how to collect delinquent payments. How you handle your situation is specific to your individual case and set of circumstances. Whether you contact your attorney, a mediator, or your local district attorney's office, I encourage you to take action. You deserve financial support in caring for your children.

FOR YOUR KIDS' SAKE

The most common reaction by a custodial parent who doesn't receive child support is to deny the other parent access to the children. Anger and resentment are understandable, but using children as a means of revenge is both unacceptable and counterproductive. Not only is visitation a court-ordered right, but children are the ones who suffer when they are denied access to a parent.

If you have financial disputes, work them out directly with your ex-spouse. Do not involve your children. Sue and Ned, unfortunately, did just that. Their two sons, Howard, 12, and Jeffrey, 14, live with their mother but see their father every other weekend. At least that was the case until Sue and Ned got involved in a full-scale property dispute.

Ned was the one who wanted the divorce and Sue clung to the house as the last remnant of their marriage. Ned was advised by his lawyer that in light of the generous settlement he had made, Sue would have to buy him out if she wanted to remain in the house. Sue felt that since the children lived in the house, Ned should consider it as a part of his providing for his children. The battle waged on for over eight months with countless angry phone calls, threats, and bad feelings. After the first month of the dispute Ned noticed that his sons seemed reluctant to spend time with him. They seemed tense and withdrawn and, when questioned, wouldn't divulge why. One day when Ned was alone with his older son, he blurted out, "Mom thinks you're stingy for not letting us keep the house. Why are you making things so hard on her? Besides, we don't want to move." The boy clearly didn't understand why his dad didn't just let them live in the house. "If we move I'll have to change schools and I'll lose all my friends," he cried. It was apparent to Ned that Sue had filled the boys with biased information. "If your mother stopped living like a queen she could afford to keep the house," Ned shot back at his son. "She's driving me to debtors' prison."

When Ned dropped the boys back at their mother's house, he met her at the door and let loose. "I'm sick of you filling the boys full of lies about me," he shouted. "You're always pleading poverty when you know it's not true. If you're so tight for money, why the hell don't you get a job?"

The animosity and fighting waged on and the children continued to suffer. It wasn't until a year after the property dispute had been settled that the boys wanted to rekindle their relationship with their father.

When you're engaged in a financial dispute with your ex, it's almost impossible to keep your anger from seeping out where your children can feel it. But using your kids as the rope in your tug-of-war can only unravel their relationship with both of you. The only things you create by involving your kids in your battle is greater stress, unhappiness, and confusion.

HELPING KIDS COPE WITH FINANCIAL REALITY

"Why can't I have a new Nintendo cartridge? Billy's mom just bought him one."

"Jill and Pam are going to the amusement park this weekend. Can I go too? It only costs twenty-five dollars."

"All the kids on my team have new cleats. Why do I have to wear these funky old ones?"

"Sally's parents are divorced and she's buying a new prom dress."

We want to give our children the best of everything: new clothes; the latest toys and games; music, art, or karate lessons; trips and vacations. But a single parent can't always give kids the extras. Living on a limited budget does have its positive side, however; one of the most valuable gifts you can give your children is a responsible attitude toward money. When I ask parents in my seminars "What do you want your children to learn about money?" the most frequent answer is "I want my child to learn to be responsible." Teaching your kids to spend wisely, live within a budget, and save are invaluable lessons that will stand them in good stead.

I am not denying the difficulty of saying no, especially when you're already feeling guilty about depriving them of the ideal family. Most people equate "no" with rejection and the last people anyone wants to reject are their own kids. "No" doesn't have to mean "I don't love you," however. Actually, despite your children's protests, saying no is sometimes the most loving word you can utter. You've seen kids who have what I call the "silver spoon syndrome." They go through life feeling entitled to everything and anything. Most of these children are in for a rude awakening when they enter the real world of hard work, struggle, and delayed gratification. One of the most loving things you can do for your kids is to help them learn to cope with the frustration of not getting what they want when they want it. Teaching them responsibility, self-sufficiency, and self-discipline while they are young gives them a solid foundation for what you, of all people, know is an unpredictable future.

Following are five steps for helping your kids cope with your new financial situation.

1. Tell your kids enough about your financial situation so they know what to expect.
2. Reassure your kids that they will be taken care of.
3. Teach your kids to save and live within a budget.
4. Avoid the comparison game.
5. Encourage your kids to earn money for extras.

Let's look at each step in greater detail.

1. TELL YOUR KIDS ENOUGH ABOUT YOUR FINANCIAL SITUATION SO THEY KNOW WHAT TO EXPECT

Your children need to be told enough about your financial situation to know what they can expect but not so much that they feel burdened by money concerns. Divorced parents commonly talk to their children about their finances. Please don't burden your kids with your financial worries. If you are under financial strain, talk with another adult to relieve your stress.

There is a fine line between telling your kids about your financial limitations so that they can understand why you're not eating out as frequently, and sharing your anxiety with them. Let your kids know that you have a limited budget and you're going to have to be more careful about spending. Remember, children who have to make do with less are not damaged. In fact, far from it. Kids need to learn that you're not the magic jinni who fulfills their every wish.

2. REASSURE YOUR KIDS THAT THEY WILL BE TAKEN CARE OF

After divorce, one of your children's main concerns is "Will I be taken care of?" Kids wonder if they will have enough food and clothing, and a house to live in. Even if it seems obvious that your kids will have what they need, they need your reassurance.

My client, Marcia, a woman who had been divorced since before the birth of her son, recalled a time when she needed to reassure her son. "I can remember driving him to school one day when he was nine and he looked over at me and asked, 'Mom, are we going poor?' I was shocked. We had lived in the same house in the same neighborhood for the past nine years, and we had always driven the same car, but nevertheless he was worried." She realized that her comment the day before about being careful about what they spent had made more of an impact than she had realized. She reassured him that they weren't poor and that he would have what he needed.

"Once he had put that concern behind we had a wonderful conversation about money," she said. This was an opportunity to remind him of the numerous ways they have fun without spending a lot of money. They spontaneously made up a game of naming all the things they liked to do that were free: giving hugs, riding bikes, taking bubble baths, laughing, playing with friends, playing tickle, etc.

3. TEACH YOUR KIDS TO SAVE AND LIVE WITHIN A BUDGET

I recommend that you give your kids a weekly allowance and let them learn how to budget their money. This should be their money and with some gentle guidance they should spend it as they see fit. One boy I know receives a weekly allowance of three dollars. When one Saturday rolled around this nine-year-old asked his mother for his allowance, then jumped on his bike and rode over to the local baseball card shop with some friends. In no time at all he had spent his entire allowance on one Nolan Ryan card. He proudly showed his mother his purchase and she reminded him that that was his spending money for the week.

The next Tuesday afternoon he came running into the house and said, "Mom, I need two dollars to go to the arcade and play video games with my friends." His mother reminded him, "That's what your allowance is for. Once you've spent it, that's it until the next week."

He shouted back, "Oh, Mom, that's not fair. Everybody else's parents gives them money. Don't be so lame!"

"It doesn't matter what the other kids' parents do," she responded. "At our house you get an allowance and once you spend it that's it until the next week." She stuck to her guns and taught him a valuable lesson about setting priorities, living within his means, and saving.

I recommend to parents that as their children get older they provide a clothing allowance so kids can learn how to budget significant amounts of money. This will also save you from being hassled for new clothes. Before I instituted a clothing allowance I used to feel like I was a twenty-four-hour-ready teller. You know the drill. "Mom, can I have fifteen dollars for a new tank top?" "I need a new pair of running shoes for track." "Mom, I saw the most beautiful dress today. Will you come with me to see it?" A clothing allowance eliminates this constant harangue.

Another benefit of a clothing allowance is that it teaches your kids about living with their mistakes. For the past six years my daughter has received a clothing allowance. Every six months she receives a set amount of money that she uses to buy clothes. Ama had just started a new pay period when she and her friend Becky went shopping. Several hours later they returned and she proudly pulled a luscious purple velvet leotard from a fancy bag with the logo of an expensive boutique. "Mom, isn't this rad? I'm going to wear it after the prom. Don't you think it's gorgeous?" I could see how pleased she was with her find and I agreed that it was beautiful. I asked her how much it cost and she innocently replied, "A hundred and ten dollars." I was surprised. "Do you realize that you just spent more than one sixth of your clothing allowance?" Once Ama realized what she had done, she was upset. "Maybe I should take it back. I really like it, but that's too much money." But when she looked at the receipt it was marked "Absolutely no refunds." She was stuck. While I felt badly for her, I held my tongue and refrained from giving a lecture. She learned much more from her mistake than from anything I could have said. Needless to say, she is now much more thoughtful about her purchases. Allowing your children to make financial decisions and to live with their wise investments as well as their mistakes is good preparation for the future.

4. AVOID THE COMPARISON GAME

Children from single-parent families frequently complain that their friends have more material advantages. You can listen to your children's complaints without feeling that you have to remedy the situation. A case in point: When Ama was thirteen she attended a local private school. Many of the kids came from wealthy families. At the time I was driving an old Honda station wagon; I can remember her pleading with me not to drive her to school because she was so embarrassed by our old car. Day after day she would come home with the latest news—how one kid had his own personal trainer, another a brand-new CD player and countless CDs, and someone else her own credit card.

Ama was clearly in awe of these children's wealth. In comparison, she felt deprived. After several months of talking about what the other kids had, Ama admitted, "Mom, even though the kids at my school are really rich, a lot of them don't seem happy. They have a lot of cool stuff, but they don't get along with their parents and they act stuck-up and spoiled. I like nice things, but money isn't everything." As you can imagine, this was music to my ears.

Don't get caught up in trying to keep up with the Joneses and providing your kids with the things their friends have. Your children also have to make choices between essentials and extras. They may not be able to do or have all the things their friends do and have. They may have to work to afford some of the things they want. But what a wonderful gift you give your kids when you teach them that life is a series of compromises and that with hard work come rewards.

One of the ways to cultivate an attitude of gratitude in your kids is for all of you to do some volunteer work. Find an organization that accepts food for the needy, take a few hours to work at a homeless shelter, or join an organization that provides holiday meals for low-income families. This will accomplish two things. First, your children will gain a sense of appreciation for all that they *do* have. Second, they will experience a feeling of satisfaction by helping people in need. Our world desperately needs a generation of children who can think about others as well as themselves.

5. ENCOURAGE YOUR KIDS TO EARN MONEY FOR EXTRAS

There is nothing wrong and everything right with letting your kids know that you will provide all of the necessities of life but that they will have to earn the nonessential frills. The analogy I use in my seminars is that your kids automatically get a coach-class ticket, but if they want to fly first-class they will have to earn the upgrade.

Allow your children to make money by doing extra chores like washing the car, mowing the lawn, cleaning the bathroom, or something else around the house. Encourage them to get a part-time job working at the local video store, baby-sitting, delivering newspapers, etc. If they want to go to camp during the summer, set a goal that they have to earn a certain portion of the camp tuition. Then let them work toward saving money for their summer experience. Not only will this help your kids to appreciate the value of money, but they will feel competent and capable as they are able to work, earn, and save.

SOMETIMES ADVERSITY IS A BLESSING

You may be amazed at how understanding and compassionate your kids can be. My daughter was scheduled to go to the Grand Canyon with her geology class. I had sent in a deposit and she was registered for the trip. But a couple of weeks before she was scheduled to leave I had a crisis in my business and realized that I couldn't afford for her to go. I was upset that I had to disappoint her, but Ama was devastated. "What do you mean I can't go," she cried. "My whole class is going! It's not fair. I can't believe you're doing this." She ran into her room and slammed the door.

When she came out a while later I apologized to her, but she was still upset. One evening, a few days later, I went into her room and sat on her bed. "I'm disappointed that you couldn't go on the trip, but there was nothing I could do," I explained with tears in my eyes. "I really wanted you to, but I just can't afford it right now. I'm really sorry!" Ama looked over at me. "Mom, don't feel like you have to give me everything," she said reassuringly. "I'm disappointed too, but you do so much for me and I know you couldn't help it." She leaned over and gave me a hug and we both cried with a sense of relief. Sometimes difficult situations bring out the best in people, including kids. Don't underestimate the strength, resiliency, and compassion of your children. Give them a chance to show you how understanding, resourceful, and responsible they can be. You will all grow and benefit from these types of experiences.

PLAN FOR THE FUTURE

Since you are a single parent it is even more important that you provide for your children in case of your untimely death. I know this may sound morbid, but what if something were to happen to you? Who would be your children's legal guardian? Who would be the executor of your estate? It's time to think ahead and make provisions for your children's welfare.

I know, I can hear your resistance. I too had a tremendous amount of resistance to making out a will, and there are several reasons for resistance in this area. First, it's difficult to accept that something could actually happen to you. Second, a will is an admission that you are getting older and will eventually die. And third, it's hard to relate to the whole idea of death and your own mortality.

But I pushed through my resistance and found an attorney who helped me draft a simple will that would provide for my daughter's care in the event of my death. The total cost for drafting the will was $125 and it was money well spent. If you don't already have a will, pick up the phone and call an attorney. Do it for your children!

So how much does money *really* matter? Not everyone has to be wealthy, but we do have to know that we can support ourselves and our family. Money matters, but hopefully only as a means for providing a secure and comfortable life for yourself and your children. Take the necessary steps to survive in the present while planning and working toward greater financial independence. Knowing that you can earn as much as you need will give you a sense of personal power. But remember what John Lennon and Paul McCartney wrote, that money can't buy you love.

Chapter 10

Building a Life of Your Own

What the caterpillar calls the end of the world the Master calls a butterfly.

Richard Bach, Illusions

You can view the end of your marriage as a chance to transform yourself or you can see it as a door slamming in your face. Either way, divorce is a life-changing event. Most people leave their marriages hoping for a better life for themselves and for their children. Time and again clients tell me they divorced because their marriage had become intolerable and they wanted a fuller, more satisfying life. I encourage you to perceive your divorce this way, as an opportunity to discover new strengths and abilities, to redefine what you want, and to establish more fulfilling relationships. Your divorce gives you a shot at a whole new life and a whole new "self." This is also a chance to become a better parent.

Following your divorce, you are faced with two major tasks. First, to help your children feel safe and secure. And second, to take advantage of the opportunity your divorce has provided you. For much of this book I have focused on the children, their needs and how to help them to make a healthy adjustment. In this chapter I'm going to focus on you—who you are now as an unmarried individual, what you want, and how you can restore your self-confidence and self-esteem.

Before you can redesign your life, you will have to meet five challenges: You must (1) free yourself from guilt, (2) reclaim your identity, (3) restore your self-esteem, (4) build a support network, and (5) rediscover your sexuality. While you probably won't go through these steps in a linear fashion, each is necessary in order to take full advantage of your second chance.

1. FREE YOURSELF FROM GUILT

Guilty, guilty, guilty is the chant divorced parents repeat in their heads. This constant reminder remains just below our consciousness. Nevertheless, its presence clouds our judgment, inhibits our actions, and interferes in our relationships with our children. Guilt is a major roadblock to building a new life for yourself and to being an effective parent.

"When Jake is about to go to his father's house, I get mean and short-tempered," said Liza, a tiny woman built like a one-time Olympic gymnast. "I'm filled with anxiety and guilt about his having to go back and forth between my house and his dad's. Subtle little things like when Jake doesn't have a warm coat because he left it at his dad's or when he's grumpy and uncooperative when he comes back to my house all add up to my feeling like a terrible parent." Liza's self-reproach prevents her from seeing herself clearly. Because she is a single parent she thinks her family is wrecked and Jake will never get what he genuinely needs. Her guilt operates on overtime and prevents her from addressing everyday issues in a rational way. "I'm extremely critical of myself as a mother," she said. "No matter what I do I always feel inadequate and like a failure."

Guilt crops up in all parents, but divorced parents seem to be plagued continually. Many of us feel we've been sentenced to a life in which we're trying eternally to make up for depriving our children of a "Leave it to Beaver" childhood. We're caught between who we think we should be and who we are, what we want to do and what we can do.

This bind can lead to two types of guilt: appropriate guilt and toxic guilt. Let me define each. Appropriate guilt occurs when you have either neglected or hurt someone or violated one of your fundamental beliefs. Acknowledging your culpability with feelings of guilt can be healthy. As the psychiatrist Helen Singer Kaplan said, "Without guilt we'd be a nation of psychopaths."

Toxic guilt, on the other hand, causes you to blame yourself for situations that are beyond your control. Toxic guilt keeps you stuck in the past, attempting to attain an unrealistic standard or striving to live up to other people's expectations. Appropriate guilt can be a psychological "red light" that lets you know you're off track, but neurotic guilt only leaves you feeling helpless and inadequate.

Let me give you an example of a time when I fell into the toxic-guilt trap. When my daughter and I first moved into our current neighborhood, I felt like the odd woman out. Most of my neighbors had been married between fifteen and twenty-five years; they had lived in the same house and their children all went to the local school. Then there was me, a single mother of a single child. A few months after we began living there Ama came in after playing with one of the neighborhood kids and asked, "Mom, why can't we be a normal family like the Johnsons?"

I felt as though I had been punched in the stomach. All my guilt demons started jumping up and down shouting, "You should have hung in there with her dad!" I just wanted to cry. Instead, I regained my composure and told her, "We *are* a normal family. Besides, would you really want us to be like the Johnson family? Remember, Jenny Johnson can't spend the night at anyone's house. The Logans are normal," I went on, "but Randy Logan's dad screams at his mom so loud that you can hear it all the way across the street." That answered Ama's question, but my old feelings of guilt and shame were still running rampant.

That evening as I walked to the video store I saw my next-door neighbors sitting around their dining room table eating dinner. The dad and the two sons were laughing as the mom brought the food to the table. The first thought that came to my mind echoed Ama's earlier question: Why can't we be a normal family? It looked so right seeing my neighbors sitting there together eating and talking. "That's the way it's supposed to be," I muttered to myself.

Even when my daughter and I did sit down and have dinner together, it always felt as though something or someone was missing. I couldn't shake the feeling that I was doing something wrong. I still believed that a real family had both a mom and a dad and I compared myself to that idealized standard of the American family. I still felt deficient and ashamed.

For years I had tried to make up for the loss and pain caused by my divorce. Unfortunately, nothing I ever did was enough to erase the effects of that long-ago decision. Periodically I would get caught in the toxic-guilt trap; each time it seemed I had been trying to live up to the impossible standard that "good parents should always put their children's needs first." But not only is that impossible, it isn't healthy, either for you or your children. Whenever you hear yourself use phrases like "I should always," "I must never," and "I ought to," you know you're being run by an archaic, unrealistic standard of perfection. You are doomed to feeling guilt-ridden and inadequate, a real failure. So what do you do when you encounter your guilt demons? Here are five guilt busters that I have found to be extremely effective, both in my own life and as tools in my seminars and support groups.

Guilt Busters

1. Identify your guilt triggers.
2. Give up the Superparent syndrome.
3. Stop overindulging your kids.
4. Take time for yourself.
5. Make a list of things you're doing right.

Now let's look at each.

1. *Identify your guilt triggers.* In my seminars and support groups I suggest that participants make a list of all the things they feel guilty about. I then ask them to read their lists to a partner. When people read their lists out loud they are often shocked by how ridiculous they sound. For example, Pamela felt guilty about leaving her children to attend her support group meeting one night a week. Daisy felt guilty that her

son's father wasn't around to take him to a father-son picnic. Audrey felt guilty that she had bought her daughter a Little Mermaid costume instead of creating a homemade Halloween costume as other mothers did. Nat felt guilty because he couldn't buy his kids treats when they were with him.

Take Action

To alleviate guilt you must do one of two things: Change your behavior or adjust your expectations. I recommend that you too make a list. Look over your guilt triggers and ask yourself, "Is there some truth in the things I feel guilty about?" If there is, then decide what changes you will make to remedy the situation. The best way to alleviate guilt is often to take action. Two of the situations in that support group required that the parents take action; the other two required that they examine their unrealistic expectations.

- Daisy brought her dilemma to a support group and started out by describing her guilt over her ex's absence from his son's life. Daisy couldn't force her ex to be involved, the group members reminded her, but she could find a substitute father to go with him to the father-son picnic. All by herself she could take action to make the situation more tolerable.
- Pamela felt guilty about going out in the evening after being away at work all day. As we talked, Pamela admitted that she actually felt all right about going out one night a week to her support group meeting. Her real concern was her children's complaints about the baby-sitter. She needed to change baby-sitters so that her children would be happier while she was away. Once she did, her guilt evaporated.

Adjust Your Expectations

Daisy and Pamela could take simple actions to alleviate their guilt, but this isn't always possible. Some guilt is caused by unrealistic expectations or beliefs. When this is the case, you need to adjust your expectations to match your current reality. For example, Audrey and Nat felt bad about themselves because they had an unrealistic idea of what to do in order to be a "good parent." Audrey felt guilty for buying her daughter a Little Mermaid costume; she believed that good mothers should always put their children and their needs first.

As we discussed this idea in a support group meeting, Audrey discovered that she had adopted her belief from her mother, but the more she talked about it, the sillier it seemed. Audrey's mother had a husband who went to work every day while she stayed home and baked cookies, prepared home-cooked meals, and had time to make handmade costumes for her children. Audrey quickly realized how different her life was and how impossible it was for her to live up to that old standard. With this insight, she could breathe a sigh of relief. Audrey now had the freedom to do what she felt was right based on the reality of her current situation.

Nat also held an impossible image of a good parent. He believed that good fathers must be good providers. As Nat explored this belief, he remembered that his own family had been very poor. There were many times when he had had to make do or go without. In fact, as a child he had suffered great hardship. Nat had made a vow that when he had kids of his own, he would give them everything he never had. As long as he held on to this standard he felt like a failure. Worse, he was tormented by toxic guilt. Once he uncovered his unrealistic belief, he could accept a more attainable standard: Good fathers sometimes buy extras for their children—when they have extra money and when they choose to and when their children really need something. By adopting a more realistic criterion, Nat was able to dispel his own guilt demons . . . at least on this issue. You can use the same approach when you discover your own unrealistic standards. Change your expectations from the impossible to the practical, based on your present life and situation.

One of the most common guilt producers is the divorce itself. Lenore, a solidly constructed young woman with straight blond hair and the fresh complexion of her Norwegian heritage, was newly divorced. During one of our early sessions she said, "When I got married I thought it would be forever. But over the years I knew I had to get out. I can remember telling my mother about my desire to leave Barry. She told me that I was being too demanding, that I expected too much of him. She kept encouraging me to stick it out."

The night before the session Lenore had attended the science fair at her daughter's school. There she saw all the mothers and fathers with their children. She started to doubt her decision and wondered what she had done to her children; they hadn't asked for this divorce. "I feel like I'm depriving them of a normal family life," she said. "I can't stop thinking that I've done something terrible to my kids and there is no way to make it up to them. Maybe my mother was right!"

Over the next several sessions Lenore and I began to dissect her guilt. I asked her what it had been like to be married. She admitted that her home had been tense, filled with anger and fighting. I pointed out how detrimental that environment is for children. We also discussed how unhappy and depressed she was during the last year of her marriage. She talked about her inability to "be there" for her children while she was under such pressure. Shining the light of reality on to her situation helped Lenore see that as a divorced woman she was a much stronger and more effective mother.

During one of our last sessions Lenore came up with the insight: "I know now that I did the right thing by leaving my husband." She added, "Both for me and my children. They are much better off not living with two miserable parents in a tension-filled home." She had realized that she was giving her kids a much healthier role model. They had seen someone in an unworkable situation who had the courage to change. "I need to keep reminding myself of that," she said. Lenore had been caught between a false ideal and what she knew intuitively was right for herself and her children. Impossible standards of perfection are often based on someone else's opinion or a deprivation you felt as a child. Until you update your expectations, you'll be vulnerable to feelings of guilt.

Take a minute and ask yourself the question, "Am I doing

my best as a conscientious parent?" If your answer is yes but you're still plagued by feelings of guilt, you need to put away the whips and chains. Yes, there is always room for improvement when it comes to parenting. And yes, when you discover something needs changing and it's within your control, you should take action, make the necessary course corrections, and move on. But that is the only positive use of guilt.

2. *Give up the Superparent syndrome.* Many single parents try to overcompensate for what they think their children have lost as a result of their divorce. They try to become both a mother and a father. Others struggle to maintain the lifestyle they had when married. For most of them that is next to impossible. If you *are* managing to maintain the perfect home, someone is suffering and most likely it's you.

   Meet Kim, who first arrived at my office running and out of breath. From the moment I met her I was struck by her frenzy. Kim gave the impression of someone on fast forward. She threw off her coat and began talking with machine-gun rapidity. As she described her life after divorce, it became clear why she was in such a hurry.

   Kim got up every morning at five o'clock to clean her four-bedroom house, do a couple of loads of laundry, and iron her children's clothes. She often prepared something for that night's dinner before she went in to wake her two children. Then she would help them get dressed and ready for school, make them breakfast, and pack their school lunches. She would shower hurriedly and get ready for work, drop her children at school, then rush to her job. Kim was head of education and training at a large metropolitan hospital, and she recently had taken on implementation of several new programs that required extra planning and preparation.

   After her divorce Kim had decided to go back to school and took classes every Saturday to get a nursing credential. Every day during her lunch break she gulped down a protein shake and rushed over to the gym to work out for forty-five minutes. At 4:45 she raced out of the hospital to pick her children up from after-school care. She then drove them to their various after-school activities, rushed home and put dinner in the oven, then dashed back to get her kids from their respective activities.

Each evening she and her kids sat down to a home-cooked meal, then she would spend time with each child, reviewing homework and helping with reports or projects. After reading several stories and tucking the children into bed, Kim went downstairs, washed the dishes, and sat at the kitchen table studying for her nursing classes. By 11:30, too weary to read anymore, she fell into bed, only to wake up next the morning and start her grueling routine all over again.

Kim was a Supermom, trying to compensate for the disruption her divorce had caused her family. She had decided to be the perfect mother and career woman. She would be the most competent at work, in top physical condition, and well-dressed; her children would excel at school, enjoy home-cooked meals, be just as well-dressed, *and* have a caring, involved mother.

Kim was the first person in her family to divorce. She was desperately trying to prove to her children, herself, and most of all her family that she could manage. She wanted the world to know that neither she nor her children were in any way affected by the divorce. Kim was determined to maintain the illusion that they were still the perfect family, but all of them were suffering under this impossible burden. Kim was running herself ragged. She was more like a robot than a loving, caring mother. Her children were under pressure to maintain the appearance of perfection. There was little room for any feelings or time for reassuring talks, let alone any fun.

The truth was that Kim couldn't maintain her predivorce lifestyle and still keep her health and her sanity. None of us can, nor do we have to. Something has to give. Your children don't need crisply ironed clothes and home-cooked meals as much as they need a relaxed parent who has time to spend with them. When you drive yourself to "do it all," you end up stretched to the breaking point and everyone suffers. It's time to give up the Superparent syndrome and concentrate on what's really important to you and your children.

3. *Stop overindulging your kids.* A guilty person is seldom an effective parent. You may find yourself rewarding your children for inappropriate behavior, spending excessive amounts of money, or letting them break rules. For example, Curtis, a divorced father of two teenage girls, felt terribly guilty that he saw his daughters only one weekend a month. He had hoped to see them more regularly, but his work had dictated that he move away. Every time his daughters came to his house, Curtis would drive them to the mall and let them charge up a storm. The girls would come home with shopping bags filled with new clothes, CDs, and sporting equipment. You name it, they bought it. When the older daughter turned sixteen he outdid himself by buying her a new car.

   Curtis was trying desperately to assuage his guilt by buying his daughters' forgiveness, but presents were no substitute for his presence. After a year of relentless spending Curtis began to resent his daughters' expectation of expensive weekends. With the support of the support group members, Curtis was able to see the hole he had dug for himself. In time he was able to shift from being a sugar daddy to having a more natural relationship with his daughters.

Too Much Slack

The absolute need to set limits for your children is often obscured by clouds of guilt. Divorced parents frequently make excuses for their children's inappropriate behavior. By letting your kids get away with murder, you do no one a favor. In fact, you are setting your children up for some hard knocks. My client Maria, herself the product of a strict and traditional Italian-style home, gave into this kind of guilt. Her seven-year-old son, Kyle, had spent the weekend at his father's house. That night when Maria asked him to turn off the television and do his homework he threw a fit. In her mind, Maria made excuses for his misbehavior. "It's hard for him to settle back into my routine after he's been at his dad's house," she thought. "Poor kid, he shouldn't have to go back and forth between two homes." Maria had a full-blown case of guilt.

She gave in and said, "Okay, you can watch one more show." When the next show was over and she asked him to start his homework, Kyle protested again, this time by calling his mother names, screaming, and crying. Maria finally put an end to Kyle's uncooperative behavior by turning off the television and sending him to his room, but by then she had let herself be pushed beyond her own limit.

All children test limits. Your guilt interferes with your setting and maintaining the necessary boundaries. When you allow guilt to color your judgment and affect your decisions, your children learn to manipulate you by using behavior that is bound to backfire on them sooner or later. Save them the agony by not letting your guilt interfere with limits you must set.

4. *Take time for yourself.* Many parents try to compensate for the pain of divorce by devoting themselves totally to their children. Giving up any life of their own, they sign up with the Martyr School of Parenting. But all work and no play makes for a dull, stressed-out, overprotective parent. "It's really tough for me to take time for myself," said Ellie, the recently divorced wife of a chiropractor. She had been her husband's receptionist, office manager, bookkeeper, and "nurse." After the divorce, she devoted herself just as ardently to her children. "For a long time I didn't do anything by myself. I couldn't even escape to the movies by myself because I was working so much at my new job and I felt guilty about being away from my kids." Ellie considered dropping out of the support group because she didn't want to be away from them more than she had to, but she eventually realized how important it was to take time for herself. "I decided to take my kids to their grandma's house on the night of my support group meeting. My mother was happy to watch them and they were glad to see her. I felt so relieved."

Ellie had forgotten that she had needs of her own. Her first step was discovering that she needed to recharge her battery. Then she had to be reminded that she was entitled to time for herself. "That took a while," she said, "but now I'm remembering how to have fun. I've stopped being a martyr and I'm in a much better mood." Ellie has more patience with her kids when she takes time to nurture herself. "I think they're actually relieved that I go out and do things," she said. Taking care of yourself is not a luxury; it's a necessity. Yes, of course your children's needs deserve your attention, but your needs require just as much notice.

5. *Make a list of things you're doing right.* When you are consumed by guilt you can't remember all the positive things you regularly do for your children and others. When I ask participants in my seminars to list ten things they feel proud of, many complain that they can think of just two or three. Only if I push them to dig deeper into their positive memories can they complete their lists.

Here are some examples that might refresh your memory and help you to start on your own list.

- "I'm proud that I really work at being a good listener," one woman said. "When my son is upset I take time to really listen to him. I try to understand what he's going through."
- "I feel good about the time I spend with my children," said a father of four. "I see my kids every chance I get and I talk to them every day."
- "I give myself a lot of credit for having had the good sense to leave an intolerable marriage," said a mother of two. "My children have a pretty good model of a fulfilled person. They see me with a satisfying career and I have a community of people who nurture me."
- "I never washed a dish during the entire time I was married," confessed one man. "Now I run a household on my own. We hang out at home and my kids invite their friends over. They seem to consider my place home."
- "I didn't think I could learn to discipline," one woman said. "My husband did the discipline while we were married; I didn't know how to make my kids take me seriously. All I

did was yell and scream and then give in. Now I hold the line."

Make a list of at least ten things you feel good about. Think of some of the everyday events, precious moments, or times when you genuinely feel that you are a good parent and doing your best. To ward off your guilt demons you must remind yourself that you're only human, that you're doing the best job you can.

2. RECLAIM YOUR IDENTITY

Once you have learned to keep your guilt demons quiet, you're ready to start the building process. The next step is to reclaim your identity. Your marital relationship may have provided definition for what you thought, how you felt, for your very hopes and dreams. In obvious and subtle ways, marriage determines habits and behavior. Your marriage gave you an anchor, someone who knew where you were, someone to check in with, and someone who cared about your well-being. When marriage ends, the entire structure crumbles. You're stripped of familiar habits, routines, and rituals and the security that they provide.

After their divorce people often feel lost or at loose ends. One of the startling realizations many people have is how much of themselves they sacrificed or lost during their marriage. Divorce provides you with an opportunity to resurrect the self you lost, an occasion to discover the new you. This can be an exciting, rich time. These are some things my clients have done to recover aspects of themselves.

- "It had been ten years since I picked up my tennis racket and thought of finding a game," Raymond said. "I went so long without playing that I wasn't sure I remembered how to serve. My wife hated tennis. She thought it was a game for snooty, rich people, so I gave it up. I used to watch matches on TV, but she even gave me a hard time about that."
- "My husband wouldn't let me wear frilly, feminine clothes," said Vicki. "I never did figure out whether he felt threatened by my looking sexy or if he just liked a more natural look. He

would complain if I wore makeup. I wanted to please him, so I dressed in casual, loose-fitting clothes. I finally gave up wearing makeup altogether. I didn't think much about it until after my divorce. One day I went into my closet and found a sexy, red, tight-fitting dress that I hadn't worn in years. I put it on and made myself up and realized how much I had missed feeling like a sexy, alive, pretty woman. I hated the organic, Earth Mother look!"

- "I think I got married and had children to avoid going out into the world," confessed Ginger, an obviously intelligent redhead who'd been a model before she married. "It was a nice safety net because I didn't know who I was or what I wanted to do. For years I pretended that I wasn't intellectual or smart because my husband was intimidated when I expressed an opinion. I recently applied to graduate school. When I got my acceptance I felt competent for the first time in my life. It's an incredible feeling. I'm becoming a fuller version of me!"

One way to define yourself is to remember who you were and what you did before you got married. In recalling your past, you will gather the strength you'll need to establish a new life for yourself. Carrie, a mother of two, came to me for therapy. She walked into my office looking dejected and unsure. Her shoulders were hunched over, her hair hung down over her eyes, and she dropped into the chair like a rag doll.

Carrie, 36, had been married to Rick, a high-powered corporate executive who had been extraordinarily critical. "I never felt like I was good enough for Rick," Carrie explained with tears in her eyes. "Nothing I did was ever appreciated. I felt more like Rick was a punishing father and I was a bad little girl rather than two married adults." Her husband had focused on her worst qualities. His acid comments had eaten away at anything solid in her self-image.

"I shut myself down during the first year of our marriage," she remembered. "Unfortunately, I stayed for twelve more years. Day by day, I felt worse about myself. I actually had the sensation of shrinking." By the time she left her marriage, Carrie's self-esteem was nonexistent. She was able to give herself credit for having the courage to leave, but now here she was on her own with two kids and she felt this big hole in her gut. "I feel like I lost myself," she complained. "Little by little, I just disappeared. I desperately need to find myself again."

Over the next several months Carrie and I worked to exorcise the negative messages she had internalized from her emotionally abusive husband. Once she was able to decrease the steady stream of negative self-talk we slowly began to uncover what she wanted for herself and her children.

I asked her to do an exercise in which she went back in time to a period before her marriage, a time when she felt good about herself. I suggested that she close her eyes and recall the experience in as much detail as possible. I asked her to remember who she was with, what she was doing. It could be a time when she felt important to someone whom she respected and whose opinion she valued. It might have been a time when she did something that only she could have done in that particular way. It could have been a time when she was getting things accomplished. Or perhaps it was in a relationship where she shared some difficult-to-express feelings and connected on a deeper level.

After sitting quietly for a few moments Carrie opened her eyes and told me about her time in a New York City art school, where she majored in photojournalism. Her senior project was a photo essay of a mental institution. "I spent every weekend for three months getting to know a group of inmates and photographing them. I couldn't believe the conditions that they lived in. Most had been abandoned by their families; some were so heavily medicated that they sat like rocks, staring into space. I was fascinated by their stories." After countless hours in her darkroom Carrie handed in what she considered her twelve best prints. A few weeks later she received notice saying that her work was to hang in a student exhibit at the Museum of Modern Art. "I couldn't believe it," she told me. "I was the only person from my school whose work was chosen. Even as I tell you, I can feel the pride and satisfaction not only from having my work recognized, but for documenting these forgotten people." As Carrie recalled this positive experience, her entire demeanor changed. Her fact lit up, she sat taller in her chair, and was more energetic.

I pointed out this dramatic difference to Carrie. "Yeah, I feel more like the person I was before I met Rick," she replied. "I'd forgotten about that part of my life. Now I can bring it back and build on it." I asked her to continue recalling positive feelings and interests she had prior to her marriage. I suggested that she record positive memories in a journal. Over the next several months Carrie reported memories of other "peak experiences," as well as recollections of long-lost interests and relationships that had been good. Once Carrie had dug down to her foundation of self-esteem she could take a clear look at who she was now, a veteran of a thirteen-year marriage and a mother of two terrific children.

Reclaiming yourself marks a major turning point. You have survived the dark night of the soul and are now coming out into the light of day. It's time to reclaim personal qualities, interests, and beliefs that may have been overshadowed in your marriage. Only by reclaiming who you are can you know what is important to you.

Redefining Yourself Exercise

This is an exercise that I assign to participants in my seminars. Read the instructions, then find a comfortable chair to sit in and close your eyes.

Get into a comfortable sitting position with your arms and legs uncrossed. Relax and become aware of your breathing. Now imagine an empty chair in front of you and picture a person sitting in front of you, someone you knew in the past and really cared for, but whom you haven't seen or talked to in at least five years. This could be a college roommate, your best friend from high school, a teacher or mentor, etc. In as much detail as possible visualize the person's features, clothing, and coloring. See this person as vividly as you can. Once you have this image clear in your mind's eye, begin to describe yourself. Remember, it's been a while since you've been in contact with one another. You want to impress this person with who you are and what you have accomplished. Tell about your interests, attributes, strengths, and accomplishments. Imagine that you are talking with an old friend for whom you cared deeply. You want this person to appreciate and respect you. Once you have visualized yourself talking with your friend, take a sheet of paper and write down all your attributes and accomplishments. This exercise will help you to get a clearer picture of who you are, what you have accomplished, and what you have to offer.

Discovering Your Cutting Edge Exercise

What psychological or emotional challenges do you face right now? What part of yourself do you want to strengthen? What qualities do you want to cultivate? What interests do you want to rekindle or pursue? What do you want to achieve in your work life? With your children? What qualities do you want in a new relationship? This inventory will give you a better idea of where you want to focus your time, energy, and attention.

3. RESTORE YOUR SELF-ESTEEM

Many people come away from divorce believing there is something fundamentally wrong with them because they couldn't make their marriage work. "My wife rejected me," one man said angrily in a seminar. "It bothered me that she fell so quickly into another guy's arms. I was so hopeful that our marriage would last; I knew we had problems, but I really thought we could work them out. My self-esteem took a beating; I was afraid that no one would find me attractive."

If you're like most people who have gone through divorce, you probably question your judgment and your ability to build a satisfying new life. For many, this is the first time in their adult lives that they are without partners. One of the first steps in rebuilding self-esteem is to get comfortable with solitude. As the theologian Paul Tillich said, "Loneliness is a word to express the pain of being alone. Solitude is a word to express the glory of being alone."

Learning to Like Your Own Company

During my interviews for this book I heard numerous people confess to having felt alone even while married. If your relationship lacked warmth, love, emotional support, and companionship, you too probably felt lonely. Loneliness has little to do with external circumstances and everything to do with how you feel about yourself. Studies have shown that people who suffer from ongoing feelings of loneliness have low self-esteem. They fear rejection, have difficulty forming close relationships, and don't like their own company.

After their divorce people often try desperately to avoid being alone. They enter a phase in which they jump immediately into a new superficial relationship, become overly involved in work, or race through a string of one-night stands. These distractions keep you from confronting the fact that you really are alone.

You have your children, of course, but you are now the only adult in the house. Until you admit to feelings of loneliness you can't do anything to alleviate the problem. Loneliness is a result of a lack of real emotional warmth. Once you admit to having this need you can begin to find ways to satisfy it.

"Being alone was hard for me in the beginning," said one of my clients. "I missed the companionship of a relationship. I missed caring for someone and having someone care for me. I missed how I felt when I was in a relationship. I used to cry a lot about being alone." She finally realized that she could be dating, but by then her priorities were different. She had a standard for a relationship and she wasn't ready to give someone that type of commitment. She was being pulled in too many directions by other demands.

"For a long time I was afraid of being alone," she said, "but I'm learning to enjoy being by myself. I'm starting to do things that make me happy and not wait for someone to rescue me. I go to the library, check out books, and read like I used to. I used to enjoy going to the movies by myself and I'm doing that again. I'm rekindling old interests, like hiking and watching soccer. And I'm discovering new ones. I just started to take piano lessons. I'm no Keith Jarrett, but I'm really enjoying myself. I really like my newfound sense of freedom."

Before you reach out to others first you have to love, accept, and appreciate yourself. In the course of marriage and divorce you've probably lost sight of who you are, what you have to offer, and what makes you happy. In my workshops I ask participants this question: "If you neglected your friends the way you neglected yourself, would you have any left?" Many people answer no.

During this period especially, you need to treat yourself with love, respect, understanding, and compassion. In effect, you need to learn how to become your own best friend. As the humorist Sam Levenson said, "Remember, my son, if you ever need a helping hand you'll find one at the end of your arm." Ask yourself what qualities you value in a friendship. Make a list of them. Cultivate these qualities in order to be a supportive friend to yourself.

Use your time alone for self-discovery. "I can't remember ever being alone in all the years I was married," said Alicia, a perky brunette with a go-for-it attitude. "We were either always together or we were with the kids." Now for the first time in years she has whole days to herself. Her ex takes the kids some weekends and she has space just for herself.

"I feel like a kid in a candy shop," she said. "Last weekend after the kids left I put on my favorite Barbra Streisand CD, went out into the garden, and cleaned out some flower beds. Then I lay in the grass and felt the sun on my skin and just breathed in the warm spring air. The kids were spending their Easter vacation with their father and I had wondered about being alone for ten days, but to my amazement I enjoyed myself. I bought food I liked to eat; I did yoga in the living room without my kids making fun of me. I began to savor being by myself. I was able to sit quietly and listen to my feelings. I felt a new sense of freedom almost like beginning my life all over again. Now I look forward to time alone. It's such a wonderful feeling to enjoy my own company."

Take Good Care of Yourself

After divorce, it is easy to feel overwhelmed by everyday demands. Without realizing it you can lose sight of your own needs. Now, more than ever, you need to learn the art of selfishness. I'm not advocating that you ignore your children and their needs and retreat to an elegant spa, but I am suggesting that you make an effort to care for yourself on a regular basis.

You're going through a major life transition; the better you care for yourself, the better able you will be to care for your children. Be gentle with yourself; do the things that make you feel good. This is a time of high stress and you need extra TLC. Pay close attention to your body, be sure to eat well, exercise, and get plenty of sleep. Make yourself a priority—that is a necessity, not a luxury.

Learning to care for yourself physically as well as emotionally will help increase your self-esteem. Make a list of at least five things you like to do. Now ask yourself when the last time was you did any of them. Make a commitment to do at least one within the next week. Start simply. Buy yourself some flowers, rent a video, take a bubble bath, go for a walk with a friend. Not only do you need it, you deserve it!

Keep a Sense of Humor

Rule number one in the Parents' Guide to Staying Sane: Don't take yourself too seriously. Cultivate a sense of humor. Laughter is healing. We tend to take ourselves and our lives very seriously. Humor can be a temporary relief from pain and worry, and laughter often permits a new perspective on a troubling situation.

I have a close friend who is also a single parent and a writer. We refer to ourselves as the Fruit Loop sisters because we act so crazy with one another. No matter how upset I may be, when I talk to Celeste I find myself laughing. The other day I had an upsetting phone conversation with Ama's father about college tuition. I handled the interaction well, but when I hung up I felt angry. I called Celeste and said, "I have a call in to Uncle Nunzio. I'm thinking of taking out a contract on Ama's dad."

"They'll lock you up," Celeste replied.

"I know. But I've thought it over and it's worth it. A clean, dry cell, three meals a day, and the chance to read good novels—how bad could it be?"

There was a long pause at the other end of the phone and Celeste finally asked, "Do you think Nunzio would do a two-for-one deal and we could include my ex? It would be much more fun to have a pal in the pen." We cracked up and my funk lifted. Try to take yourself and your problems lightly. Being able to laugh at yourself makes hard times tolerable.

Cultivate an Attitude of Acceptance and Self-Respect

We are all doing the best we can with what we know. I remind parents regularly that if they knew better, they'd do better. There is no such thing as a perfect person or a perfect parent, perfection being out of reach for mortal human beings. Just because you make mistakes or fail at something doesn't mean that *you* are a failure. To succeed in life you have to participate. Now is not the time to retreat into your shell. You need to take risks and get involved in your new life.

Most of us are hard on ourselves when we make a mistake or feel insecure. We often become self-critical, thinking that beating ourselves up will help us to change. The truth is that before you can change your behavior, you must accept where you are now. Only then can you take the steps necessary to make the change. Imagine what you would do if one of your children felt frightened about going to school for the first time. You'd probably pick him up, wipe away his tears, and reassure him. This same strategy needs to be applied to you. You are embarking on a new journey. Like any pioneer, you need proper provisions; in this case, love, support, acceptance, patience, and understanding.

The more caring, gentle, and accepting you can be with yourself, the faster healing will take place. Patience is in great demand and in short supply, but now, more than ever, you need to be kind to yourself. A friend once taught me a chant that I still use when I am overly critical and impatient with myself. Repeat this phrase over and over again to a simple melody of your choice: "I love myself. I am gentle with myself." As you do you will change your inner attitude and adopt a more accepting attitude.

In the chapter on getting an emotional divorce you learned to recognize your Doomsday voice. Now I'd like to introduce you to your nurturing inner parent or friend. Yes, you do have one. That part of you may not be as visible or developed as you would like, but the only way to cultivate it is to listen and encourage its presence in your life. The next time you are feeling apprehensive, imagine how you would treat a child who came to you feeling the same way. For example, imagine you are going out with someone for the first time. You're feeling nervous. What would you need to hear to make you more comfortable? A supportive parent or friend might say, "Relax, your date is probably just as scared. You're a wonderful person and you have a lot to offer. You have a great sense of humor, you're intelligent, you're interesting. Just be yourself and you'll do just fine." Wouldn't this kind of support be helpful?

You can awaken this nurturing, supportive part of yourself even though your efforts may feel awkward at first. Becoming your own best friend or supportive parent means treating yourself with every bit as much tenderness and compassion as you would a troubled buddy. Just imagine that you are the most supportive, reassuring confidant anyone could have. This kind of internal support enables you to cope with even the most difficult situations.

When you're making important changes and taking big risks, the last thing you need is a critical voice giving you a running commentary on everything you are doing wrong.

"I took my son on a vacation to Club Med thinking that there would be a lot of single parents and single people there," Lois explained during a support group meeting. But when they got to Ixtapa she found she was the only single person in the entire club. "I felt so alone and out of place," she remembered. "I thought the couples were looking at me with pity thinking, 'Poor dear, she doesn't have anybody.' I wanted to spend the entire week in my room."

Her son went off to play with the other kids, so she really was on her own. "I stayed in my room and read a book, but after a couple of hours I realized that I was hiding," she said. "I remembered what you had said during group about being supportive of yourself. I asked my nurturing parent to give me a pep talk. If I ever needed her, now was the time. I heard myself saying, 'Lois, it took courage for you to come down here on your own. I give you a lot of credit. Remember, you've always made friends easily. The first step is to get out where the people are. I know you can do it. Give it a try. If you're too uncomfortable you can always come back up to this dark, cinder block cell.' "

She finally decided to venture out. "I put on my bathing suit, walked down to the pool, and sat down next to a friendly couple who immediately started chatting with me. I thought to myself, 'What a wonderful relationship they have.' I felt incredibly jealous."

Lois spent the rest of the day swimming, playing volleyball, and taking wind-surfing lessons. Once she had gotten out of her room she had a great time. That night she made herself go to a dance. She was the only single person there, but she danced with staff members and enjoyed herself immensely. The next morning at breakfast the friendly wife of the couple she had met the day before sat down at Lois's table and confided how miserable she was in her marriage.

"As I listened to her, my feelings of shame began to melt away," Lois said. "I remembered why I decided to get divorced, how much my life had improved, and how well I was doing on my own. After all, I could afford to take us to Club Med and was enjoying being on my own."

Change happens more easily when you have support. Think of yourself as your own best friend. When you are in a difficult situation, imagine what a supportive parent or friend would say or do. Then do the same thing for yourself. It's much easier to face challenges, change old habits, or take risks when you feel some inner support.

Get in the Habit of Giving Yourself a Message of Love and Appreciation

Most people spend too much time thinking about their shortcomings and what they've done wrong. In an average day the average person thinks fifty thousand thoughts. Unfortunately, the majority are negative and self-critical. How much better to shift the focus to incorporate self-love and appreciation. This concept may sound strange and perhaps may even make you feel uncomfortable. From early childhood most of us have been taught to be cheerleaders for others, not ourselves. In order to make the necessary changes, you need to lead some cheers for the valuable, unique, courageous person that you are. Imagine how different your life would be if every morning when you awakened you gave yourself a message of love and appreciation. It could sound something like "I love me, I value me." Consider giving yourself this message several times a day, like a psychological vitamin pill.

As you get into this habit you will notice a greater sense of inner calm. And as you get more comfortable with internal support you will find it easier for you to build a network of supportive friends.

4. BUILD A SUPPORT NETWORK

These are some of the sweetest words you'll ever hear:

> "How are you doing? If you need to talk I'm available."
>
> "I know being on your own can be overwhelming and I just want you to know that I'm here for you."
>
> "Why don't you bring the kids over and leave them with me for a few hours and take a break?"
>
> "Your kids are lucky to have you for a parent. You're really doing a great job helping them to make the adjustment."
>
> "Why don't we play hooky today and do something fun?"

Now ask yourself the following questions: When you're upset who do you talk to? When you have a decision to make and you need someone to help you kick an idea around, to whom do you turn? When you need a break from your kids, who do you ask? When you need to share your deepest fears, concerns, and hopes, to whom do you reach out?

If you are like most people your answer to many of these questions is your friends. Friendships can take many forms, from childhood friends to people who share a common interest, to neighbors, co-workers, older people, or those you consider kindred spirits. A single parent needs a community of support. One of the most difficult aspects of being a single parent is the feeling of isolation. Cultivating a circle of friends helps break the isolation barrier. "One of the things I find most difficult about being a single parent is not having another adult to share in the decision-making process," said Beth, a once-shy homebody who blossomed after divorce. "Sometimes I really feel like the Lone Ranger. I need someone that I can discuss the everyday things that come up, from Amy's cough to where to get a baby-sitter when I have out-of-town meetings. I don't think I could make it without my friends. They're my lifeline."

A network of friends is vital to divorced parents, but nurturing a friendship can be difficult when you have too many demands on your time. Many parents who go through divorce pull up the drawbridge and focus all their attention on their children. For your sanity and emotional well-being, you must cultivate adult friendships. Friends are an essential part of self-care. "I learned networking," said Karen, an independent New Englander who was slow to warm up, even to me, her therapist. "At first I would rather have made an appointment with a dentist than asked anyone a favor. But I found that other mothers can be wonderful when you let them know what you need. I started out by practicing on safe people. I'd take a deep breath and force myself to ask, 'Would you watch my son for a couple of hours while I run errands?' I was continually amazed at how truly generous and giving people were. The school officials, teachers, and my neighbors all pitched in when I needed help. I think that building a support network is one of the most important things a single parent can do."

Try to stay in touch with other parents, especially those with children close to your children's ages. They will provide you with a reality check when you are certain your child is truly troubled, the only kid in the world who refuses to sleep in his own bed. Having a network of other parents as friends decreases that horrible sense of alienation and eliminates your fear that you're the only one who is confused, conflicted, and unstable. The reality is that most parents are crazy a good part of the time, whether they have a partner or not!

Divorce Isn't Contagious

When it comes to friends divorce often separates the wheat from the chaff. "Friends who were married avoided me because I was single," one woman said during a support group meeting. "A couple of my friends suddenly didn't have time to see me. Maybe they perceived me as a threat. Either they thought I would go after their husbands or my divorce was contagious. I don't know. But a special few were really there for me."

She had learned the meaning of a true friend. Several who she considered close were really fair-weather friends. When times got tough they went south. "I learned to cherish the ones who stood by me," she said. "I've also started to develop a few new single women friends." When old friends drop out of your life as a result of your divorce, you know it's time to cultivate new ones. This can be painful, but their lack of commitment says more about them than it does about you. Use the time to branch out and cultivate some new relationships.

For men, reaching out for new friends can be even more challenging, especially if they relied on their wives to organize their social lives. Get creative in finding ways of reaching out. Either rekindle old friendships or start new ones.

You may have to take the initiative. Your old friends may be waiting to hear from you now that you have started a new life. Or you can meet new people at work, at your health club, at your children's school, in classes, or at political rallies. The possibilities are endless. Keep an open mind and you'll be amazed at the amount of support available.

Choose friends who support your growth but also challenge you. "I have a few very close friends," said Gladys, a chic, rail-thin public relations director for a social service agency. "They don't let me get down on myself. They point out all the great things I'm doing and help me to recognize my strengths. A lot of the time I don't believe them and I argue with them, but they don't let me get away with my crap." Gladys's friends let her know when she's being hard on herself and losing her perspective. "I'm always amazed that after knowing all they know about me they love me just the same," she said. The joy of having good friends is part of building your new life. Even when you enter a new romantic relationship, the love and support your friends afford you is irreplaceable. Cherish and honor your friendships and they will add richness to your life.

Where Do I Get My Support Exercise

Make a list of the resources in your life. Take a moment and think about what currently serves as your support system, in terms of physical as well as emotional support. Do you get the help of kind words from family members, your children's school, neighbors, friends, co-workers, other parents, a therapist? Ask yourself, "Do I have enough support in my life?" Once you have made your list, see if you need to strengthen or expand your support system. If you do, make a commitment to make the necessary changes.

5. REDISCOVER YOUR SEXUALITY

After divorce, confidence is shaken to the core. You begin to question your judgment. "How could I have been so blind?" "How could I have been so stupid?" "I don't know if I'll ever be able to trust myself again." You wonder about yourself as a sexual partner, you question your emotional capacity, you doubt your desirability. Your natural tendency may be to vow celibacy, run out and buy a nun's habit or priestly vestments and head for the nearest monastery. But now isn't the time to crawl back under the covers. The only way to regain your self-confidence and self-respect is to jump back into life. No, I'm not suggesting that you devote your waking hours to finding your soulmate or that you become a regular at your local singles bar. What I am suggesting is that you spend time with the opposite sex (or the same sex, if that is your sexual orientation) and start to regain your self-confidence as an attractive, desirable man or woman.

There will probably be several hurdles to overcome when you enter the dating world. "How do I meet someone?" you will ask. "Between a demanding career and taking care of my kids how can I find time?" "Is it possible to be a good parent and be sexually active?" If you are asking yourself these kinds of questions, take heart. You're not alone. Here are some comments from participants in my support groups and counseling practice. You'll probably recognize yourself in the concerns they are expressing.

- "It's great to be a woman again. I'm about to turn forty and I feel like my life is just starting to come together," one woman confided during a counseling session. "But entering the dating world with a purple scar from a C-section on my stomach, stretch marks, and one breast about a half an inch lower than the other is terrifying. I'm scared that men won't find me attractive when they realize that I'm a mother. Believe me, I'm sexy and fun and I love to laugh, but when I'm with my kids I'm a mother a hundred and fifty percent. It's hard to blend the two."

- "The beginning was the worst," one man confessed. "I was damaged goods. I felt like anyone who went out with me was getting a wreck. My brother fixed me up with a blind date and we all went out together. The woman was attractive, bright, and funny. She was everything I like, but I felt like an alien from outer space. I didn't know what to say or do. It took a long time before I felt comfortable going out. It's not like when I was in my twenties and there were women everywhere. Now it's almost impossible to meet people. I'm working, I have a daughter, and I'm a lot more selective. This is really hard. I'd much rather be in a relationship."
- "It's wonderful to feel sexy and alive again," said another woman. "I have had several great affairs, but I can't connect that part of me with being a mom. Good moms aren't supposed to be sexually active with men other than their children's father. And I'm afraid that if a serious suitor does come into my life I'll throw myself away all over again. I'll say, 'Who do you want me to be?' and try to be just that."
- "There're just not enough hours in the day," said still another. "I'm a nurse. I get up at five A.M. By the time I get home and take care of my daughter I'm too tired to even think about going out. Dating sounds great in the abstract, but do you think they could deliver the guys to my house?"

Despite your trepidation, rediscovering love and sex are essential to building your new life. Everyone has misgivings about reentering the dating world, especially since we have experienced the pain and loss of ending an important relationship. You have to take yourself by the hand and move past your discomfort and ease yourself back into the world.

One of the best ways to meet people is by doing what you enjoy. Join the Sierra Club, get involved in a political campaign, volunteer at a homeless shelter, take a class at your local community college. Doing the things you love will bring you in contact with people who share a common interest. Have you ever noticed that people who are passionate about something are always more attractive? The key to meeting people is to leave your house, unless, of course, you want to limit your circle to plumbers, repairmen, gardeners, or Avon ladies.

A common pitfall for people reentering the singles world is eliminating perfectly nice people on the basis of unrealistic expectations or standards. Keep an open mind. The goal isn't to meet Ms. or Mr. Right but to rediscover yourself as an attractive, desirable sexual being. You can find satisfaction in a variety of relationships. "I have a boyfriend I've been dating for two years," Nora explained. "Our relationship is never going anywhere, but it has its advantages. He's not demanding, he likes my kids, he doesn't compete with their father, and I have someone in my life. I recognize the disadvantages; he definitely has some issues with intimacy. But I've come to accept the relationship for what it is. Maybe this is all I want right now."

Then There's the Kids!

There is one extra element that can make dating even more challenging: the children. "In the beginning I felt like I had never been out on a date in my entire life," said an exceptionally pretty participant in one of my seminars. "I felt like such a novice that I couldn't understand why anyone would ask me out. It was really strange. Men did find me attractive and I did start dating, but having children in the house made dating even more awkward. I felt torn; it was great to be responded to as a woman again, but I wasn't willing to compromise my kids for my need to go out. My concerns now are so much different than before I had children."

Parents often find that dating has changed dramatically. They have to make new compromises. "When I was involved with a man sexually I would see him only when my children were away or I would go to his house," said a woman whose unhappy fifteen-year marriage had made her ultracautious about emotional commitment. "I didn't want my children to be involved in my dating until I met someone I was really serious about. I've managed to be a good mom and have a social life too." Making a satisfying social life is difficult but crucial. Despite your children's protests about your going out, they are relieved when parents have lives of their own. Kids don't want you to focus all of your time, attention, and energy on them. When you acknowledge and attend to your own needs, you provide your children with a healthy role model.

"In the beginning I had these fantasies of meeting Mr. Right and becoming a new family," said Darcy, a young woman who had married right out of high school. "I would introduce my daughter to my dates and she would get attached to them. There was a time when I was seeing two men at once. Josie, who was six at the time, knew that serious boyfriends stayed overnight. I never thought much about it until one morning when she asked me if that was Gerald or Daniel in the bathroom. At that point I realized that I had to stop acting like an adolescent and be more responsible. I realized that it wasn't just me. My daughter was also affected by my actions. After that, I stopped having dates sleep over while Josie was home. I had to be more responsible."

Most single parents choose not to introduce their dates to their children until they are seriously involved. "I keep my dating life completely separate from my kids," one man said. "Now that I've been seeing the same woman for eight months and we're planning on living together I have gradually introduced my children to her." There is a delicate balance between keeping your dating private and letting your children know that you have a healthy social life. Your children may be matter-of-fact about your dating, but by waiting to involve a new person in their lives you save your children from having to face another unnecessary loss.

Go Slow

"I really took my time before I got seriously involved in a new relationship," one woman said at a support group meeting. "I didn't know what I was doing; I was stuck in the old pattern of wanting to take care of somebody and wanting him to take care of me. I decided to take some time for myself before I got immersed in someone else's life again. I finally feel secure enough to be in a relationship without losing myself completely. I'm thirty-seven and not the gorgeous young chick I was when I met my husband, but I certainly know a whole lot more about myself and what I want. And I wouldn't trade that for anything in the world."

In the year following divorce most people have one of two reactions: either they avoid dating altogether or they embark on a quest to find a new partner. For many, the natural tendency is to lose themselves in a new relationship. Despite this impulse, it is essential that you take some time to get to know yourself. Find out who you are and what you want before you jump back into another committed relationship. This is a period of tremendous personal growth. Take the time to nurture your strengths, abilities, and interests. Use this second chance to ignite your joy and passion. When you are content and intensely involved in your own life, you are more likely to attract another mature, whole adult. The better you know yourself, the more you will bring to your next relationship.

Divorce opens up many opportunities. What you make of your new life is up to you. You can use this time to examine the mistakes you made in your marriage, redefine what's important in relationships, and discover the direction you want your life to take. You are beginning a new life, but now you are stronger and more confident than you were before. Whether or not you choose to have another partner in your life, you will always have yourself. *Carpe diem*, seize the day. Use this second chance wisely.

Chapter 11

What Kids Have to Say

A child's life is a piece of paper on which every passerby leaves a mark.

Chinese proverb

This book wouldn't be complete without a word from the children. The children and young adults you are about to meet range in age from eight to twenty-two. The youngest was two when his parents divorced and the oldest was seventeen. These children come from various socioeconomic and ethnic backgrounds. Some live with mothers who are barely able to keep up with expenses; others are from affluent families and shuttle between two well-maintained homes.

Despite their diverse backgrounds, these young people had two things in common. All were eager to talk about growing up with divorce in the hope of clarifying for themselves what the experience had meant. And they also wanted to help other children avoid some of the pain they had suffered. Their names, too, have been changed to protect their privacy, but I have retained their wisdom by relaying their vivid descriptions in their own words.

One thing was clear: No matter how their parents ended their marriages, the divorce played a crucial role in these children's lives. No matter their age, economic background, or custodial arrangement, that event left an indelible impression. Many of these children welcomed their parents' divorce as an end to a tension-filled home life, but the divorce itself was, and continues to be, a defining experience in their lives.

What is it like to grow up in a divorced family? The children you are about to meet will shed some light on what they found to be helpful and hurtful. Let's hear what they have to say.

FINDING OUT ABOUT THE DIVORCE

"My parents never told me anything," recalled Claudia, a round-faced nine-year-old. "One day I came home from school and my father's things were gone. I was scared. I wasn't sure where my dad had gone or whether I'd get to see him again. It would have helped if he had told me what was happening. Of course it still would have been hard, but not as hard as having him just vanish."

In some families children aren't informed about their parents' decision. No explanation is offered. Many parents favor secrecy and their children pay the price.

Allan, 18, was only seven when his mother and father divorced. Looking back, he realized that the way his parents handled the situation was awful. "No one said anything. At first I thought we were moving. Then I thought that I was going to just be by myself with my mom. I finally figured it out for myself. They acted like I wasn't going to be affected by the whole thing." For a while he felt as if his dad were his ex-dad. "I was very sad," he remembered. "I cried a lot. Finally my mom explained that she and my dad couldn't live together anymore, but that my dad would still be in my life. I wish she had told me sooner so that I didn't feel so worried. Having separate homes sounded okay as long as I knew I could still see my dad."

Claudia and Allan express the frustration of many children who are left in ignorance. Letting them know about the divorce wouldn't have changed the situation, but it would have mitigated some of their fears. Telling them the why of the decision and describing the new living arrangement would have helped them cope with the imminent changes.

Other children recalled a better experience. They were given a clear explanation of their parents' decision. As difficult and as painful as it was to hear the life-altering news, all of these kids felt relieved.

"My mother sat me down and told me she and my dad were getting a divorce," said Linda, a seventeen-year-old high school senior who was thirteen when her parents divorced. "She was more upset than I was. She said that my dad was going to get an apartment in the area and that I could go back and forth between the houses whenever I wanted to.

"They thought that I would take it a lot harder, but I knew from the beginning that it was the best thing. Of course, it wasn't a happy time, but I didn't feel sad." Linda's parents had fought constantly. If they hadn't told her they were going to separate she was going to tell them to get a divorce. "They just weren't happy," she recalled. "All the fighting and violence was too much. It was upsetting to hear my parents screaming at one another. So the divorce wasn't a shock to me. I was waiting and waiting for it to happen." For Linda the news came as a relief. The stress between her parents had been causing her to spend more and more time away from home; the divorce offered a welcome respite from living in a war zone.

For Carlos, 15, the news came as a surprise. His parents did tell him and his sister about their decision, but Carlos was left with many unanswered questions and a lot of confusion. "They sat my sister and me down in the den," he remembered. "It was just after Thanksgiving and I thought they were going to tell us my dad had lost his job. They told us on a Saturday night about ten minutes before I was going out. My dad did most of the talking and my mom was crying. My father was the one who wanted the divorce. He said that he and my mother were having problems and that things weren't working out between them. He told us that he was going to move out for a while and eventually it was going to lead to divorce. They never fought so I had no idea that anything was wrong.

"That night I went to a party and I remember feeling really out of it. I wish they had told us more details and had left more time for us to ask questions, but I guess they just wanted to get it over with. I was thinking wild thoughts like I'm going to have two houses and two more parents when my real parents get remarried. . . ."

Parents who keep their children in the dark about serious marital conflicts don't prepare them for the reality of what's to come. That, combined with insufficient opportunity to ask questions, can add to their stress. Let your children know about your decision to divorce and what they can expect, at least in the immediate future. Keep in mind that talking to your kids is an ongoing process. Open communication is necessary if they are to cope successfully with this dramatic change in their lives.

EFFECTS OF DIVORCE

In interview after interview children gave credit to the divorce for their greater sense of independence. Laurie, 17, was nine when her mother and father separated. "At first I was angry that I had to take care of myself," she said. "My mom would leave for work before I left for school, so I would wave good-bye and wait at home until it was time for me to leave. It used to be that my mother would wave good-bye to me every morning. Then, all of a sudden, I was home waving good-bye to her. I had to get used to coming home after school and being alone. I was just a kid; I didn't think I should have to do that. But I learned at an early age to depend on myself. I think these experiences really prepared me for later life."

Jason, now 22, was just eleven when his parents divorced. He views divorce as positive. "I've learned a lot about independence and that no one is going to do it for me," he said. "I've learned that my life is what I make it; I have to take charge of it and make it work. My ideals and goals are realistic. I grew up in a very realistic setting; I wasn't jetting off to ski in Colorado as many of my friends were. All my dreams have been small dreams that I've been able to realize through hard work. . . . My parents' divorce made me grow up. I learned a whole lot at a very young age."

There were times, however, when being left on their own felt more like a burden than a gift. Alicia's parents divorced during her junior year in high school. "I was under a lot of pressure at school, plus all the emotional stuff going on," she recalled. "I was used to having my mom and dad figure things out for me. Now it was time to decide about college and I had to do the whole thing myself. I'd go to my mom and she couldn't help me, so I'd go to my dad. But they were both so caught up in getting their own lives together than I was left to do it all. There are a lot of colleges I would have rather gone to, but I made a decision just to get the whole thing over with. . . . When I had to send in my college applications, my mom would say, 'Why don't you ask your dad for the money?' My dad would send me back to my mom. I felt lost in the shuffle.

"Ever since they got a divorce I've made sure I've had a job," said Alicia, now eighteen and a college freshman. "My dad used to give me money all the time, but now I don't see him that much. I've been working a lot and saving money. And I've been trying to do more things on my own so I don't have to depend on them so much. Basically, I'm setting myself up in case I have to take care of myself."

Alicia may have been a legal adult but her air was that of an abandoned child. In fact, her parents had abandoned her, both emotionally and financially. "My parents' divorce made me more self-sufficient," she said, "but it's been really hard."

What one takes away from conversations with these young adults is that divorce is rarely all good or all bad. Dark clouds often do have silver linings—each of these children found at least one thing positive in what others consider a bad experience.

THE BURDEN OF PARENTIFICATION

Allowing children the privilege of responsibility is a far cry from burdening them with unsuitable emotional demands. In the wake of divorce, relationships between parents and their children often become inappropriately intense. Parents are tempted to turn to their kids for reassurance, companionship, or solace. The children, however, resent being robbed of their childhood.

"I didn't want to be my mother's 'friend,' " remembered Anna, a fourteen-year-old only child. "I felt smothered. My mom got really possessive and leaned on me too much," she said. "I was the only person in the world who she truly loved so there was a lot of pressure on me. I felt for her, but I didn't want to be responsible for her. That really was the worst part about the divorce, having to cater to her. It was a major chore. She wanted me to keep her company. I didn't really want to be that close with her, but I felt obligated. I had to give up my own life to take care of her. I was only eleven. All my friends were off having a good time and I had to stay home and baby-sit my mother. Things didn't really improve until she met someone else that she loved. It was hard being the only person in her life."

Children are acutely sensitive to their parents' emotional states, but this is even more true for children of divorce. Ruth, now 16, was three when her parents divorced. She recalls her elementary school years with sadness. "My mom was really moping around the house a lot and she wasn't really there for me," she said. "I never could tell her when I was upset because I would just upset her more. I had to hold everything inside. When I was in sixth grade and my friends were going out, my mom wanted to keep me at home. When I was about thirteen we went to a therapist because it seemed like she didn't want me to grow up and go away. She wanted to keep me little. . . .

"Looking back, it would have been so much better for me if she could have thought about what I needed and not been so spaced-out. She was always in her own world. I wish she had talked to me about my life or asked me about how I was feeling or what I needed. I didn't need a friend; I had plenty of those. What I needed was a mother." Ruth has a difficult time expressing her thoughts and opinions and has become a people pleaser. She has a poorly developed sense of self and is unsure of herself. Ruth struggles in her personal relationships and shies away from close friendships.

It was apparent from talking with these children that they felt obliged to assume the role of friend or confidant. They expressed a certain amount of bitterness about being forced to take care of their parents.

CAUGHT IN THE CROSS FIRE

When I asked children about the most difficult aspects of their parents' divorce, a common answer was ongoing parental battles. "It was bad enough that my parents fought like cats and dogs while they were married," recalled Randy, 16, who was a kindergartner when his parents finally separated. "But the battles raged on even after they divorced. I had hoped it would get better once they lived apart, but in some ways it seemed worse."

Randy expressed the sentiments of many. Time and time again these innocent victims would recall the pain of witnessing arguments and fighting between two people they loved.

"The worst part of the divorce was the fighting," remembered Martine, a tall, bright-eyed college sophomore. "The huge blowups and all the petty ones. It made me sad that they treated each other so badly. I remember a time when my mother pulled out a butcher knife. I knew that she was just holding it because she was frustrated, but it was scary to see her that mad. Mostly, though, it was the yelling that made me nuts. My dad would come over and he and my mom would get into these arguments. Our house was very big and open and their voices would echo. There was no getting away from the sound. The only relief was if I took my dog for a walk or went to my friend's house. But I knew I had to go back and it would just happen again. I felt like a refugee from my own home. I never understood why they were still doing this to one another; the fighting never did any good. Now that they were divorced why couldn't they let things go? But they didn't. They still argue about everything and they've been divorced for eight years." Martine's parents probably didn't want to estrange their daughter, but, in fact, that's precisely what they did. She seldom leaves college for visits home.

Robin, 8, complained that her mom and dad can't talk on the phone for more than two minutes without bickering. "It makes me get a knot in my stomach when I hear them fighting," she said. "Sometimes I just want to get away from both of them. I hate hearing them hurt each other. I just wish they'd stop."

There were times in some of these children's lives when they would have preferred not seeing their noncustodial parent in the hope of avoiding the inevitable conflict. "The last time my dad picked me up my parents got into a fight," explained Sonya, a pudgy eighth grader whose teachers worry about her being so withdrawn. "My mom started yelling at him and my dad accused her of not letting me have a relationship with him. He said he was going to get his lawyer to make her give me time with him. They were both screaming at the top of their lungs. I couldn't stand it. I felt like I was being torn in two. I ran upstairs and slammed my door and turned my music up really loud so I didn't have to hear them fighting.

"It makes me not want to even see my dad if they are going to argue," Sonya continued. "It's not worth going through that to spend time with him. When my mom and dad fight they put me right in the middle. I just want to get really small and disappear into the woodwork. I think I do a pretty good job; I pretend I'm not there. I hate hearing two people I love being so cruel to one another. I get headaches listening to them. I wish they would stop!"

As you hear from these pain-filled examples, marital conflicts take a tremendous toll on children. Children who are subjected to this kind of insensitivity are frequently depressed and withdrawn. They seem to be the only ones in the family who understand that nobody wins!

CAUGHT IN THE MIDDLE: WHEN IT'S NOT SAFE TO LOVE BOTH PARENTS

Children are very sensitive to the messages they receive from one parent about their relationship with the other. They need to feel free to love both, but some I interviewed felt pressure to pledge their allegiance to only one. "I usually take my mom's side in things," confessed Jon, a shy high school junior. "My brother and I are sort of like the jury. We have to figure out whose side to take. It's kind of weird. But mostly we stick with my mom."

Madeline, an energetic twelve-year-old, describes a similar situation. "My mom doesn't want me to spend time with my dad," she said. "When I'm with him I notice all the things that are bad about him because I know when I come back from seeing him I will get the third degree. It's not just the questions, it's the way she asks. I know she doesn't approve of my dad and she's just waiting for me to give her more evidence to build her case about why he's such a terrible person. I end up getting mad at her because I don't have any space to have a relationship with my father. I just wish she would stop putting her nose in my private business.

"It just seems like more of a hassle to see him," Madeline continued. "I feel pulled apart! I want to love my dad, but I think I have to wait until I leave home and am on my own. I just can't imagine doing it while I'm still living with my mom."

Madeline has been forced to pledge her loyalty to her mother despite her longing for a relationship with her father. Sometimes the pressure to take sides is more indirect than this, but don't think for a minute that children aren't aware of what is being asked of them.

"I can tell that my mom doesn't want me to spend time with my dad," said Jeff, a lanky thirteen-year-old with sandy blond hair. "My mom would never tell me not to see him, but I get these subtle messages. Whenever I say I'm going over to my dad's she gets this look that lets me know she doesn't like it. I don't think she likes my sister and me having another life that doesn't include her. I guess she doesn't want my dad to have good times with us."

Not only are these children deprived of an independent relationship with both parents, but they are angry about the pressure to take sides. This is a no-win situation for everyone involved.

MISSION IMPOSSIBLE

Children of divorce are frequently asked to spy. Nell, 19, is a self-assured young woman who recalls with clarity her parents' divorce when she was in junior high. "When my father remarried I had problems with my stepmother," she said. "My mom would grill me about my dad's new wife. She would use my struggle with my stepmom to say bad things about her when, in fact, she didn't even know her. It turns out that my stepmother is great, but my mom would use every opportunity to find out what my dad's new life was like.

"I can remember how she'd waited until we were driving in the car to question me," Nell went on. "I'd feel trapped and obliged to answer. As I got older I started to tell her to shut up and stop asking me stuff. I finally told her that if I wanted to tell her something I would. It wasn't like she was concerned about my dad and wanted to know if he was happy. That would have been different."

These children are also asked to keep secrets. "My dad claims he doesn't have any money and then he takes off to Hawaii for three weeks," explained Amanda, 16, whose parents divorced when she was fourteen. "It's true that my dad's a hard person to get along with. My mom won a lawsuit for fifteen thousand dollars and she hid it from my dad. She put half in my name and half in my sister's name so my dad wouldn't know about the money and try to get it from her. I felt kind of weird about it, but my mom doesn't have much money and she needed to keep it for herself. I guess it was all right to help her. . . .

"When my dad got a new apartment he bought all this nice, new, expensive furniture and I told my mom about it," Amanda continued. "I guess she brought it up to my dad and he got mad at me. He gave me the full lecture about how what he buys is his business and that I shouldn't tell anyone. I sure learned my lesson. Now I just keep my mouth shut. I don't say anything about what anyone does."

When children are pressured to reveal the private details of their other parent's life or to keep secrets, they are put in the awkward position of betraying one parent to please the other.

THE BURDEN OF CARRYING MESSAGES

Serving as message bearer was high on the children's list of divorce horrors. "Not only did my parents keep their feud alive after their divorce," says Roberta, 15, who's been dealing with her parents' divorce for seven years. "For a long time they made me deliver these evil messages. I felt more like a telephone than their child. I hated being used and then catching hell when I told them something they didn't want to hear."

James, 22, whose parents have been divorced for ten years, shares similar feelings. "There was a lot of name-calling back and forth between my parents," he said. " 'You better remind your father to pick you up on Friday. You know how unreliable he is.' 'Tell your greedy mother that I'm not going to send her check on the twenty-fifth instead of the tenth.' Tell your father . . . Tell your mother . . . It went on and on. I hated carrying messages."

Unfortunately many of the children I interviewed reported being used this way. "My dad was cheating my mom out of child support," I was told by Larry, a high school sophomore. "He wasn't giving her enough money to take care of my brother and me. My mom's a teacher and her salary was cut, so she didn't have as much money to buy us food. For a while we were just barely making it. My mom told my brother and me that whenever she asked my dad for money or even to pay the child support he skimped her on. So she wanted my brother and me to talk to him instead.

"The next weekend when we went to my dad's house we told him that we needed money for food," Larry continued. "He got really mad and yelled that he just put the check in the mail and maybe it got lost. I didn't believe him. He's always making excuses. I know there's another reason why he doesn't have a lot of money. My brother and I found drugs at his house. We found crack pipes and drug stuff in his closet. My brother and I know that the money is probably going up his nose, but we can't say anything to him. It's his life and I can't make him stop, but I feel bad about it."

Larry was not only forced to carry unwanted messages but he had to assume an adult role in his family. He and his brother had to live with the disturbing knowledge of their father's drug habit.

THE EFFECTS OF CRITICISM

Several children I interviewed shared one similar sentiment: "The worst part of divorce was that I expected things to improve, but my parents just continued to criticize one another." In too many families hostilities between parents didn't diminish after divorce. Battles between parents continued to flare up, criticism and negative comments snowballed, and the children suffered.

When I asked Sandy, 17, how her parents got along now that they were divorced, her response was "They don't. The hard thing for me is that they bad-mouth one another to me. My mom will put my dad down. She'll say, 'Your father is a cheap bastard when it comes to you. He'll lie about not having enough money but when it comes to fixing up his Corvette he finds the money.' My dad bags on my mom too. Sometimes when my sister and I are at his house he'll make fun of my mom and talk about her like she's stupid. He says things like 'Your mom's a real financial wizard. She never did have any brains when it came to money. You should see how she screwed up her income taxes. She's never going to be able to manage.' I hate him when he says things like that. Mostly I try to ignore their sniping. Sometimes I walk out of the room if they won't stop. I told my mom and dad that it bothers me, but they can't seem to control themselves."

Sandy's words were echoed by Patrick, 13, whose parents have been divorced since he was three. "My mom always criticizes my father in front of me. She'll call him stupid and a religious fanatic. She comes down on him really hard. I have to sit there silently and let her get it out. It's like she has this nasty streak inside of her.

"She puts my dad down. No matter how much I tell her I don't want to hear it she goes on, as if I hadn't said a word. I really resent her for that. Sometimes the criticism is more subtle and my mom will just slip something in with this bitter tone in her voice. She blames my dad for everything. 'Because of your dad . . .' I can always tell by her voice that she's criticizing him, sometimes it's in the undertone of what she says. I hate it. I love my dad and to hear someone say things about someone you love hurts. Plus, I know it's not true. What she says is straight-out lies. I also feel badly that she thinks so badly of my dad."

Fortunately, there are parents who don't make negative comments about their ex-spouses in front of their children. For a better understanding of the value kids place on abstention from criticism, listen to the appreciation expressed by Helen, a twenty-two-year-old film production assistant who credits her divorced parents with having done several things right. "My mom actually went through hell and high water with my dad," said Helen, "but she always lets my brother and me create our own opinion of my father. She would never speak badly of him and vice versa. She says, 'I have my experiences with him and you'll have yours. Hopefully, they will be positive.'

"My mother encouraged my brother and me to have our own thing with our dad. If I ever felt angry it was because *I* was feeling it, not because she was making me feel it. I was really free to form my own opinions about each of my parents without any pressure from either of them."

Helen went on to explain yet another way in which her mother made the divorce easier on her and her brother. "My mom was very conscientious about telling us about the good times she and my father shared. She would tell us about how they met, how excited they were when they found out she was pregnant with each of us, and about how much in love they were. When my mother talks about why she and my dad split up she explains it as a difference in backgrounds. My father was born in a Latin culture and is very traditional and my mother is a liberated Jewish woman from New York. My mother talked about their differences but never made my father out to be a bad guy. I really respect and appreciate both my parents for putting our needs first and letting us love them both."

I can't find a clearer statement of what happens when parents criticize one another than the words of twelve-year-old Alex: "I have both my mom and dad inside of me. When my mom says something bad about my dad it's like she's saying something bad about me."

LIFE *WITHOUT* FATHER

For many of these kids, divorce represented the end of their family as they had known it and also the loss of a relationship with their fathers. As Pedro, a twenty-three-year-old graphic designer, looks back, he recalls the pain of growing up without a male role model. "The worst part of my parents' divorce was that I missed my dad," he said. "When he wasn't there I always felt like something was missing. I guess my father decided that his business was more important than watching my brother and me grow up.

"I was seven when my dad split and I really needed him. My mom never remarried and it was hard without a male role model in my life. When I hit adolescence, I had a hard time changing from a boy to a man. I didn't have enough contact with my father to know how a man was supposed to act. I hated him for leaving me. Fifteen years later my father and I are starting to connect on an emotional level. I'm trying to take up where we left off."

Many of the children I interviewed did have regular contact with their fathers. Their experiences were myriad.

"My dad just lived around the corner from my mom and me,

but somehow it just wasn't the same as having him in our house all the time," said Laura, 14, who was eight when her parents separated. "I stayed overnight with my dad at least once a week, but when I went back to my mom I always missed him. A few months after my dad moved out he bought me a music box. He put it in a sports bag and gave it to me. For the longest time I carried that bag around with me everywhere I went because it smelled like him and I wanted to keep him close to me. I really missed him." Children will frequently cling to gifts and belongings of the noncustodial parents as a way to feel close and connected when away from them.

Alison's relationship with her father improved dramatically after her parents separated. "My dad used to be really impatient and uptight," she said. "He wasn't nice to my mom. He would get angry in a flash. He would blow up over nothing. My sister and I were scared of him. I hated the idea that they were getting a divorce but in a way it was better because we didn't have to be around all that tension." Alison, now fifteen, was surprised at her father's postdivorce attitude. "I never thought that this would happen, but when I have problems or need help with really personal stuff I talk to my dad," she said. "We've become friends." It is not uncommon for the parent-child relationship to improve as a result of divorce. Sometimes the absence of stress and marital tension allows parents to be more their real selves and to develop more open relationships with their children.

For some children, divorce brings additional stress. Joseph, now 17, recalls that his parents really had to split up. "A few months after my dad moved out I found out that he was gay," he said. "It was the second shock of my life. The divorce was the first one. At first I felt betrayed. It took a while for me to grasp the concept of what being gay was. I hoped gayness wasn't hereditary. Once I found out that it wasn't I got worried about who he would be hanging around with and AIDS. It just made things harder like having divorced parents wasn't bad enough. I tried to look at it like 'I have a special dad,' but still that was one more thing that made me different. By now most of my friends know that my dad is gay and they don't care. Especially my best friend, he's really cool about it."

Joseph not only had to cope with the news of his parents' divorce, he was faced with an additional factor. Yet despite an already difficult situation Joseph's father remained a big part of his son's life. "All in all, things worked out better than I expected," Joseph went on. "I see my dad more now than when we lived together. It may not actually be more time, but when we're together he really pays attention to me. So I still have my dad in my life, and he can be who he really is. I think both he and my mom are happier."

NO MORE HAPPILY EVER AFTER

Most young children expect to grow up with both a mother and a father in a happy family that will last forever. Our children learn about living happily ever after from books and television and they cling to the media's promise of security and stability. Divorce, however, forces even the youngest children to take a hard look at the reality of marriage, commitment, and family.

The children and young adults with whom I spoke all said their attitudes toward relationships had been altered by their parents' divorce. Many of these children had a much healthier and far more realistic view of marriage than their peers from intact families. Heather, 18, was eleven when her parents divorced. She shared her thoughts on marriage. "Most of my friends have divorced or separated parents. I think my generation is going to get married a lot later and be a lot more sure. I don't think we're going to get married just to get married. I've seen the mistakes that my parents made. Hopefully, I can avoid them. Number one, I'm going to wait until I feel really passionate about getting married. If it takes until I'm fifty, that's okay. My parents' lack of communication has made me realize how important it is to keep the communication going so you can work together. Because marriage is constant work.

"I don't think I'll give up so easily," Heather went on. "Sometimes it's going to be a struggle, but marriage is a life commitment. Imagining that once you have the ceremony everything is going to be like a Walt Disney movie is crazy. I know better than that."

Pedro, the twenty-three-year-old graphic designer who grew up with an absentee father, has a lot of trepidation when it comes to marriage. "Marriage scares me more than death," he says with a laugh. "I lived with a woman for four and a half years and not once did I think about marrying her. I can't see myself married, yet the idea of getting married is very appealing. I think I'd be a good husband and a great father, but it's hard to imagine making a commitment to a woman and spending the rest of my life with her. People change and there's a lot of space to change in the course of a lifetime. My changing; that's my ultimate fear.

"The divorce my parents went through was miserable," he explained. "I saw what they did to each other. I saw what it did to my brother and me. My parents have started new relationships and those failed too. Does that mean that they're failures themselves or is it something about our society and the times? I'm not sure. The only thing I know for sure is I'm scared as hell to get married."

Meg, 17, saw both parents remarry within a short time after their divorce. Her point of view differs only slightly from Pedro's. "I think you should be at least thirty before you get married," she said. "People change drastically as they grow. I don't want to do what my mom did, drop out of college and just marry someone. My mom wanted to be a physical therapist, but she gave that up. Now she really regrets giving up that part of her dream; she's starting over from scratch at forty-six. I'd have to be really mature and ready. I'd have to know what I wanted out of life before I would get married. I don't ever want to be in my mom's position.

"I think marriage is a sacred thing and I definitely want to get married, but I think you have to be really careful. It's so easy to fall in love and think that this is it. I hope I can remember what I learned from my mom and her experience and do it differently." A childhood spent with divorced parents does not doom kids to unsatisfying, failed relationships as adults. Each of these young adults expressed a sense of caution about marriage and commitment. They realize that marriage is going to require work; they want to have a strongly developed sense of self before they enter into a partnership. This is a healthier and more mature perspective than their parents' generation had. Most of us grew up believing in happily ever after.

THE SILVER LINING

When I asked these children for the benefits of their parents' divorce, the two most frequently mentioned were improved parent-child relationships and greater happiness for their parents. "My house is a much nicer place now," said Diane, 18, a tall young woman with curly blond hair. "It's just much more comfortable. My dad is really uptight and strict and it was tense when he was around. What I've learned since the divorce is that my mom and dad never communicated. They didn't really tell each other how they were feeling. They were married, but they weren't really together. That's why it turned out the way it did.

"While my mom and dad were married she was totally stressed-out. She never talked about anything; she kept it all to herself. For a long time she had trouble with her jaw. At times she couldn't eat. She held all that tension inside and it was making her sick. She went to doctor after doctor and took all kinds of pills, but nothing helped. Since the divorce my mom feels better than she ever has been. Her jaw problems have completely cleared up.

"The divorce was tough for her in the beginning but she's decided that she really wants to be her own person. She does things now she never would have done with my dad. She enrolled in classes at college and has built a group of friends rather than just being the submissive wife. She's doing things she always wanted to do. My mom married my dad when she was twenty-one. She gave up her real life to be with him. They're both much better off being divorced."

Chris, now 17, was four when his parents ended their marriage; his mother remarried two years later. When I asked Chris about the benefits of divorce, he recalled, "When my mother remarried my family got bigger. I feel loved by more people. My stepdad's whole family is now my family. I have another dimension of learning by being with them. I have another view of the world. I have two sisters from my mom and stepdad's marriage and they have enriched my life immensely. Besides, it's a lot friendlier now. My parents have more distance. Their only bond is us children and there's no regrets there; they know they got together for a good reason.

"I think I've come through the divorce and stuff pretty okay," Chris continued. "I've learned a lot from it. My mom and I were talking the other day and she was asking me if the divorce has messed me up in any way and I don't think it has. I think my family worked and I've gotten a lot of support. It's not perfect; it has its quirks. But I don't know anyone who has the ideal, perfect family. Actually, I know kids in a two-parent family who are really messed-up. So I'm not sure it's whether you come from a divorced family or a two-parent family that makes the difference. I think it has more to do with who your parents are."

ADVICE FOR DIVORCING PARENTS

At the end of each interview I asked the same question: What advice would you give parents to make divorce less painful for their kids? "Never, ever, put your child in the middle of your arguments or bad feelings," stated a twelve-year-old emphatically. "Don't tear your kids apart by involving them in your battles. Absolutely do not communicate through your kids; if you have something to say to the other parent, tell them directly."

A young man who spent most of his childhood with a distant, uninvolved father offered, "I think it's really important to have a mother figure and a father figure. Parents should promise their kids that they will be there for them. The mom or dad may not want to be there for each other, but they should still be there for their kids."

"Be honest with your kids," counseled a twenty-one-year-old. "Tell them in a straightforward way what's going on, how it happened, and why you are getting divorced. Let them know the divorce wasn't their fault. Be there for your kids; let them talk to you. Parents should let their kids ask as many questions about the divorce as they want to. And I think that kids need a lot of reassurance from their parents that they both love them and they aren't going to disappear.

"If parents fight, kids won't want to talk to them as much," he added. "Kids really need someone to talk to about the changes, no matter how old they are. Without that, it's really hard to get back to your own life and feel secure. And finally, don't criticize the other parent. If every time your son wants to talk about his feelings you put down his mom or dad, your kid isn't going to want to talk to you."

A ten-year-old suggests, "Don't argue. If you're going to argue, don't do it around your kids. Parents shouldn't involve their kids in their fights at all, in any way. Some people don't care if their kids are standing there listening to them use bad language. That's not fair to kids. When parents do that their kids grow up thinking that they can't love both their parents. Just keep it easy so that kids can see either parent whenever they want to."

And one final piece of advice from a twenty-year-old: "Friendly divorces are hard to come by. But when you see your parents communicating it feels really good."

THE FUNCTIONAL DIVORCE: WHEN DIVORCE IS POSITIVE

The media depict the typical divorce as a battle royal. In fact, high levels of hostility are not typical. Research does not support the stereotype that most divorcing couples are out for blood, that they engage in protracted legal combat, want revenge, destroy their children and families, and want their former spouse to rot in hell. This extreme applies to 25 percent or less of divorcing couples. The majority do communicate and cooperate at least about their children.[1]

Not one of the children I interviewed enjoyed his or her parents' divorce and many expressed sadness, but they all acknowledged the rightness of the decision. Several of the children I interviewed experienced what I call a "functional" divorce. They were spared the stress of divorce warfare. They were not asked to take sides; they were allowed and in many cases encouraged to love both parents; they did not hear scathing criticism. These kids have open, easy access to both parents. Their parents put their children's needs above their personal feelings and made every effort to create a healthy, loving postdivorce environment.

As I spoke with these children I was struck by their awareness of their parents' effort on their behalf. These children felt respected, protected, and cherished. And although there were some rough spots during the process, they didn't see their parents' divorce as an obstacle to their future happiness, dreams, or success as adults.

While none of their parents would describe the task of building a parenting partnership as easy, each exercised tremendous self-discipline. They made a commitment to work for the higher good. They were able to separate their relationship as parents from their relationship as a couple. They put their children's welfare over their need to control or hurt one another. Few of these parents would describe themselves as friends but all were able to cooperate successfully as parents. Their priorities were to minimize the trauma of divorce for their children and to continue being responsible parents. This required a certain degree of maturity and restraint and a lot of deep breathing, but these parents felt unanimously that their hard work was worth the effort.

Most children are strong and resilient. If divorce is handled constructively they will bounce back and thrive. Josh, 18, is a good example of what it's like to grow up in a healthy postdivorce environment. His mother and father separated when he was seven and his sister was five. "My parents weren't the fighting kind," he says. "My mom and dad called us into their bedroom and my dad told us that he was going to move into his own apartment nearby and that we would be with him half the time and with my mom the other half.

"The reason they gave was that they just weren't happy with one another anymore. Although they had loved each other when they married, that love had changed. I can remember my mother saying, 'Your father is a wonderful man, but he's just not the man for me.' Eventually, I understood what she meant; my mom and dad are really different. Now that I think back it's hard to understand how they stayed married as long as they did. My dad is into a ritzier lifestyle. He and his new girlfriend are yuppies. They like material things and prestige. My mom and her boyfriend are more into art, nature, and exercise. They care more about people than things. Now that he's divorced, my dad seems like he's more where he wants to be. My mom and dad together never could have done what they're each doing separately. I can see that they're much better off being divorced.

"My father was the one who initiated the divorce, and I have to give my mom a lot of credit. She never put him down or tried to turn me against him. I don't remember ever hearing them fight. I know they must have, but they never did it in front of me. I feel pretty lucky. Even though we don't all live together I think they've really given me a solid foundation.

"My life seems pretty normal for this day and age. Most of my friends come from divorced families. Of course, I would have liked to have had an old-fashioned–type family, but that was out from the start because both my parents worked.

"I know a lot of kids whose parents are still married and in many ways I think I'm much more mature than they are. I listen to friends talk about their relationships with their parents and mine is so much better. I know it may sound strange, but I don't have any regrets about my parents' divorce.

"I definitely want to get married and I hope I can stay married for a lifetime, but life doesn't always work out the way we plan it to. That's the most important thing I've learned. My parents and I made the best of our situation."

Now let's meet a young woman who credits her parents' respectful relationship with her healthy self-esteem. Marsha, now 20, was nine when her parents divorced. She will graduate from college with a degree in biology. "My mom and dad are opposites," she said. "My mother is British and kind of prudish and my dad's totally different; he's totally outgoing. They have different values and they just didn't get along in an affectionate way. At first I really was mad that they got divorced, but now I don't believe in staying together for the kids. I would feel like I was gypped out of a decent family life if I found out later on that it had all been fake. The divorce worked out for the best, anyway. The money was the only bad part; everything else was fine. I get my dad's attention when I'm with him, and my mom's attention when I'm with her, so it's the best of both worlds.

"I had lived in the same apartment all my life, so when my dad first moved out we arranged that my brother and I would go to his place every weekend. It was like that up until I left for college. Of course, there were times when I wanted to be with my friends instead of my dad, but he was cool about that. My friends were always welcome at his house too, so it was pretty loose. The only bad part was that we mostly spent weekends with my dad. He was the fun one and my mom was more of the business one, so I saw my dad more as a rescuer and my mom as the disciplinarian. That sometimes created stress between my mom and me.

"The funny thing about my parents is that after the divorce they became pretty friendly. They really get along well now. Neither of them have remarried. Even now my mom is always invited to my dad's house for Thanksgiving and Christmas. I think it's great because I still have both my parents. I'd much rather have it this way than have the kind of parents who don't talk to one another. I can't imagine what it would be like if they stayed together. They'd probably be throwing plates at each other. They get along so much better now because they both have lives of their own.

"My parents' divorce changed me a lot," she added. "I learned that nothing is perfect or lasts forever."

Several of the children I talked with witnessed one parent calling a halt to intolerable behavior on the part of the other parent, thus modeling for their kids' respect, responsibility, and independence. Sarah, 18, saw her mother assert herself and leave a stifling, unfulfilling marriage. "I think my mom felt squelched. She needed to have her own voice. She said one of the reasons she decided to get a divorce was because she wasn't being a good role model for my brothers and me. She wanted us to have a better image of how a woman could be. If we continued to see her submit to our dad, we might do the same thing she did. That was certainly a factor in her wanting a divorce.

"My dad was outwardly Mr. Mild Manner," she said. "He's a professor and usually all calm, cool, and collected. But any minute he would fly into a rage and yell at my mother. I remember hearing it echoing through our house. Once I dreamed that my father turned into a werewolf. His anger was really scary and our house was always so tense. There were times when there was a forced okayness, but there was still a lot of stress. I think I lived with a lot of fear. I was afraid of my father. If I was goofing around with one of my brothers, he would scream, 'Sarah, John! What's going on down there?' We would freeze. We couldn't ever be silly. Since the divorce we can have fun.

"For a long time I wanted them to pull it together or at least fake it. But as I got older I realized that divorce was actually better because they stopped fighting. I can remember after the divorce sitting at the dinner table with my mom and my brothers and acting goofy. I think she was so glad to be silly. We could laugh and talk and it was really nice. Since their divorce I can be more honest with my father rather than being afraid of him."

WHEN DIVORCE IS THE ONLY SOLUTION

Many of the parents I work with in my private practice, support groups, and seminars say their divorce was the only answer to a painful, unfulfilling marriage. When children are involved, couples usually make every effort to reconcile their differences. Parents usually consider their decision carefully before deciding to divorce. However, when there are irreconcilable differences, you must do everything possible to create a healthy postdivorce environment for your children. Parents who can put themselves in their children's shoes and can attend to their children's needs and feelings give them the best chance at emerging from divorce in sound psychological health.

In the forefront of your mind must be the questions: How can we uncouple without destroying our children and our family? How can we become ex-spouses without becoming ex-parents? As you consider these questions, heed these children's wisdom.

Chapter 12

Healing Our Children/ Healing Ourselves

If we are peaceful, if we are happy, we can blossom like a flower, and everyone in our family, our society, will benefit from our peace.

Thich Nhat Hanh, Being Peace

Her husband had left her for a younger woman and she wanted to kill him. "I hated his guts," this woman told the members of her support group. "All I could think about was making him pay for the pain he caused me. After he did that I didn't think he could be a good parent. I made him out to be the bad guy and I made it impossible for him to see his kids." But in her heart of hearts she knew he was a good father. He was a creep to her, but he loved his kids. Using them to get back at him was causing them a lot of pain, and she couldn't handle that. So she made a conscious decision to be civil and respectful to him as the children's father.

"There were many times when I wanted to drive by his new house and smash all the windows or leave a vicious message on his answering machine," she said. "But I used every ounce of self-control I could muster. I just kept repeating to myself, 'My goal is what's best for my children. My goal is what's best for my chil dren.' That became my mantra. Whenever I was about to lose it, I would take a few deep breaths and repeat it again. Keeping myself from hurting him was probably the hardest thing I've ever done, but I did it for my kids. And it's been worth all my hard work. They still have their family."

This woman epitomizes the kind of restraint necessary to a functional divorce. She chose healing over hurting, she chose her children's well-being over revenge, she chose peace of mind over anger. Learning to cooperate with your ex-spouse is probably the greatest challenge you will ever meet. You may want to strike back even as you understand how important it is that you work *with* rather than against your ex-spouse. But if you want to protect your children, you have to restrain your destructive impulses. Then, with a calm spirit, you can discover solutions to the complex issues that arise from your divorce.

Your divorce and what you make from it are in your hands. Your attitude is the key to healing yourself and your children. There are healthy divorces where both children and parents come through the crisis well-adjusted with nurturing family relationships. And there are toxic divorces where relationships are destroyed and psyches are damaged. You, and only you, can make the difference.

This book isn't a panacea for postdivorce. There is no universal cure because each divorce is unique. You will have to adapt the various approaches offered here to your situation. The techniques I recommend have been "kitchen-tested" by me and the hundreds of parents in my private practice, support groups, and seminars. Experiment. Choose the ones that work for you.

ACCENTUATE THE POSITIVE

Your perceptions are powerful and you always have a choice about how you perceive something. Rather than thinking of your divorce as a personal failure, you can perceive it as an opportunity for growth. As the well-known adage teaches, you can look at a glass half filled with water and describe it as half full, which will focus your energy in a positive direction, or see it as half empty, which will send your energy downward and produce negative feelings.

Virginia Satir, the pioneer of family therapy, once said, "Life is your current view of things. Change your view and you change your life." Your attitude is like a carnival mirror that can alter your perception of reality. Train yourself to look for the positive.

In every one of my seminars I tell this story about the industrialist Andrew Carnegie, one of the wealthiest men in turn-of-the-century America. When he came to this country from Scotland as a small boy he worked at a variety of odd jobs. Through hard work and perseverance he became the largest steel manufacturer in the world. At one point he was said to have forty-three millionaires working for him.

A reporter interviewed Carnegie and asked how he had managed to hire forty-three millionaires. Carnegie responded that those people hadn't been millionaires when they first started working for him, that they had become wealthy under his guidance. "How did that happen?" the reporter wanted to know. "People are developed the same way gold is mined," Carnegie replied. "Several tons of dirt have to be removed to get an ounce of gold; but one doesn't go into the mine looking for the dirt, one goes in looking for the gold."

Carnegie's observation describes one way you can approach your divorce and your interactions with your ex-spouse. You can look for the flaws and imperfections. Or you can look for the gold. The more good qualities you seek, the more you will find. A shift in your attitude that allows you to look for the positive is a good step forward. Negative situations don't have to be responded to negatively. The choice is yours!

THE PATH OF THE WARRIOR

Your relationships are your teachers; they lead you to self-awareness and inspire you to make better choices. Use your relationship with your ex-spouse to strengthen yourself.

Many divorcing couples view each other as the enemy. The writer Carlos Castañeda tells a story about how enemies can be the greatest teachers. Don Juan, a Mexican *brujo,* was a man of knowledge and Castañeda's teacher. When he was young, Don Juan's own spiritual mentor had apprenticed him to an abusive, dangerous ranch foreman. At one point the foreman tried to kill Don Juan. After some time Don Juan escaped and returned to his teacher, shocked at having been placed in such a horrible, life-threatening situation. But his teacher was firm; he knew what Don Juan needed to learn and he had put him in exactly the right place to learn it. Don Juan was sent back to the "petty tyrant" and told to stay centered no matter what the foreman did to provoke him.

After a few years of living in this hell Don Juan learned the warrior's skill of keeping his center, no matter the provocation. In instructing Castañeda in the way of the warrior, Don Juan explained, "The warriors who succumb to the petty tyrant are obliterated by their own sense of failure and unworthiness. . . . Anyone who joins the petty tyrant is defeated. To act in anger, without control and discipline, to have no forbearance, is to be defeated."

For many of us, our ex-spouses are petty tyrants. We don't have to like them, but we can learn to appreciate what they have to offer. Once you have adopted this attitude, you'll no longer need the relationship with your ex as your teacher, nor will you attract others like it. Your divorce and the process that follows, like Don Juan's ranch foreman's, will have given you the opportunity you needed to grow and become strong.

Your goal is to heal. Every time you maintain your center and prevent a discussion with your ex from turning into a fight, you promote your own and your children's healing. Whenever you act for the greater good, whenever you exhibit self-control, integrity, and dignity, you automatically increase your self-esteem and self-respect. Use your divorce as a learning experience.

MODELING

Children learn by imitation. Your actions speak much louder than anything you can ever say. You model for your children on a daily basis. How you treat your children's other parent, how you reorganize your life, how you cope with stress and face money woes become the basis for your children's approach to life.

The family is a child's first and most important classroom. If we want our children to act with respect and dignity, then we have to treat them and others with respect. If we want our children to have integrity, then we must be honorable and trustworthy. If we want a world of peace and harmony, then we have to model cooperation and creative problem solving, both with our children and with our ex-spouses.

Kids are keen observers. Nothing goes unnoticed. Parents are a powerful force in molding their characters, beliefs, and values. When you make a commitment to a functional divorce, you teach your children to confront life's serious problems with respect, compassion, and integrity. Your kids learn that even though you and your former spouse are no longer married, you have the maturity to cooperate in their best interest. That is a powerful message. The way you relate to life's challenges is a daily lesson in human possibility.

Caring for yourself is difficult when so much of your life has been organized around caring for others, but the point is that you have to do something to refill your tank. The people who are most effective in coping with conflict and stress are those who take good care of themselves. When you take time for yourself, you give your kids the message that you value and respect yourself. You are a model for your children's self-esteem. Research confirms that self-esteem isn't something that is taught, but rather something that's "caught," most likely from constant exposure. Parents with healthy self-esteem tend to raise children with a similar level of self-worth.

When you nurture yourself, you have more resources to nurture others. Being a parent is hard even in the best of circumstances, but you have the additional challenge of being a divorced parent. For everyone's sake, take good care of yourself. When you honor yourself, you give your kids an example of a fulfilled, vital, caring person.

THE MYTH OF THE INTACT FAMILY

For most people, divorce came with a sense of failure and shame. The divorced person hasn't lived up to his or her own or society's expectations.

Society clings to the ideal of the intact family and continues to view divorce as pathological, a sign of inadequacy on the part of the individual. Although growing up with divorce is becoming more common, the children still carry a social stigma. Think for a moment about the language frequently used to describe children of divorce. How often have you heard someone say "Poor child, she comes from a 'broken home.' " In fact, there are millions of dysfunctional marriages in which relationships have been broken for years. To call a divorced home "broken" assumes that nonbroken homes are terrific. Sometimes they're not. Society's view of divorce as pathological must change. There must be room to consider divorce a positive solution to an unworkable situation. When that happens, the stigma of growing up with divorce will fade.

The form the family takes doesn't determine the health or toxicity of relationships. There are dysfunctional intact families, dysfunctional divorced families, functional intact families, and functional divorced families.

Many children grow up in dysfunctional but intact families. In some, the marriage died long ago and the parents are going through the motions and suffering in silence. Others are riddled with abuse, both physical and emotional. Many of these families maintain the seamless veneer of denial that only perpetuates the myth. In these families everyone suffers, yet they sustain the traditional form of what a family is supposed to be. These families are intact, but are they healthy, nurturing environments for adults or children? Of course not.

Like it or not, families *are* changing. The old ideal of Ozzie and Harriet or the Huxtables of *The Cosby Show* represents a shrinking segment of the population. But as long as society clings to the myth of the intact family, alternative family forms will not be fully acknowledged and integrated into the mainstream.

We must shift our view to see families not as static objects but as a process. Families are living organisms that grow and change and sometimes split apart only to reorganize anew. When we embrace this perspective, then divorce can be appreciated as a healthy choice. When families are seen as a process, the concept of intact or "broken" becomes irrelevant. Families can simply be families. And when this happens, society can concentrate on promoting the family's health and growth regardless of its form.

THE FAMILY OF THE FUTURE

We are living through a period of historic change in American family life. We are in a process of sorting and reassessing. The present chaos is essential to the next step in family evolution. Unfortunately, the process of change is seldom pretty. Take the transformation of a lowly caterpillar. He creeps along until he's ready to go into his cocoon. Entomologists, those who study bugs and insects, say that once inside he undergoes a period of fluidity in which his tissues sort of liquefy and then completely reorganize. When he emerges he is a butterfly, but for a brief period he is a most unattractive puddle. The moral, of course, is that discomfort is a necessary part of metamorphosis, whether in the individual, the family, or society as a whole.

Whenever massive social change occurs, the natural tendency is to retreat to the familiarity of the good old days. But in spite of tremendous resistance from traditionalists there *is* no going back. What these people don't understand is that traditional family values can be accommodated in new family forms.

The answer to their intolerance and fear is the creation of functional, healthy divorced families. You are a pioneer, forging a new model of relating based on mutual respect, love, and integrity. You must have patience and courage. Eventually social and political institutions will revise their policies to acknowledge alternative families.

THE NEED FOR SUPPORT

"I was in sixth grade and it was right around the time my parents got divorced that my best friend Randy's father died of a heart attack," recalled Marina, a twenty-three-year-old medical student. "All the kids at school made cards to cheer her up. When I went to see her, she told me how her relatives had come over to help her and her mother get through the loss. I can still remember walking home and feeling furious as I walked home. I had lost my dad too, but no one came to comfort me. Not one person called to say they were sorry, no one came to see how we were doing. We were on our own. I couldn't understand why there was such a big difference between a person dying and a family dying. To me, it was all kind of the same."

Divorce is the only major family event for which there is little or no recognition. When there's a death in the family, relatives and friends rally around. When a baby is born, a great fuss is made. Marriage, graduation, adoption, important homecomings—all inspire celebration. But when you divorce you are left alone.

Our culture treats divorce as a threat to the institution of marriage. Many act as if it is contagious; they don't want to get too close to the diseased couple. Divorcing couples deserve as much support and love as they start a new life as they received when they first married. Divorcing families need a supportive community, a network of people they can turn to for advice and encouragement. If you aren't already involved in a single-parent's support group, I recommend that you explore what's available in your community.

This isn't the time to put on your Lone Ranger costume and ride alone off into the sunset. You and your children are in the midst of a family crisis. If you are like most, you feel overwhelmed and discouraged. You need reassurance as you navigate this new terrain. Contact the YWCA or YWHA, your local social service agency, or call your church or synagogue.

Our society has not as yet learned how to embrace this major life transition, so you have to reach out for your own support. One single father was determined to be involved in a divorced father's group. After a futile search for an existing group, he placed an ad in the local newspaper and started his own. The first meeting had four other divorced fathers. A month later he had twelve other men who made a commitment to meet for two hours once a month. Be creative. But no matter what it takes, find some support.

Social worker Elizabeth McGonagle in Ballston Spa, New York, developed a support group for children who were experiencing divorce. The goals of her program are to reassure them that they are not alone and that they can survive the ordeal, and to teach them to cope with the changes in their families. You may want to consider implementing a similar program in your children's school. A list of resources in the back of this book includes information about national organizations that offer support.

THE POT OF GOLD

You may not be able to imagine a time in the future when you are not furious with your ex-spouse. You're probably more focused on uncoupling and establishing a separate identity than on thinking about the continuity of your lives and how you will remain interconnected. But your children are the thread that connects you, one that survives over time and space.

Time has a magical way of helping us to transcend the trauma of divorce; it lets us refocus on the wonderful beings we once created together. When I divorced my daughter's father I never wanted to see him again. I wished that he would drop off the face of the earth. Thirteen years later our eighteen-year-old daughter, Ama, was about to be graduated from high school. Ama and I decided to invite her entire family, my relatives as well as her father's. My ex lives in another state and although we have frequent phone conversations I hadn't seen him in five years. Needless to say, I had mixed feelings about his attending her graduation. But as I sat between my ex-husband and his mother at the ceremony and watched our daughter step forward to receive her diploma I was filled with a sense of gratitude that all those years ago we found one another and came together to produce this wonderful young woman. Any residual regret melted away as through tear-filled eyes I watched her march down the aisle in her purple cap and gown carrying her head high with a sense of pride and accomplishment. I glanced over at her father and he too had tears in his eyes. He flashed me a smile and gave me a thumbs-up. I passed him a Kleenex and we both burst out laughing at how sentimental we still were.

Once the ceremony was finished we made our way to the reception area. After a round of refreshments and far too many photographs of the graduate with various family members, all returned to my house for a celebration. As the afternoon wound down Ama's father found me talking to some friends and announced that he and his mother were about to leave for their hotel. They said their good-byes to my family, then Ama and I walked them out to their rented car. I gave Grandma Eve, who is now very frail, a big hug and told her how glad I was that she had come to share this special day with us. We helped her into the car and I turned to say good-bye to Ama's father. We both looked over at our daughter, embraced, and cried in one another's arms. I cried for what we once had, I cried with gratitude for what we had produced, I cried with relief at how well our daughter had turned out despite our divorce, and I cried with joy for our having shared this special moment with one another. My ex looked at me with tears streaming down his face and said, "You have a lot to be proud of. I just want you to know that you're a terrific mother and you've done a great job with Ama. We may not have been able to make our marriage work, but we sure made one terrific kid." Ama stood there watching us appreciate one another in an entirely new way and taking in this moment of healing. All the hard work and my commitment to cooperation was paid off in that instant of recognition. My daughter did have a family who loved, honored, and cherished her. And this was my precious proof that it *is* possible to raise solid, healthy children in a divorced family.

Notes

Introduction

1. Much of the material in this section was obtained both in conversation with Joan B. Kelly, Ph.D., as well as from her articles published in *Family Law News* and *Family and Conciliation Courts Review.*
2. Judith Wallerstein and Sandra Blakeslee, *Second Chances: Men, Women, and Children a Decade After Divorce* (New York: Ticknor & Fields, 1989).
3. Mavis Hetherington, K. Camera, and D. Featherman, "Achievement and Intellectual Functioning of Children in One-Parent Households," in *Assessing Achievement,* ed. J. Spence (New York: Freeman, 1981).
4. B. Berg and R. Kelly, "Measured Self-Esteem of Children from Broken, Rejected and Accepted Families," *Journal of Divorce* 2 (1979): 363–370; and Joan B. Kelly, "The Adjustment of Children After Divorce: Are Negative Effects Exaggerated?" *Family Law News* 15, no. 1 (Spring 1992).
5. A. J. Cherlin et al., "Longitudinal Studies of Effects of Divorce on Children in Great Britain and the United States," *Science,* June 7, 1991, p. 1386.
6. J. Block, J. Block, and P. Gjerde, "The Personality of Children Prior to Divorce: A Prospective Study," *Child Development* 57 (1986): 827–840.

Chapter 1. Helping Your Kids Cope with Crazy Times

1. Ken Magid and Walt Schreibman, *Divorce Is a Kid's Coloring Book* (Gretna, LA: Pelican Publishing Co., 1980).
2. Judith Wallerstein and Sandra Blakeslee, *Second Chances: Men, Women, and Children a Decade After Divorce* (New York: Ticknor & Fields, 1989).
3. Honorable Silvia Cartwright, "21st. Century Family Law Pro-

spective," *Family and Conciliation Courts Review* 27, no. 2 (December 1989).

Chapter 2. Games Parents Play

1. Adapted from Donald A. Gordon, Ph.D., and Jack Arbuthnot, Ph.D., *Children in the Middle* (Athens, OH: The Center for Psychological and Family Law Alternatives, 1990).
2. John Bradshaw, *Bradshaw on the Family* (Deerfield, FL: Health Communication, 1988).
3. Judith Wallerstein and Sandra Blakeslee, *Second Chances: Men, Women, and Children a Decade After Divorce* (New York: Ticknor & Fields, 1989).
4. A study by Kathleen A. Camara and Gary Resnick of Tufts University, "Interparental Conflict and Cooperation: Factors Moderating Children's Post-Divorce Adjustment," in *Impact of Divorce, Single Parenting, and Stepparenting of Children,* ed. Mavis Hetherington and J. Arasteh (Hillside, NJ: Lawrence Erlbaum Associates, 1988).

Chapter 3. Getting an Emotional Divorce: How to Stop the Battle with Your Ex

1. Adapted from a process used by Jack Canfield and Georgia Noble in their Self-Esteem Seminar.
2. Quoted by Abigail Van Buren, *Los Angeles Times,* February 16, 1992.

Chapter 4. They Said It Couldn't Be Done: Building a Parenting Partnership

1. Isolina Ricci, Ph.D., *Mom's House, Dad's House: Making Shared Custody Work* (New York: Macmillan, 1982).
2. C. R. Ahrons and R. H. Rogers, *Divorced Families* (New York: Norton, 1987).
3. Mavis Hetherington and J. Arasteh, eds., *Impact of Divorce, Single Parenting, and Stepparenting of Children* (Hillside, NJ: Lawrence Erlbaum Associates, 1988).

Chapter 7. Where's Poppa? Keeping Both Parents Involved

1. S. J. Hewlett, *When the Bough Breaks* (New York: Basic Books, 1991).

2. Frank Furstenberg, Jr., and Kathleen Mullan Harris, "The Disappearing Father? Divorce and the Waning Significance of Biological Parenthood," Department of Sociology, University of Pennsylvania, March 1990.
3. Quoted in Tamar Lewin, "Father's Vanishing Act Called Common Drama," *The New York Times,* June 4, 1990, p. A18.
4. Judith Brown, "Grief," at the conference of the American Orthopsychiatric Association, Chicago, 1978.
5. S. J. Hewlett, *When the Bough Breaks* (New York: Basic Books, 1991).
6. Judith Wallerstein and Sandra Blakeslee, *Second Chances: Men, Women, and Children a Decade After Divorce* (New York: Ticknor & Fields, 1989).
7. Adapted from M. G. Cohen and G. Newman, *101 Ways to Be a Long-Distance Superdad* (New York: New American Library, 1989).

Chapter 8. Making It Legal: Choosing an Attorney and Other Issues

1. I would like to thank Hugh McIssac, Glen Hardie, Forest Mosten, J. C. Hirsch, and Joel Edelman for their help with this chapter.
2. Kenneth Kressel, *The Process of Divorce* (New York: Basic Books, 1985).
3. Joan B. Kelly, Ph.D., "Long-Term Adjustment in Children of Divorce," *Journal of Family Psychology* 2, no. 2 (1988): 137.

Chapter 9. Money: How Important Is It?

1. Greg J. Duncan and Saul D. Hoffman, "A Reconsideration of the Economic Consequences of Marital Dissolution," *Demography* 22, no. 4 (November 1985): 485–97.
2. U.S. Census Bureau, *Child Support and Alimony* (Washington, DC: U.S. Census Bureau, 1990), p. 7, table E.
3. Lucy Marsh Yee, "What Really Happened in Child Support Cases: An Empirical Study of the Establishment and Enforcement of Child Support Orders in the Denver District Court," *Law Journal of Denver* 57 (1980): 21–36.
4. Susan Faludi, *Backlash: The Undeclared War Against Women* (New York: Crown, 1991).

5. D. J. Hernandez, "Demographic Trends and Living Arrangement of Children," in *Impact of Divorce, Single Parenting, and Stepparenting on Children,* ed. Mavis Hetherington and J. Arasteh (Hillsdale, NJ: Lawrence Erlbaum Associates, 1988).

Chapter 11. What Kids Have to Say

1. Joan B. Kelly, Ph.D., "The Adjustment of Children After Divorce: Are Negative Effects Exaggerated?" *Family Law News* 15, no. 1 (Spring 1992).

Suggested Reading List

Books for Parents

Bateson, Mary Catherine. *Composing a Life*. New York: Plume, 1990.

Beal, Edward W., M.D., and Gloria Hochman. *Adult Children of Divorce*. New York: Delacorte Press, 1991.

Belli, Melvin, and Mel Krantzler. *Divorcing*. New York: St. Martin's Press, 1988.

Berman, Claire. *Adult Children of Divorce Speak Out*. New York: Simon & Schuster, 1991.

———. *Making It As a Step Parent: New Roles, New Rules*. New York: Harper & Row, 1986.

Bernstein, Anne C. *Yours, Mine, and Ours: How Families Change When Remarried Parents Have a Child Together*. New York: Norton, 1989.

Bird Francke, Linda. *Growing Up Divorced*. New York: Ballantine Books, 1983.

Bradshaw, John. *Homecoming: Reclaiming and Championing Your Inner Child*. New York: Bantam Books, 1990.

———. *Bradshaw on the Family*. Deerfield, FL: Health Communication, 1988.

———. *Healing the Shame That Binds You*. Deerfield, FL: Health Communication, 1988.

Bret, Doris. *Annie Stories: A Special Kind of Storytelling*. New York: Workman Publishing, 1986.

Briggs, Dorothy Corkille. *Celebrate Your Self*. New York: Harcourt Brace Jovanovich, 1977.

Clarke, Jean. *Self-Esteem: A Family Affair*. Minneapolis: Winston Press, 1978.

———, and Connie Dawson. *Growing Up Again*. Center City, MN: Hazelden, 1989.

Cohen, Marilyn. *Long-Distance Parenting: A Guide for Divorced Parenting*. New York: New American Library, 1989.

Crum, Thomas. *The Magic of Conflict*. New York: Simon & Schuster, 1987.

Einstein, Elizabeth. *The Stepfamily: Living and Learning*. New York: Macmillan, 1982.

Faludi, Susan. *Backlash: The Undeclared War Against Women*. New York: Crown, 1991.

Fassel, Diane, Ph.D. *Growing Up Divorced: A Road to Healing for Adult Children of Divorce*. New York: Pocket Books, 1991.

Fisher, Roger, and William Ury. *Getting to Yes: Negotiating Agreement Without Giving In*. New York: Viking Penguin, 1981.

Gardner, Richard A. *The Boys and Girls Book About One-Parent Families*. New York: Bantam Books, 1988.

———. *The Boys' and Girls' Book About Divorce*. New York: Bantam Books, 1983.

———. *The Parents Book About Divorce*. New York: Bantam Books, 1977.

Ginott, Hiam G. *Between Parents and Teenagers. New York: Macmillan, 1969.*

———. *Between Parent and Child*. New York: Avon Books, 1956.

Grollman, Earl A. *Talking About Divorce and Separation*. Boston: Beacon Press, 1975.

Jampolsky, Gerald. *Teach Only Love: The Seven Principles of Attitudinal Healing*. New York: Bantam Books, 1983.

Jeffers, Susan, Ph.D. *Feel the Fear and Do It Anyway*. New York: Harcourt Brace Jovanovich, 1987.

Kalter, Neil. *Growing Up with Divorce*. New York: The Free Press, 1990.

Marston, Stephanie. *The Magic of Encouragement: Nurturing Your Child's Self-Esteem*. New York: Pocket Books, 1992.

Miller, Alice. *For Your Own Good: Hidden Cruelty in Childrearing and the Roots of Violence*. New York: Farrar, Straus & Giroux, 1983.

———. *Prisoners of Childhood: How Narcissistic Parents Form and Deform the Emotional Lives of Their Gifted Children*. New York: Basic Books, 1981.

Newman, G. *101 Ways to Be a Long-Distance Superdad*. Mountain View, CA: Blossom Valley Press, 1984.

Olds, Sally. *The Working Parents Survival Guide*. New York: Bantam Books, 1983.

Peck, M. Scott. *The Road Less Traveled: A New Psychology of Love, Traditional Values, and Spiritual Growth*. New York: Simon & Schuster, 1978.

Ricci, Isolina, Ph.D. *Mom's House, Dad's House: Making Shared Custody Work*. New York: Macmillan, 1982.

Rogers, Fred, and Clare O'Brien. *Mister Rogers Talks with Families About Divorce*. New York: Berkley Books, 1987.

Rosin, Mark B. *Step-father's Advice on Creating a New Family.* New York: Ballantine Books, 1987.

Samlin, Nancy. *Loving Your Child Is Not Enough: Positive Discipline That Works.* New York: Viking, 1987.

Satir, Virginia. *The New Peoplemaking.* Palo Alto: Science & Behavior Books, 1988.

———. *Your Many Faces.* Millbrea, CA: Celestial Arts, 1978.

Shahan, Lynn. *Living Alone & Liking It.* New York: Warner Books, 1981.

Simon, Sidney, Ph.D. *Getting Unstuck: Breaking Through Your Barriers to Change.* New York: Warner Books, 1988.

———. *Forgiveness: How to Make Peace with Your Past and Get On with Your Life.* New York: Warner Books, 1990.

Sinetar, Marsha. *Do What You Love: The Money Will Follow.* Mahwah, NJ: Paulist Press, 1987.

———. *Elegant Choices, Healing Choices.* Mahwah, NJ: Paulist Press, 1988.

Smedes, Lewis B. *Forgive & Forget.* New York: Pocket Books, 1984.

Stearns, Ann Kaiser. *Living Through Personal Crisis.* Chicago: Thomas Moore Press, 1984.

Steinem, Gloria. *Revolution from Within.* Boston: Little, Brown, 1992.

Teyber, Edward, Ph.D. *Helping Your Children with Divorce.* New York: Pocket Books, 1985.

Trafford, Abigail. *Crazy Times: Surviving Divorce.* New York: Bantam Books, 1982.

Vaughn, Diane. *Uncoupling: Turning Points in Intimate Relationships.* New York: Vintage Books, 1990.

Viorst, Judith. *Necessary Losses.* New York: Simon & Schuster, 1986.

Visher, John, and Emily Visher. *Stepfamilies: A Guide to Working with Stepparents and Stepchildren.* New York: Bruner Mazel, 1979.

———. *How to Win as a Stepfamily.* Chicago: Contemporary Books, 1982.

Wallerstein, Judith, and Sandra Blakeslee. *Second Chances: Men, Women, and Children a Decade After Divorce.* New York: Ticknor & Fields, 1989.

Books for Children

Blume, Judy. *It's Not the End of the World.* New York: Dell, 1986.

Brown, Laurence, and Marc Laurence. *Dinosaurs Divorce.* New York: Little, Brown, 1968.

Cleary, Beverly. *Dear Mr. Henshaw.* New York: William Morrow, 1983.

Fassler, Diane. *Changing Families: A Guide for Kids and Grown-Ups.* San Francisco: Publishers Group West, 1988.

Girard, L. *At Daddy's on Saturdays.* Morton Grove, IL: Albert Whitman, 1987.

Ived, S. *The Divorce Workbook.* Burlington, VT: Waterfront Books, 1985.

Krementz, Jill. *How It Feels When Parents Divorce.* New York: Alfred A. Knopf, 1984.

Lasher, M. *My Kind of Family: A Book for Kids in Single-Parent Families.* Burlington, VT: Waterfront Books, 1991.

Mayle, P. *Why Are We Getting Divorced?* New York: Harmony Books, 1990.

Sanford, D. *Please Come Home.* Highlands, CO: Multnomah Press, 1988.

Vigna, J. *Saying Goodbye to Daddy.* Morton Grove, IL: Albert Whitman, 1991.

Resources

ORGANIZATIONS FOR PARENTS

Advocacy Groups

These groups will provide support, information, and reports about divorce, how to help your children, and how to collect child support.

Association for Children for Enforcement of Support
1081 Jefferson Avenue, #204
Toledo, OH 43624
800-537-7072

For Our Children's Unpaid Support
P.O. Box 2183
Vienna, VA 22180

National Child Support Advocacy Coalition
P.O. Box 420
Hendersonville, TN 37077

National Council for Children's Rights, Inc.
2001 O Street NW
Washington, DC 20036
800-547-NCCR

U.S. Department of Health and Human Services
Office of Child Support Enforcement and Reference Center, 4th Floor
370 L'Enfant Promenade SW
Washington, DC 20047
Provides information, booklets, and a national newsletter.

Children's Legal Rights

Children's Defense Fund
122 C Street NW
Washington, DC 20001
202-628-8787

Children's Legal Rights Information and Training
2008 Hillyer Place NW
Washington, DC 20009
202-332-6575

Children's Rights Groups
693 Mission Street
San Francisco, CA 94105
415-495-7283

Organizations to Help Find Missing Children

Child-Find
P.O. Box 277
New Paltz, NY 12561
1 800-I-Am-Lost

National Center for Missing and Exploited Children
1835 K Street NW, #600
Washington, DC 20006
202-634-9821 or 800-843-5678

Child Support Enforcement

Association for Children for Enforcement Support
1018 Jefferson Avenue, Suite 204
Toledo, OH 43624
419-242-6130

EXPOSE (for military spouses)
P.O. Box 11191
Alexandria, VA 22312
703-255-5844 (day) or
703-255-2917 (evening)

Federal Parent Locator Service
U.S. Department of Health and Human Services
Family Support Administration
Office of Child Support Enforcement, 4th Floor
370 L'Enfant Promenade SW
Washington, DC 20047
202-252-5443 (Federal Locator Service)
202-252-5343 (Family Support Administration)
202-475-0257 (Department of Health and Human Services)

For Our Children and Us Inc. (FOCUS)
60 Lafayette Street
New York, NY 10013
212-693-1655

National Child Support Enforcement Association
Hall of the States
444 North Capitol Street NW, Suite 613
Washington, DC 20001
202-624-8180

National Institute for Child Support Enforcement (NICSE)
7200 Wisconsin Avenue, Suite 500
Bethesda, MD 20814
301-654-8338

Booklets on How to Collect Child Support

"Child Support: Methods of Collecting Everything You're Entitled To" Resources
P.O. Box 5019
155 East C Street
Upland, CA 91786
Send $7.00 for a booklet that will take you step by step on how to collect child support.

Handbook on Child Support Enforcement
Consumer Information Center
Department 628 M
Pueblo, CO 81009
Send for a free handbook.

Support Groups

Family Enterprises America
333 Seventh Avenue
New York, NY 10010
212-967-2740

Fathers Are Forever
P.O. Box 4804
Panorama City, CA 91412
818-846-2219

Fathers for Equal Rights
P.O. Box 010847, Flagler Station
Miami, FL 33101
305-895-6351

Gay Fathers Coalition
P.O. Box 50360
Washington, DC 20004
202-548-3238

Joint Custody Association
10606 Wilkins Avenue
Los Angeles, CA 90024
310-475-5352

Mothers Without Custody
P.O. Box 56762
Houston, TX 77256
713-840-1622

National Congress for Men
c/o Fathers for Equal Rights of America
P.O. Box 2272
Southfield, MI 48037
303-354-3080

National Council for Children's Rights
2001 O Street NW
Washington, DC 20036
202-223-6227
Promotes education for parents and schools on children and divorce.

National Council for Men
223 Fifteenth Street SE
Washington, DC 20003
202-Fathers
A clearinghouse for men's support groups and resources nationwide.

Parents Without Partners
8807 Colesville Road
Silver Spring, MD 20910
800-637-7974

Parents Anonymous
National Office
2230 Hawthorne Boulevard, Suite 208
Torrance, CA 90505
800-421-0353
In California 800-352-0386

Victims of Child Abuse Laws (VOCAL)
P.O. Box 11335
Minneapolis, MN 55411
612-521-9714
A support group for parents falsely accused of child sexual abuse during a custody dispute.

ORGANIZATIONS FOR CHILDREN

Banana Splits
Elizabeth McGonagle
Ballston Spa Central Schools
Ballston Spa, NY 12020
518-885-5361
A school-based program for children who are experiencing divorce.

Big Brothers / Big Sisters of America
230 N. Thirteenth Street
Philadelphia, PA 19107
215-567-7000

International Youth Council
c/o Parents Without Partners
8807 Colesville Road
Silver Spring, MD 20910
800-637-7974

SUPPORT FOR STEPFAMILIES

The StepFamily Association of America
602 E. Joppa Road
Baltimore, MD 21204
301-823-7570

The StepFamily Foundation
333 West End Avenue
New York, NY 10023
212-877-3244

ADDITIONAL RESOURCES

"Bill Your Ex" Kits
3960 Laurel Canyon Boulevard, #437
Studio City, CA 91607
800-828-2299
This is a kit that includes thirteen payment coupons, invoices, past-due notices, and return envelopes. It costs $14.95 and is a businesslike way of reminding you ex-spouse about delinquent payments.

The Written Connection
2633 E. Indian School Road, #400
Phoenix, AZ 85016
800-334-3143
This is a kit to make writing to your children easier.

Index

Note

I welcome any comments, questions, or suggestions you may have regarding the material I have presented in this book.

Stephanie Marston is available for lectures, conferences, workshops, and speaking engagements throughout the country. For further information please contact Raising Miracles Educational Seminars, 134 East Santa Fe Avenue, Santa Fe, New Mexico, 87501; 505-989-7596.